# Modern Christian Assembly Stories

Gary Nott
With Foreword by Canon Martin O'Connor

Brilliant
PUBLICATIONS

We hope you and your pupils enjoy the assembly stories in this book. Brilliant Publications publishes many other books for use in primary schools. To find out more details on any of the titles listed below, please log onto our website: www.brilliantpublications.co.uk.

**Other assembly books**

| | |
|---|---|
| Brilliant Stories for Assemblies | 978-1-903853-49-8 |
| More Brilliant Stories for Assemblies | 978-1-90578-074-7 |
| Class-led Assemblies | 978-1-90578-014-3 |
| 50 Fantastic Assembly Stories for Key Stage 2 | 978-1-78317-102-6 |

**Other titles**

| | |
|---|---|
| Into the Garden of Dreams | 978-1-89767-576-2 |
| 100+ Fun Ideas for Creating a Happier Classroom | 978-1-90578-076-1 |
| 100+ Fun Ideas for Transition Times | 978-1-90578-034-1 |

Published by Brilliant Publications Limited
Unit 10
Sparrow Hall Farm
Edlesborough
Dunstable
Bedfordshire
LU6 2ES, UK

Website:     www.brilliantpublications.co.uk
Tel:         01525 222292

The name Brilliant Publications and the logo are registered trademarks.

Written by Gary Nott
Illustrated by Chantal Kees
Cover by Chantal Kees

© Text Gary Nott 2016
© Design Brilliant Publications Limited 2016

Printed ISBN:   978-1-78317-228-3
ebook ISBN:     978-1-78317-229-0

First printed and published in the UK in 2017.

The right of Gary Nott to be identified as the author of this work has been asserted by himself in accordance with the Copyright, Designs and Patents Act 1988.

Pages 7–195 may be photocopied by individual teachers acting on behalf of the purchasing institution for classroom use only, without permission from the publisher or declaration to the Publishers Licensing Society. The materials may not be reproduced in any other form or for any other purpose without the prior permission of the publisher.

# Contents

| Story | Main theme | Page |
|---|---|---|
| Foreword by Canon Martin O'Connor | | 5 |
| Introduction | | 6 |
| David and Arthur's Story | Autism/Difference | 7 |
| Katherine's Story | Bullying | 11 |
| Joshua's Story | Second chances | 15 |
| Mr Ripple's Story | Taking risks | 19 |
| Evan's Story | Disability/Difference | 23 |
| Tom's Story | Mistakes | 27 |
| Mr Carmichael's Story | False accusations | 31 |
| Scarlett's Story | Bullying | 35 |
| Archie's Story | Safeguarding | 39 |
| Mrs Groves' Story | Death | 42 |
| Billy's Story | Embarrassment/Humour | 46 |
| Aaron's Story | Putting people on a pedestal | 50 |
| Marley's Story | Fitting in | 54 |
| Daniel's Story | Racism | 57 |
| Mr Jenkins' Story | Making time for Jesus | 61 |
| Cameron, James, Jasmine and Derek's Story | Phobias | 65 |
| Henry's Story | Family breakdown | 69 |
| Mr Peters' Story | Getting things out of proportion | 73 |
| Conrad's Story | Labelling | 77 |
| Eddie's Story | Alcohol abuse/Desperation | 81 |
| Mr Johnson's Story | Child protection | 85 |
| Matthew's Story | Disability | 89 |
| Karnel's Story | Slippery slope | 93 |
| Scott's Story | Disability/Children's mental health | 96 |
| Ethan's Story | Humour | 100 |
| Mrs Barley's Story | Pride | 104 |
| Nadia's Story | Vulnerability | 108 |
| Father Liam's Story | Disappointment | 113 |
| Serena's Story | Medical conditions | 116 |
| Mr Terry's Story | Valuing what you have | 120 |
| Mr Duncan's Story | Making time for God | 124 |
| Benny's Story | A way out of trouble | 128 |
| Danny's Story | Being overweight/Difference | 131 |

## Contents

| Story | Main theme | Page |
|---|---|---|
| Samaya's Story | Honesty is the best policy | 135 |
| Nicola's Story | Divorce | 139 |
| Harry's Story | Annoying habits | 142 |
| Darren's Story | Safeguarding | 145 |
| Comfort's Story | Girl power!/Equal opportunities | 149 |
| Lottie's Story | Adoption | 152 |
| Luke's Story | Dementia | 156 |
| Mr Reynolds' Story | Rejection | 159 |
| Gary's Story | Christmas/Humour | 163 |
| Dominic's Story | Getting out of bother | 165 |
| Mickey's Story | Making mistakes without thinking | 169 |
| Daniel's Story | Homesickness | 173 |
| Anna's Story | Overcoming tragedy | 177 |
| Archie's Story | Keep trying | 180 |
| Ashan's Story | Peer pressure | 184 |
| Damien's Story | Respecting others | 188 |
| Tommy and Jacob's Story | Falling in and out of friendship | 192 |

# Foreword

Storytelling is the essence of human communication: through sharing our own story, and being drawn into others', we grow in understanding, self-knowledge and wisdom. Research suggests that we make sense of much of the world around us by organising our observations in story form; that is, we humanise or personalise information in order to grasp more fully its meaning for us.

Jesus of Nazareth was the story teller par excellence! His parables are as fresh and instructive today as when those gracious words first fell from his lips. His ancient stories continue to give deep meaning to modern lives.

In this collection of stories, Gary Nott deploys the very best techniques of storytelling. Using modern situations and idioms, which are familiar to children, he communicates the wisdom found in Jesus' parables.

Everyone has challenges and problems in the routine of daily life: sometimes we refer to them as Crosses we have to bear. These stories powerfully illustrate The Master's example and encourage those who are burdened to imitate him in his determination to do The Father's will. Perseverance – that is a lesson which Christ teaches us – to keep going despite the heavy burdens we may have to carry from time to time.

I regularly witness whole-school assemblies at St Bede School where both pupils and staff are captivated by the wondrous story-telling of this inspirational headteacher. I am very pleased to commend his collection of stories as a powerful resource for the transmission of Christian values.

Canon Martin O'Connor, Chadwell Heath, England

# Introduction

I have always found collections of assembly stories to be like recipe books. I would use one or two but the vast majority would not appeal. When I was first a Head, I bought lots of collections – only to use just a handful of tales. It was an expensive business. I wanted to write a book where you would want to use most, if not every story contained within. As a headteacher of 20 years' standing, I have led lots of assemblies, hundreds. Since 2012, I have been the headteacher of a faith school. This brings with it a new dimension. Assemblies are explicitly Christian in nature. That said, I now realise that my assemblies earlier in my career, when leading non-denominational schools, fell short of the requirement that they too should be broadly Christian in make-up. They weren't. They were largely secular. I didn't have the confidence to make a link to the Christian traditions. The stories in this collection all can be used to convey a Christian message. For some tales, the link is made in the teacher's notes and can be explored once the story is told. Other stories have the Christian message explicitly conveyed during the telling of the story through a Bible reference. I make reference to Collins' *The Rainbow Good News Bible* (2009) throughout.

However, the stories in this collection have a dimension that is even stronger than the Christian one. They are all modern stories. They deal with issues that children in the 21st Century can relate to: bullying, racism, embarrassment, peer pressure, disability, breakdown of family life, death – and the list goes on. Some will make your children laugh, whilst others will prompt them to reflect deeply. I hope that the stories are good stories rather than good stories for primary aged children. As such, your staff will enjoy them as much as the pupils.

Although the stories are primarily aimed at KS2, I have used them with KS1 and KS3 too.

# Teacher's Notes
# David and Arthur's Story

## Background
My youngest son has autism. At the time of writing, he can't talk. He communicates with sign language and uses an i-Pad to summon up images in order to show what he is trying to say. He began by attending a 'normal school', but we came to believe that a special school was right for him. Some other parents of children with disabilities are strong advocates of a mainstream education for their child. It can often be a very difficult decision to make as parents naturally worry about getting it wrong. Whilst children are quick to accept others, despite their differences, not all parents of able-bodied children are as generous. I once had a father say to me, 'I don't want my child taught in the same group as a disabled child.' It took me some time to come to terms with this statement.

## General theme
How do children with disabilities make us feel? Are we embarrassed, do we feel awkward, show sympathy, or do we see the child not the disability?

## What do Christians believe?
Jesus sought out the lame and the afflicted. He believed that their place was with Him. God creates the people we are: 'You created every part of me; you put me together in my mother's womb. When I was growing there in secret, you knew that I was there – you saw me before I was born.' (Psalms 139:13,15) It is by His design that we are who we are. 'I have come in order that you might have life – life in all its fullness.' (John 10:10)

## Prayer
*Loving Father, you made us in your image. Thank you for loving each and every one.*

## The story
How does anyone feel when they start a new school? Is it easy to know how Arthur was feeling? Can the children hazard a guess?
What sort of a person is David? Why would he make a good friend for Arthur?

## PSMC links
- Is Arthur disabled? (Be prepared for some disagreement.)
- How are disabled people viewed in society?
- Can anyone share the story of someone with a disability? How does that person meet life's challenges?

© Gary Nott and Brilliant Publications Limited
*This page may be photocopied for use by the purchasing institution only.*

Modern Christian Assembly Stories

# David and Arthur's Story

David enjoyed school. A tall lad with a shock of red hair, he was likeable. He had attended St John's Primary since Year 2. He hadn't known anyone when he first came. He had cried a lot then. But now he was in Year 4 and knew lots of the children in his year, and had friends in other parts of the school, too. David had been upset before half-term when his best friend Mark had moved away from St John's. But his mum had said he would see Mark again in the holidays. 'Besides,' she added, 'you'll be okay – you have lots of other friends too.' It was true. There were Ashish, Mary, Raiyan, and plenty of others.

When the children returned after half-term, Mark's desk stood empty. This made David feel a little funny inside; he was, after all, missing his friend. Mr Fitzpatrick, his teacher, said a new child would be starting soon, but not quite yet.

When his mum picked him up that day, the first thing she asked was, 'So, who new joined your class today?'

'No one,' answered David. He repeated what Mr Fitzpatrick had said. 'Someone will be starting soon, but not quite yet.' The week passed, and the next, but still no one came.

David heard his mum speaking with the other mums after school one evening: they were grumbling and one mum remarked loudly, 'I won't be happy if he comes; he will take up all the teacher's time.' David wasn't sure who they were talking about and asked his mum on the way home.

'I think the new boy joining your class has special needs,' said Mum. David wasn't sure what special needs were. Wasn't everyone special? At least, that was what Mr Fitzpatrick said. Didn't everyone have special needs?

David rushed into class on Monday morning; he had finished all his homework and was keen to show Mr Fitzpatrick. There at Mark's desk stood a new boy, who was tall and thin. He had a faraway look; like he was listening out for something. There was a new adult too, standing next to him; David wondered who it could be. Mr Fitzpatrick entered the classroom and clapped his hands. The class went quiet.

'Good morning everyone,' he said. 'I have some exciting news. We have a new member of the class today. Arthur is joining 4F.'

Arthur. It was an odd name. David had never met anyone called Arthur before, though he had heard of King Arthur, of course.

'We all have special things about us that we will want to share with Arthur today,' continued Mr Fitzpatrick. 'And we will want to learn about him too. I already know that he likes dinosaurs and Peppa Pig. He has a brother and two sisters.' Mr Fitzpatrick suddenly looked ill at ease. 'But,' he said, 'one of the really special things about him is that he doesn't talk. When I say, doesn't, what I mean to say,' said Mr Fitzpatrick, looking rather uncomfortable again, 'is that he can't.'

'Can't talk,' blurted out Candice. 'Really?' The class were quiet. They hadn't met a classmate before who couldn't talk. It was odd. Different. Arthur looked like he hadn't heard anything. He was smiling, looking away. The children didn't know what to say next. There was an awkward silence.

Mr Fitzpatrick came to the rescue. 'Arthur uses an i-Pad to make sentences from pictures and words,' he said. 'We can read these on the computer screen to understand what he is thinking. Anyway,' he added, 'time to get on with our day. Now then, who managed to finish the homework?'

The morning came and went. Arthur had a

lady who worked just with him. She was called Mrs Brock; she was friendly and David liked her. At lunchtime, David and his friends tried to talk to Arthur, but it wasn't easy. He acted like he couldn't hear them and the children didn't know what to do. He wouldn't look at their faces. Arthur ran off and wandered around the edges of the playground. David watched him. He seemed to be very excited. He was making lots of noise, whooping and babbling; and jumping up and down, waving his arms. He seemed happy enough, David thought.

On the way home David told his mum that they had a new boy in class who was different. 'I know,' she said. 'He's autistic; it's a shame.'

Autistic. David hadn't heard that word before. He asked Mum what it meant. But Mum was in a hurry as they were late for David's Beavers that night. They hurried off and were swallowed by the darkness.

Later, after Beavers and tea, David logged on to the computer. 'Dad, how do you spell autistic?' he asked.

'A-U-T-I-S-T-I-C, I think,' mumbled Dad, thinking hard. David typed the word into the search engine and pressed the search key. Lots of information appeared. Some of it David couldn't read; most of it he didn't understand. But one page caught his eye. It said, children aren't autistic, but they do have autism. David wasn't sure what it meant. But it sounded important. He printed it off and put it into his homework diary.

The next day at school, David tried to speak to Arthur again. But it was no good; he just ran away. David ran after him. Arthur ran faster. He was a good runner, better than David.

By the end of the week, David had almost managed to keep up with Arthur as he sped across the playground. Arthur whooped and babbled excitedly but David had no idea what he meant. David went to talk to his friends. He enjoyed chatting and joking with them.

They made each other laugh with their jokes. David wondered what Arthur would say, if he could talk. David remembered when he had first come to the school and knew no one. He remembered how sad he had felt. David stopped chatting and ran to find Arthur again. He chased after him but still couldn't catch him. Arthur was laughing.

For the final activity on Friday afternoon, the children would sit down on the carpet and talk about what they had learnt during the week. That week, Raiyan had learnt to find the area of a shape. Everyone clapped. Aaron had learnt that the Earth orbits the sun. Again, everyone clapped. David clapped along with everyone else. Then Mr Fitzpatrick said, 'What about you David, what have you learnt?' David took a deep breath. He knew what he wanted to say. But dare he say it? He reached for the paper in his reading diary.

'I have learnt that people aren't autistic but that they have autism.' There was a hushed silence. Everyone looked at Arthur. They had heard their mums say that he was autistic. But

Arthur didn't seem to be paying attention; the children had started to think that Arthur didn't listen when others spoke.

'Wow,' exclaimed David's teacher. 'Quite right. But do you know what that means?'

'Not really,' said David, 'but I think it's important.'

'Well,' said Mr Fitzpatrick, 'let me see if I can explain. David tell me something you have learnt about Arthur this week.' That was easy, thought David.

'He's a brilliant runner,' he said, with a smile. 'Far quicker than me.'

'Well,' said Mr Fitzpatrick, 'that's right. Arthur is lots of things – amongst other things, he is a fast runner. He has autism so he finds some things difficult that we find easy. But that doesn't tell us who he is or what he is. The things that he can do, say far more about him than the things he can't. He has autism like you have red hair, David. It's just one of the many things about you, just one. There are many others; things that are more important. When we talk about you we don't start by saying, "Here's David, he's a redhead."'

'Mr Fitzpatrick,' Mrs Brock said, 'Arthur has something to share.' Everyone looked. Arthur had made a sentence with pictures and words on his i-Pad: it read, 'I like school.'

---

On their way home, David's mum, asked about his day and David told her about the conversation he had had with Mr Fitzpatrick. 'Hmm,' said Mum, 'I see. It's like Aunt Lucy. Some people say she is diabetic. But she prefers to say that she has diabetes. Saying she is diabetic doesn't tell us about all the things she can do, just the things she has trouble with. It's a label that can be unhelpful.' A label: David thought he got it but sometimes it was hard to understand the complicated stuff. Maybe when he was older, it would make more sense. David thought some more about Arthur. Arthur was complicated too but David liked him and Arthur liked school. That made David feel good.

'Isn't it wonderful that Arthur comes to your school,' smiled Mum. 'It reminds me a bit of that story in the Bible.'

'Which one?' asked David.

Mum said, 'The one where the friends care for someone so much that they want him to join everyone else at Jesus' side. Their friend is different. Their friend is special. Just like your friend Arthur.' David couldn't think what story Mum meant but later that night he took to his computer again. He searched for 'Jesus special friend' and this is what he read:

*One day when Jesus was teaching, some Pharisees and teachers of the Law were sitting there who had come from every town in Galilee and Judea and from Jerusalem. The power of the Lord was present for Jesus to heal the sick. Some men came carrying a paralysed man on a bed, and they tried to take him in front of Jesus. Because of the crowd, however, they could find no way to take him in. So they carried him up on the roof, made an opening in the tiles, and let him down on his bed into the middle of the group in front of Jesus. When Jesus saw how much faith they had, he said to the man, 'Your sins are forgiven, my friend.'*
(Luke 5:17–20)

The friend in the story was different. He couldn't walk. Just as Arthur was different; he couldn't talk. But like the man in the story, Arthur belonged with everyone else. Not somewhere else and certainly not outside, unable to get in. That made David smile. He realised that he wasn't missing Mark anymore. He had a new best friend.

# Teacher's Notes
# Katherine's Story

## Background
I wrote this story when one of my teachers, who had been promoted within the school, received an anonymous note saying she was only successful because she was 'best mates with the Headteacher'. She was devastated. We had to handle matters very carefully in school. She was advised to contact her professional association, who said it was a common occurrence – unsigned, nasty mail, they said, was on the increase – but that it was actually an offence in law. We never found out who sent the note but, at her insistence, we addressed it publicly within the team; she was heartened by the messages of support that she received from colleagues. Nevertheless, the note left her feeling extremely distressed; she would be sick before work and her confidence was dented.

## General theme
How do people react to others successes? Some people are pleased for others; others are jealous – in their mind, the success that they see others enjoying, should be theirs.

## What do Christians believe?
Christians believe that all good things come from God. As such, they should not be jealous of others' achievements. Jealousy is a sin. It means that we are focussed upon ourselves rather than God. We should try to be more like Jesus. Love is what matters: 'Love is patient, love is kind.' (1 Corinthians 13:4)

We are all asked to be 'modest' and not to lord it over others, as the Bible says the Scribes and Pharisees did.

## Prayer
*Heavenly Father, help us when we have feelings of jealousy in our hearts. May we remember to share in the joy of others, not envy it. Give us loving hearts always.*

## The story
Who do the children think sent the note; there is a suggestion. Can they be sure?
What would they have done?
Do they see Katherine as a victim, or is she a heroine?

## PSMC links
- With modern social media, there are lots of ways of sending someone unkind messages: texts or emails, and of course some people like to rely upon what is called a poison pen letter.
- Is this a form of bullying?
- Why do some people like to put others down? What makes them act in this way?
- What would you say to a bully? How could you make them change their ways?

© Gary Nott and Brilliant Publications Limited
*This page may be photocopied for use by the purchasing institution only.*

Modern Christian Assembly Stories

# Katherine's Story

Katherine was really excited when her teacher announced that a Head Girl was going to be appointed in Year 6 at the end of the autumn term. She had worked hard these past few months and she knew her family were counting on her to do well at school, so she carefully planned out all that she would have to do to earn the job.

She spoke to her cousin, who was older than her, for some advice. 'Always work hard and find out as much as you can about what the job involves,' she was told.

Katherine decided to speak to her teacher, Mrs Kelly, to ask her what the job would be about. Speaking with Mrs Kelly was easy. Katherine really liked her and they had got on well from the first moment that they had met. Mrs Kelly outlined what the job would entail: 'You must be a good listener,' she said. 'You must work hard. You must have great ideas. And finally, you must always be kind to the other students.'

Katherine sighed. It was a tall order. She talked it over with Mum, who said, 'You're a great listener. Remember when Nanny was depressed, very sad, and you sat with her. You listened to her for the whole wet, dark afternoon in November and she felt better afterwards.'

This was true.

'You always work hard,' added Mum. 'Remember those weeks before your Year 5 summer tests, when you did a little bit extra every night. It wasn't always what you wanted to do, but you did it.'

'But', sighed Katherine, 'you have to have great ideas.'

'Katherine,' said Mum, 'you have tremendous ideas. Who thought of us sponsoring a child abroad, when their family didn't have enough money to send him to school? You! And, who suggested to all our neighbours that we have a street party for the Royal Jubilee. You!'

It was true, thought Katherine; she had done these things. 'But,' she said, 'you have to be kind to everyone. Do you think I am?'

'I do, but why not ask your friends to see what they think?' her mum suggested.

Katherine texted Lucy. 'Do you think I am kind?' she wrote.

'Sure you are,' bleeped the reply on her phone, just seconds later. 'Remember who cheered me up when we lost our cat? You.'

She emailed Billy. 'Do you think I am kind?' she typed.

'You are the kindest person, I know,' pinged back the response. 'Remember the time when I couldn't do my homework? And I got into a right state? You helped me. And I got all the sums right!'

Katherine felt better. But what would Sally think? Sally was a girl in Katherine's class who Katherine thought didn't like her much. She never seemed to smile at Katherine, or appear friendly to her. Katherine thought she was kind to Sally. But what did Sally think?

After much thought, Katherine decided to go for the job of Head Girl. There were to be interviews and she had to write a letter of application, where she had to say why she would be the right person for the role.

The day of the interview came.

Katherine was nervous.

Mum was nervous.

Even Nanny, who now lived in Australia, was nervous.

Mr Smith, the Headteacher, was doing the interviews, alongside Mrs Kelly. Mrs Kelly smiled at Katherine as she walked into the

# Katherine's Story

## Bullying

Headteacher's office. Katherine sat down and her interview began. It seemed like a lifetime, but after 15 minutes of answering hard questions like – 'What would you do if someone was in trouble because they had done something wrong?' – the interview was over. Katherine breathed a sigh of relief.

At the end of the day, there was a special assembly. First it was announced that David Kerrigrew had been appointed Head Boy. Everyone clapped, David beamed. Then Mr Smith announced, 'After some tough interviews, our Head Girl is ... Katherine Davies.'

---

In the days that followed, Katherine was happier than she had ever been. So was her mum, and Nanny in Australia was keen to tell all her friends of how proud she was of Katherine. On Friday, just as they were getting ready to go home, Katherine went to her tray to collect her things. There, on top of her reading book, was an envelope. A brown envelope. It was sealed. There was nothing on the front. Katherine took the envelope back to her desk and opened it. She stopped dead in her tracks. For what she read made her heart stop and her spirits plummet.

The letter inside simply said:

> You are only Head Girl because you are Mrs Kelly's best friend!

It wasn't signed. Katherine burst into tears. She felt foolish afterwards. Everyone noticed. Mrs Kelly tried to be kind, but it was no use. Katherine was upset beyond words. Who had sent the letter? Was that what people really thought? Her friends? The worst thing was that she didn't know who had written the note. She looked up at Peter; it couldn't have been him. No, surely not. Then she saw Lucy. No, Lucy wouldn't do such a thing.

It was a long walk home.

Mum was kind as she always was.' Look,' she said, 'in life there are people who don't find it easy to enjoy other people's successes. When something good happens to someone else and not to them, they find it hard to cope. Often, they don't like themselves feeling this way but they can't seem to help it, even when they try.'

Mum continued, 'What did you say to Mr Smith and Mrs Kelly when they asked you what would you do if someone had done something wrong?'

Katherine thought hard, past her tears.

'I said I would tell them I was disappointed but that I would forgive them,' said Katherine.

'Exactly,' said Mum. 'So, as hard as it is, you must do that now.'

When she went to bed that night, Katherine found the Bible on her pillow opened at a page. Mum had put it there. This is what she read:

> *At once Jesus made his disciples get into the boat and go ahead of him to Bethsaida, on the other side of the lake, while he sent the crowd away. After saying goodbye to the people, he went away to a hill to pray. When evening came, the boat was in the middle of the lake, while Jesus was alone on land. He saw that his disciples were straining at the oars, because they were rowing against the wind; so some time between three and six o'clock in the morning he came to them, walking on the water. He*

© Gary Nott and Brilliant Publications Limited
*This page may be photocopied for use by the purchasing institution only.*

*was going to pass them by, but they saw him walking on the water. 'It's a ghost!' they thought, and screamed. They were all terrified when they saw him.*

*Jesus spoke to them at once. 'Courage!' he said. 'It is I. Don't be afraid!'*
(Mark 6:45–50)

Katherine felt better at once. With the Lord by her side she would have the courage to keep going and at the same time she would have the strength to forgive the person who had been so mean to her. With God's help, she would not be afraid!

# Teacher's Notes
# Joshua's Story

## Background
I once took a call from a Pupil Referral Unit (PRU), asking me to admit a child who had displayed challenging behaviour in his previous mainstream school. He was, I was told, ready to return to a 'normal' school. I had taken calls like this before and I was wary. I asked what he had done to warrant exclusion and being sent to a unit for children with behavioural issues. He had, said the head of the PRU, started a fire in his previous school. My blood ran cold. What would my governors say? What would the parents say, if they got wind of it? I prevaricated. I had learnt that if I stalled for long enough, the authorities would eventually tire of the obstacles I was putting in place and send the child elsewhere. The boy never did come to my school. It was not my finest hour. Here was someone needing a second chance and I wasn't prepared to give it.

## General theme
Second chances! Some experts say that the best indicator of future behaviour is past behaviour. This can be a counsel of despair. Most of us have made at least one serious mistake in the past – something we need to forget. Without that second chance, our lives may well have turned out differently.

## What do Christians believe?
The Christian faith is based on second, third and fourth chances. God's mercy is deep. Lots of people in the Bible are given second chances: Joshua, Jonah, David, to name a few. Is there ever an end to God's mercy? No. Eventually, if we have been called to forgive someone over and over and there is seemingly no chance of change, then we have to move on. Do you have to be sorry to merit a second chance or is it acceptable to make mistakes in life?

## Prayer
*Forgiving Father, you teach us that there is no limit to the number of chances we get. You will always forgive those who are truly sorry and turn to you. Help us to treat other people in this way too. When we have been wronged, give us the grace to accept the apology given to us and reach out with the hand of friendship.*

## The story
Should Joshua have known that no good could come of taking matches to school? Was he unlucky? Were there bits in his story that made the children feel sorry for him? Can the children agree on what they were?

## PSMC links
- In life, can we identify the wrong choices that people make? Is it so easy to spot them when it is us who are faced with the choice? Did Joshua deserve his second chance?
- Can the children share a mistake that they made in the past? Were they found out and what happened then? Have they ever been given a second chance? Did they make the most of it? Does someone who constantly makes mistakes and doesn't appear to learn from them deserve further chances?

© Gary Nott and Brilliant Publications Limited
*This page may be photocopied for use by the purchasing institution only.*

# Joshua's Story

Fire! He had been fascinated with it from a long time back. He would sit and watch his dad set light to rubbish at the bottom of the garden. 'Come back Joshua!' his father would say. 'Don't go too close!'

'Build it higher, Dad,' he would implore. And, he would sit and watch as the flames danced ever higher, sparks flying, spitting, crackling, the smell pungent; the smoke billowing into the cold dark night and lighting up the garden; the heat prickling his face and arms – it made him feel alive, excited.

Fire. He loved it and was fascinated by it.

They travelled around a lot due to Dad's job. Never in a place for more than a year; in four years, he had been to as many schools. He found it difficult to make friends, for he wouldn't be staying long, he knew that. What was the point in 'getting in' with someone? He found lessons hard. He was not naturally bright and the teachers despaired when they saw how much he had travelled. They all had different ways of working. Just as he got used to things, they would be off again, to a different rented home. Then he came to Beechwood. The kids there looked down their noses at him, thought he was rough. The teachers were no better, just thought he was stupid – not capable of anything.

He had seen the box of matches on the table one evening, after tea. Mum usually kept them out of reach. But there they were, oddly out of place. He didn't have time to think, just to act. He took the box and stuffed it into his pocket. Later, while he was watching TV, Mum came in and said, 'Did you see the matches? I need them to make a cup of tea.'

'No,' he lied.

'Dad must have taken them when he went to work,' she complained. 'Bother, I'll need to nip out to buy some more.' When the door slammed, he took the matches out of his pocket. He was bubbling over with excitement. He had matches. No one knew, just him. He took one out and struck it against the blue grit strip. It lit with a hiss and he watched it burn bright. He let it burn down to his fingers, and then just before it would burn him, he quickly blew it out. That was the start. The start of his 'bad time': a time when he would push those around him to the edge. He stuffed the matches in an old shoebox and hid it under his bed, behind some toys. Mum didn't go there, so they would be safe.

The next day at school, Miss Grimes was giving him a hard time. He couldn't see what she meant when she showed the class how to find the area of a compound shape. He didn't even know what a compound shape was. She was not amused.

'We have already looked at this,' she said, 'you're not keeping up. You don't concentrate. How am I meant to teach you if you won't concentrate?'

She kept him in, made him sharpen pencils. The other kids laughed. He didn't like them – not any of them. He felt alone, different. That afternoon the teacher asked to see his mum. Moan, moan, moan – would she never stop? Then it was Mum's turn, she told him that she felt let down. She knew it hadn't been easy for him – what with all the moving – but he had to try harder.

That night, he got the matches out of the shoebox. He slept with them under his pillow. In the morning, Mum called for him to hurry up and get ready for school. He turned to look back at his room to check he had his homework. Then he saw the matches – he didn't have time to hide them under the bed

*Modern Christian Assembly Stories*

**16**

© Gary Nott and Brilliant Publications Limited

*This page may be photocopied for use by the purchasing institution only.*

# Joshua's Story — Second chances

again, so he put them in his pocket and skipped down the stairs.

Mum ruffled his hair as he went into school. He didn't like it when she did that. The other kids would see and he had a difficult enough time with them as it was.

He went into class. Miss Grimes was standing at the front of the class. As soon as she spotted him, she was on his case. 'I hope you have completed your homework Joshua Calderdale,' she barked.

Later that morning, he couldn't get the maths again. She shouted at him. He started to cry, 'You're always on at me!' he choked, in temper.

'Don't take that tone with me,' she retorted. 'Go to the toilets and compose yourself. Then come back with an apology.'

He slipped out.

He was miserable.

Nothing was going right. He hated this school – Miss Grimes and the other kids.

He felt in his pocket for a tissue. His fingers felt something unexpected: the box of matches. He had forgotten they were there. He took them out and found a match. Then, without thinking too hard about it, he struck it. He let it burn down to his fingers. Ouch! It hurt but he almost enjoyed the sensation of pain, as it took his mind off his upset. He instinctively let go of the lit match and it fell into the waste-paper basket. He looked down. He realised that tissues sitting there had caught alight. He stood staring at them, fascinated. Suddenly the flames caught the wooden panelling underneath the basins, blistering the paint; taking hold gradually but insistently. He panicked. Things were out of control. This wasn't a fire like Dad made. It was different – wild! He hurried for the door. Where to go? Back to the classroom? No! He had to tell someone what he had just left behind. He sped towards Mrs Bishop's office. She was stood there talking to her secretary. 'Fire!' he blurted. 'There's a fire.' She looked at him, at his wide eyed stare, and she just knew. She strode

© Gary Nott and Brilliant Publications Limited
*This page may be photocopied for use by the purchasing institution only.*

Modern Christian Assembly Stories

towards the fire call point and smashed it. All of a sudden an ear-piercing shattering alarm began to wail and children from all corners of the school filed out into the playground. There was a hushed chatter as the children swarmed out through the doors. A fire drill, they had one each term; nothing different about that, just routine. Mrs Bishop would announce it had gone smoothly, job done! Except – there was something different about this drill because there they were, standing around waiting and not filing back inside.

The children began to chatter, some more loudly. The klaxon persisted.

Then on the breeze came the sound of a siren. Faint at first, then stronger, closer – sounding like it was closing in on them. Two fire engines swept into the playground. Lights flashing, hoses unfurling, firefighters running towards the toilet block.

All the while, Joshua stood watching: his small world, like the hoses, unravelling, spiralling around on the playground tarmac.

He stood separate, apart from everyone else. The fire crews rushed into the toilet block where Joshua could see flames dancing at the windows. Then as quickly as it had started, it seemed to be over. The firefighters spewed out on to the playground, shouting to one another. 'Job done,' as Mrs Bishop would have said.

The Headteacher turned, she looked all at once relieved and angry. Her eyes rested on Joshua. His number was up!

___

Joshua was sent to a special school for problem children. The funny thing was that he liked being there, in the Pupil Referral Unit – the PRU, as it was called.

The teachers were kind to him, helped him with his reading. For the first time in ages, he felt like he belonged. He was making progress – slowly but surely. Some of the other kids' behaviour was shocking; they were naughty – like, really naughty. They would swear and spit, punch and kick. Joshua was the model student: polite and hard-working.

Then Mr Stairns thought he was ready, ready to go back to a normal school. He made some calls.

The first Headteacher he spoke to said 'No.' How did he know that Joshua wouldn't set fire to his school? 'The best indicator,' he said, 'of future behaviour was past behaviour,' whatever that meant. The second Head said 'No.'

The third didn't even return the call. Mr Stairns despaired. Joshua didn't belong in a special unit. He wasn't a bad lad. He had made one mistake; he couldn't go on paying for it forever. Someone would have to give him a chance, a new start.

Joshua prayed. He prayed like he had never prayed before. He wanted to stay at the PRU. He felt like he belonged – that he was finally somewhere where he wasn't bottom of the pile.

Then the call came. Mrs Thomas of Cherry Trees would take him.

Mr Stairns told him that he would feel nervous – that was natural. That he was going somewhere different. He told him he was to take courage. Joshua was looking past Mr Stairns to the board behind his desk. There were phrases writ large: 'You are the author of your own life story!' he read. Then he saw a reference to a Bible passage; it said simply:

*The Lord's unfailing love and mercy still continue; Fresh as the morning, as sure as the sunrise.* (Lamentations 3:22–23)

All at once he felt better. He knew he was ready for the challenge. It was a fresh start. Like the phoenix that rose from the fire, he would start again. He was moving on – stronger!

# Teacher's Notes
# Mr Ripple's Story

## Background
I have never been brave enough to do a 'Pets' Assembly' but I did have a colleague once who did – it was chaos; the old adage never work with children or animals never seemed more apt than on that morning! I did, however, respect her greatly for taking a risk. I have always preferred to play it safe.

## General themes
Taking a risk. God's wonderful kingdom and the variety of pets that people possess.

## What do Christians believe?
The Bible encourages us to take risks. We read the parable of the man going on a journey, who called his servants and entrusted his property to them. To one he gave five talents, to another two, to another one, to each according to his ability. Then he went away. He who had received the five talents went at once and traded with them, and he made five talents more. So also he who had the two talents made two talents more. But he who had received the one talent went and dug in the ground and hid his master's money.

God so cared for the animals on his Earth that he instructed Noah to take two of each creature into the Ark with him. Nevertheless, animals are used and abused by mankind and this is a source of great sadness to Christians.

## Prayer
*Father, we thank you for the wonderful creatures that share this planet with us. May we live in a way that does not endanger their existence. May we remember and carry out our responsibility to take care of them. We thank you especially for the pets we have now or had in the past – for the joy and love we share and the memories we have of them.*

## The story
Mr Ripple has the best of intentions. But, to his dismay, the assembly began to unravel in front of his eyes. Not to worry, the children greatly enjoyed it. He was rewarded for taking a risk and doing something a little bit different. Life is like that sometimes: it can surprise us.

## PSMC links
- How do we show that we love animals? For example: taking care of our pets; sponsoring/ adopting animals in the wild; and visiting zoos.
- Why do some people mistreat animals?
- Why is it difficult to take a risk?

© Gary Nott and Brilliant Publications Limited
*This page may be photocopied for use by the purchasing institution only.*

# Mr Ripple's Story

Mr Ripple, Jaeda's teacher, wore jumpers that were too tight for him. A burly man with an already red face, he always looked fit to burst – 'overexcited', Jaeda's mum called it. The children were enjoying their first term with him: Mr Ripple made lessons fun. As the weeks wore on, they got used to his ways and he to theirs. Autumn turned to winter, winter to spring. Easter came and with it some hot weather. Mums and Dads said they had never known an April so warm. The class knew their teacher well by then but he was about to prove that he still had the ability to surprise them. During the year, they had listened to and watched a number of class assemblies. Some they enjoyed; others they didn't. As they approached the end of the spring term, it was their turn. That is when Mr Ripple chose to reveal a surprise: their assembly was to be different. They had been studying God's wonderful creation in RE. Mr Ripple called them together one afternoon on the carpet, and explained that he would like them to present God's wonderful kingdom of animals to the rest of the school. They were all to bring their pets in to show, and if they didn't have a pet, now was the time to buy one or borrow one. 'Really,' questioned George; 'bring our pets into school?'

'Yes,' nodded Mr Ripple, 'the more the merrier.'

'Does Mr French know?' asked Harry. Mr French, the Headteacher, was not a man to get overexcited.

'Yes, he does,' replied Mr Ripple, 'and, as Larry would say, "he's cool with it."'

Larry, the difficult child of class 4R, was impressed. Maybe Mr French wasn't so bad after all.

There was much chatter amongst the class in the coming days. They each had to prepare a short piece to read to the school explaining why their pet was special to them. Even the boys, who didn't generally like writing, were keen to type up something – albeit short. Mollie Davies had cried. She didn't own a pet and her parents had said they had no intention of buying one just for a school assembly. Mr Ripple told her not to worry. He would be bringing his pets in on the day, so she could talk about one of them. Mr Ripple had a ferret, a gerbil and a chinchilla. Mollie didn't know what a ferret was, or a chinchilla, so she decided to write about gerbils.

They had a rehearsal the day before. They each brought in a cuddly toy to represent their pet. The rehearsal went well. Mr Ripple was pleased and so were Class 4R.

The next day dawned hot again. Many of the children came into school in short sleeves and shorts. They came armed with their pets. There was a great buzz in the playground as the other children saw what was going on: dogs on leads; cats in carrying cases; fish in tanks; hamsters in cages; and more. Duncan had brought his auntie's goat whilst Sally Parker had outdone everyone for she had brought her pony. They all filed directly into the hall as Mr Ripple said there wasn't enough room in the classroom for them.

What a noise: barking, meowing and, not forgetting, neighing!

The children took their seats at the front of the Hall. Mr Dibbs, the caretaker had opened the doors and windows to cool things down. One by one, the classes marched in and the parents took their seats at the back of the Hall. They were ready.

Mr Ripple welcomed the children and parents. It was an assembly, he said, to celebrate the wonderful world of God's

**Modern Christian Assembly Stories**

creatures.

Mollie started. She was talking about Mr Ripple's gerbil. His name was Percy. She got him out of his cage; Mr Ripple showed her how. She held him tightly. Her hands were sticky and she was nervous. Percy may have sensed that she wasn't used to handling gerbils. He nibbled her finger, lightly. She let him go in fright and he fell down to the floor and made a beeline for the edge of the hall. He scurried along, then quickly climbed up the apparatus. The watching classes were startled. Was that meant to have happened? They thought not.

Mr Ripple hopped from one foot to the next. 'Would you like to continue?' he said eventually to Mark, who had brought his Alsatian to school. Mark knew all about his dog. He loved him and could talk at length about him. Troy, the Alsatian just sat obediently, glancing from Mark to the audience and back again. This was better, thought Mr Ripple. He glanced up. Percy was still sitting on the apparatus. How was he to get him down? He couldn't worry about that at the moment; he would have to get through the assembly. Why, oh why, had he ever let Mollie take Percy out of the cage?

Next up was Jimmy who was talking about his pet cockroaches. He had two. He knew them apart, he said, because of their different colourings. He wanted an unusual pet and his dad had suggested roaches. They ate all sorts of leftovers and would run about on his hands and arms.

'Should I get them out?' he asked, opening the tank.

'No,' said Mr Ripple firmly. 'Better not. Leave them be.'

They moved on. Flossie was talking about her fish. They were all different colours – fantails and guppies. She explained that one day, one had jumped out and it was only by chance that her mum had spotted it out of the tank, fighting for air.

Suddenly Mark leapt up with a scream. Startled, Troy began to bark. Mark was flicking at his leg, frantically – hopping up and down.

'A cockroach,' he screeched, ' it's on me.' He slammed his foot down with a thud. There was a crunching sound. He had squashed one of Jimmy's roaches under foot. The watching children didn't know what to do. Some, who realised what had happened, began to groan and laugh. Others were just wondering why Mark had jumped up and started to do a war dance. They didn't get that he had killed one of Jimmy's roaches. Mr Ripple did. He sighed.

Jimmy wailed, 'You've killed him! That was Freddy!'

Mr Ripple ushered Jimmy off the stage, back towards Mrs Dobbs, the Learning Assistant, who put her arms round him and gave him a comforting squeeze. There was suddenly the sound of water pouring onto the floor, as if it were gushing from a broken pipe. It was Sally's horse, standing legs apart; it was peeing. The children began to laugh. Mrs Philips, who was sitting nearby got the children up and moved them away from the pool of pee that had started to form on the hall floor. Mr French moaned loudly. Mr Ripple glanced up. Out of the corner of his eye, he spied Duncan's goat; it was eating Dianne Jenkin's cardigan, which was draped across the back of her chair. Diane had yet to notice.

It had seemed like such a good idea for an assembly. Fun, Mr Ripple had thought. He looked up to the heavens and mouthed a little prayer. Opening his eyes, he was just in time to see Percy scurry under the door into the neighbouring kitchen. He heard the cook shriek. What a day!

The assembled children, who had been watching, burst into applause. It had been the most enjoyable assembly they had seen for some time. They had been sitting up, straining to see all that was happening. Mark's Alsatian began to bark again when he heard the children clapping for it had frightened him. Giving Mark the slip, he bolted for the open door that led to the playground. Mark was in hot pursuit. It didn't seem to matter, anymore.

'To finish,' said Mr Ripple, 'we have a short reading from the Bible about God's marvellous kingdom.'

Petra Blake read:

*God looked at everything he had made, and he was very pleased. (Genesis 1:31)*

Jaeda's mum told her that she thought it was a brilliant assembly. 'Very entertaining,' she said. 'And Mr Ripple's jumper,' she added, 'had never looked tighter.'

# Teacher's Notes
# Evan's Story

## Background
I once had a child develop Tourette's syndrome. It was painful to see. But what amazed me was how good the other children were about it. They didn't laugh or make a fuss. They seemed to realise just how uncomfortable it was for the boy involved. OFSTED inspections have come to loom large over schools: teachers worry about something going wrong. The incident in this story would be every teacher's worst nightmare: a child swearing during a lesson observation!

## General theme
How do we react when others face a difficulty which, on the surface, might be quite amusing? Are we compassionate or are we superficial, laughing along with the others?

## What do Christians believe?
Christians believe that we should always react to the misfortunes of others with kindness. Jesus took pity on those who were different, lost or unwell. He never turned away from anyone in need.

## Prayer
*Lord Jesus, through the example of your earthly life, you taught us how to live. May we open our eyes to those around us who are in need – they may be in need of our friendship, our time, our love, our compassion. We thank you for your unending love that never fails.*

## The story
How did the children in the story react to Evan?
Why did the inspector focus upon them, not Evan?

## PSMC links
- Tourette's syndrome is a condition that affects a small number of children and adults. Not all swear, but some do.
- It is hard to imagine a condition that would make children want to laugh more than this one. The shock factor would be enormous! But children can be overwhelmingly kind and resist the urge to laugh at others' afflictions. Strangers, young or old, are not always as generous.

# Evan's Story

Class 6G were a lively bunch: full of characters, they had a mischievous sense of fun. Their teacher Mr Morris suffered in silence. A calm man, he tried not to let things get to him. And, mostly, he succeeded. That said, Jamie and his friends had been known to push him close to the edge. But Mr Morris always seemed in control. Until, that was, the term when Evan went what Lucy Jane called 'weird'.

Mr and Mrs Peters, Evan's parents had been the first to notice, obviously. Evan was beginning to twitch. All would be normal. He'd be chatting about something and then he would do it: just twitch, like a shiver had run across him or he had been hit with a small charge of electricity. He told his parents he couldn't help it: that he knew he was going to do it, but couldn't stop himself.

Evan was sent to a paediatrician (a doctor who specialises in children). He was diagnosed with Tourette's syndrome. It was a long word, which Evan couldn't say properly; he struggled to say 'paediatrician' too.

The paediatrician explained that it was like having an itch that had to be scratched. 'You don't,' he said, 'want to twitch, because you know people don't do that – but that's exactly what makes you do it. You can't resist the urge to do something that people just don't do.'

'Will he get better?' asked his parents, naturally more than a little concerned.

'Probably not,' said the paediatrician. 'It is not caused by feeling anxious, but it may well get worse when Evan is feeling tense or upset about something. He may well be able to stop for a while, but he won't be able to keep it up. It's too tiring. He'll end up giving in. If it gets worse, we can think about giving him some medicine to help. But for the time being, let's see how it goes.' And then, when Evan was safely out of earshot, he added (rather unhelpfully), 'it could be worse.'

Evan's parents were upset but they didn't let Evan see that.

Worse, how could it be worse?

His parents were worried about how the kids at school would react. Some laughed, to begin with. It was odd, different. Was Evan mucking about? Then they realised he wasn't. Some still laughed. But once Mr Morris had explained to them that this was something Evan could not control, they got over it. It wasn't funny for Evan – anything but.

However, other people that saw, who didn't know him, were less kind. They would point and stare.

For a while it continued as it had been – twitches, worse when he was stressed.

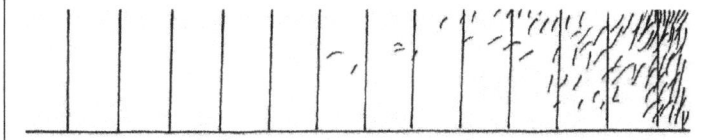

Then one day he started to shrug his shoulders. At first, just once or twice. Was this something new? Evan's parents hoped that they were imagining it but no, he had started to shrug his shoulders too.

His parents took him to see a different paediatrician. He was softer, less abrupt. They preferred him.

The paediatrician explained that Evan might do other things, especially when stressed.

He prescribed some medicine that might help but it wouldn't take the problem away. They would all have to live with it.

'We have to just get on with it,' said Dad. 'What choice do we have?'

The first time that Evan barked in assembly, the other children all turned round to see who was playing the fool. It was Evan. He was twitching. Yes, he had barked; he did it again. Like a small dog. Mrs David continued with her story; she just kept on talking. It was as if someone had told her to expect this. They couldn't have? Could they?

Some of the other kids had laughed. It was funny. Someone barking in assembly: like someone farting, but even funnier. But it was Evan. Most of the kids realised that it wasn't funny. It was Evan, their friend: a boy who couldn't help it. It wasn't funny at all.

Things continued for a while, in much the same way. Twitches, shrugs, the odd bark. The kids were getting used to it.

'Funny how kids adapt,' remarked Evan's mum, 'much better than we adults.'

Evan didn't understand what she meant. The kids at school accepted him for what he was but he could tell he made the adults there feel uncomfortable. Some didn't know how to handle it; some even told him to sit still.

Then something happened, something unexpected. The school had a telephone call to say that they were going to have an OFSTED inspection. Mrs David called the whole school into the hall in the afternoon to say that the inspectors would be with them for two days. She told the children that they should act as they normally would; that she expected everyone to be on best behaviour. It was important.

That night, Evan took home a letter informing his parents that there was going to be an inspection.

'Well,' said his Dad, 'just remember Evan, they are coming to look at the teachers, not you.'

Evan's parents were worried. They knew he didn't do well when he was worried or anxious. They thought about not sending him in. They thought hard, prayed hard. It didn't seem right to shut their son away. They were proud of him. Proud of all the things he could do but, most importantly, they were proud of the way he dealt with his Tourette's syndrome. Proud that he kept going every day; that he didn't give in, even when the going was tough. Their son, they proudly told their friends, had a disability. And he got on with it, despite that disability. It wouldn't beat him.

The teachers were on edge. This, the children sensed, was important. There were three inspectors. They arrived in the playground when the children were filing into class. Mr Morris explained that they would spend some time with Mrs David before visiting classrooms.

The children were nervous.

Would an inspector come to their class?

Mr Morris had planned an exciting morning.

He was full of praise and seemed to be pumped. He was full of enthusiastic smiles and kept saying 'Well done.'

Break time came. The children whooped as they ran around the playground.

Then, when they were lining up, one of the inspectors suddenly appeared and tagged along with them as they entered class.

The children sat down. They wanted to do their best for Mr Morris as they were fond of him. He tried hard and he cared. They had had teachers who didn't; they knew the difference.

He spent a few minutes in discussion with the inspector, nodding in Evan's direction.

Mr Morris started the maths lesson. It was co-ordinates. They had done it before and were able to answer the questions easily. Then Mr Morris threw in something new, something they had not met before.

Then Evan said it. In a loud voice he moaned, 'Why do we have to do this again? It's effing boring.'

Which strictly wasn't true. They had never done this before.

The class fell silent – they knew that Evan had crossed a line.

He twitched; shrugged his shoulders; and, flexed his jaw.

What would Mr Morris do? He suddenly looked nervous.

But before he had time to say anything, Evan opened his mouth again. The class waited for him to speak. 'If I had wanted to do this, I would have brought some effing earplugs with me,' he blurted out.

No one knew what to do.

Jamie Duggan began to laugh; Jack and Oliver joined in.

Evan didn't look bothered.

He twitched.

Did Mr Morris twitch?

'Okay, class,' he said, 'back to work. Jamie, get a grip!' Jamie couldn't stop laughing. He was in stitches.

The rest of the class were superb. They just carried on as if nothing had happened. Mr Morris relaxed. The inspector just sat, stony faced. He didn't look surprised that Evan had said what he had; neither did he look pleased. He was giving nothing away. But he seemed to be looking at them, the class, rather than Evan, which was odd, because they hadn't been the ones to swear.

The bell went.

The children put their things away.

Jamie was still laughing but to himself, quietly.

The next day Mr Morris called the whole class together. He said people with Tourette's syndrome sometimes swear. They don't mean to; they know you aren't meant to; they just can't resist the urge to say something inappropriate. He looked at their blank faces. It was all a little odd.

The inspector, he said, had been pleased with what he saw. There were children with Tourette's syndrome. The important thing was that the class showed they cared for Evan, took care of him. That, said the inspector, was the important thing. He had called it, said Mr Morris, 'a life lesson'.

So impressed had the inspector been that he left something for Mr Morris to read the class. This is what he read:

*You are the people of God; he loved you and chose you for his own. So then, you must clothe yourselves with compassion, kindness, humility, gentleness and patience. Be tolerant with one another … . (Colossians 3:12–13)*

The children weren't sure what the inspector was trying to say. 'I think,' said Mr Morris, 'he's trying to say that we are all wonderful as we are. That includes Evan, and anyone else who has a disability.'

Evan opened his mouth, ready to say something. Mr Morris held his breath. Then Evan closed his mouth. The class smiled.

# Teacher's Notes
# Tom's Story

## Background
Tom was my school's photographer for over 20 years. A lovely man, fond of jokes, he confided in me that he had cuffed an irritating boy one day on a shoot. He was full of remorse but he could not turn the clock back. The Headteacher of the school skilfully managed the situation and Tom emerged unscathed – well relatively, for there were some sleepless nights!

## General theme
We all make mistakes – especially in the heat of the moment. To err is human, to forgive, divine.

## What do Christians believe?
There but for the grace of God, go I. We all get things wrong from time to time. Jesus died so that our sins might be forgiven. He even forgave the friend and follower who betrayed him, Judas. The Christian message is based on forgiveness.

## Prayer
*Lord, it sometimes feels like we can do nothing right. It sometimes feels like the world is against us. When we have been blamed for something we didn't do or say; when someone loses their temper with us for no good reason. But however we are feeling, you are with us always. We turn to you in good times, and in bad and are assured of your never ending love.*

## The story
Why had Tom acted in such a way that day?
Do the children have sympathy with Tom or the boy? Can they explain their choice?
Why had Tom's wife been annoyed with him?
Who needs to forgive Tom in this story? Who most of all?
Why was Tom retiring?

## PSMC links
- We all make mistakes – some small, some large.
- We all look for forgiveness. Do we always find it?
- Can any of the children think of a time when they haven't felt as if they have been forgiven?

# Tom's Story

Tom had been a school photographer for over 20 years. A jolly man, he could always coax a smile from the child sitting expectantly in front of him. He liked children and they, in turn, warmed to him. He enjoyed nothing more than sharing a joke with the Headteacher, once the shots had all been taken. He loved his jokes. Tom was a popular figure: everyone liked him.

For a while, life had been getting tougher. He had arthritis in his hands; it made them swollen, lumpy. It was uncomfortable holding the camera because his fingers didn't seem to want to do what was needed. He had been thinking of calling it a day, retiring. He would be sad to go, for he enjoyed what he did; he would miss the children, their beaming smiles.

Tom had always enjoyed coming to St Joseph's. The teachers were friendly and worked hard; he could see that. But the children were challenging, always pushing at the edges. They smiled for Tom, but they fidgeted and played about when waiting to have their picture taken. Why couldn't the teachers keep them in order?

When he thought back to that day, it had seemed like any other. He had loaded the car up with his equipment, listened to the radio on the way to the school. True his hands were particularly painful for the weather was cold, it being a December day; cold and heat both made his hands worse – it was the same for anyone with arthritis. The doctor had given him medication and it helped a little, just a little. He remembered that he hadn't taken his medication that day; he had been in a hurry because he had woken late.

Children, thought Tom, as the teachers

*Modern Christian Assembly Stories*

© Gary Nott and Brilliant Publications Limited

*This page may be photocopied for use by the purchasing institution only.*

brought their classes in turn into the hall for their photo, they had changed. He was 'old school'. When he had first started out in this job, the boys and girls had been more polite – better behaved. This year at St Joseph's the children seemed to be worse than he remembered. Mr Jenkins, who Tom had known for many years, was struggling to get his class quiet. Two boys were fighting at the back of the line; Mr Jenkins had to pull them apart. It all seemed pretty hairy to Tom. One of the lads seemed particularly cheeky – loud and leery. When it came to the boy's turn in front of the camera, he played the fool to his watching friends. He refused to sit round and face the camera properly. Then he pulled a face just as Tom pressed the camera button. Tom would have to retake the boy's photo.

As he rose from the chair, the boy looked at Tom and mouthed 'Loser!' Tom saw red. Instinctively, he reached out and cuffed the boy round the ear.

'You can't do that,' cried the boy. 'He hit me, you all saw it. You're in for it, old man.'

Tom was shaken. The kid had asked for it. But, he knew enough about schools to know that he had just made a serious mistake. You couldn't hit kids, even a simple cuff around the ear. Things weren't like they had been when Tom had been a boy himself.

Mr Jenkins sped over. 'Tom,' he said, 'I think we had better see Mrs Jacobs. I'll get Mr Peters to watch my class.'

Once inside the Headteacher's office, Tom cut a forlorn figure. 'Tom,' sighed Mrs Jacobs, 'whatever were you thinking of?'

'I don't know,' he stumbled,' I just saw red – the kid was being difficult. I'm sorry'.

'Go home Tom,' she said, 'I have a difficult conversation to have with the boy's mother.'

Tom packed up his equipment. He desperately wanted to get out. He felt as if everyone at the school was watching him, pointing at him, talking about him. His hands were hurting. He looked at them and realised he was shaking. The day had darkened. He felt sick to his stomach.

Driving home, he couldn't believe he had been so stupid. It had all happened so quickly. How he would love to have that time back. But he couldn't go back – there was no rewind button on life.

He unpacked the car and went into an empty house. His wife was out shopping. What would she say? She would struggle to believe that he had been so stupid.

He poured himself a stiff drink and sat down by the phone. It was not long before it rang. It was Mrs Jacobs. She had spoken to the parent, who was not happy; she had talked of involving the police but Mrs Jacobs had persuaded her to meet in school the following day with Tom and her.

The police! He hadn't thought that she might involve them.

'Of course, she would,' said his wife, when she came home. 'It's common assault. You hit the boy, you could be arrested.'

His wife was angry with him. What had he been thinking of? It was the same question that Mrs Jacobs had put to him. He realised that he hadn't been thinking at all. Tom felt flat.

The next day he drove to the school with his wife. She stayed in the car whilst he walked in. He felt awkward and embarrassed. The secretary greeted him, 'Oh Tom,' she whispered, 'of all the boys, you had to pick Darren Gibson – his mother is a battle-axe. She isn't here yet but go into Mrs Jacobs; she's waiting for you.'

'Tom,' said Mrs Jacobs,' how are you?'

'Not too good, truth be told,' he replied.

'Let me do the talking,' the Headteacher said. 'The mother can be a tricky customer.'

They waited. There was a knock at the door. The secretary showed in a short woman with a sharp face. Tom put his hand forward to shake, but she didn't take it. She sat down and promptly started shouting. Her Darren was a good boy. He had no right to hit him. The photographer had been out of order. She was within her rights to go to the police. She began to sob. Tom sat there, feeling under attack. She was angry, her eyes wide; her tone shrill.

'Surely,' said Mrs Jacobs, 'we could avoid involving the police.' She was sure that Mr Patrick (that was Tom's name) would want to make amends. 'Tom,' she said, 'you are sorry aren't you?'

'Yes,' said Tom suddenly finding his voice. 'Very.'

'You need to apologise to my son, not me,' spat the mother. 'Let's get Darren in here.'

Darren was sent for. He was clearly enjoying the drama. He wore a fixed grin and stared at Tom. He mouthed the word 'Loser' again when facing the photographer, who was trembling now. Tom gritted his teeth. He was feeling angry again. No, this wouldn't do. He wanted this to end. 'I'm sorry Darren,' he said. 'Please accept my apology.'

'How do I know that you aren't going to do it to some other kid?' said the mother.

'I'm retiring,' said Tom. The words surprised him, but it seemed the right thing to say. He had had enough. 'However,' he said, 'before I do, please let me take some professional shots of you and Darren – free of charge, of course.'

Tom and Mrs Jacobs looked at the mother. Would it be enough?

'Free of charge?' she repeated

'Absolutely,' said Tom.

'We'll leave it at that, then,' she said.

'I have my kit in the car,' said Tom. 'If Mrs Jacobs could possibly find us a space?'

'Certainly,' said Mrs Jacobs, relieved that the matter appeared to have been concluded.

They were the most difficult photographs that Tom had ever taken. But he took them. Darren went back to class and the mother turned on her heels.

He slid back into the car. 'Well?' said his wife.

'No police,' he said,' just some photos to print.' He was feeling a huge sense of relief.

'Let's go home,' she said, squeezing his hand. As they were pulling out of the car park, Mr Jenkins came running towards him. He had a Bible in his hand.

'Read the page I've marked,' he said. 'Goodbye Tom and good luck!' Later that day Tom read:

*If you forgive others the wrongs they have done to you, your Father in heaven will also forgive you. (Matthew 6:14)*

With the Darren business finished, Tom felt like a weight had been lifted from him. He wouldn't bear a grudge against the youngster. Tom was worth more than that. Instead, he would embrace his retirement: now he thought about it, he was somewhat looking forward to a well-earned rest … .

# Teacher's Notes
# Mr Carmichael's Story

## Background
Schools are busy places. I know as a Headteacher that I should never be on my own with a child. But this is impractical. If a child arrives at my door I can't easily send for another adult each time. I do sense how vulnerable I am, particularly when a child is sent to me to be disciplined. Through my professional association, I am made aware of the allegations that are made against colleagues: some are substantiated but many are eventually judged to have been fabricated, usually because a child had a grievance against the adult concerned. By the time someone's name is cleared, their reputation is usually in tatters and there is no way back for them to the position that they occupied previously. Too often people assume that there is no smoke without fire – but the smoke does damage enough.

## General theme
Do we react when someone is accused of something? Do we immediately assume guilt or do we keep an open mind – waiting to listen carefully to all those involved before coming to a judgement. Is it possible to forget what someone has been accused of if they are then found to be innocent?

## What do Christians believe?
Jesus was falsely accused of many things. He was tried and sentenced to death. Christians believe that we must be slow to come to conclusions about people when they are accused of wrong doing. Just because people claim that someone has done wrong, it does not make it so. Jesus is, for Christians, the best example of someone falsely accused.

## Prayer
*Lord Jesus, you were the friend of outcasts: those people who weren't offered companionship, those people others didn't want to be seen with. May we follow your example and never cast anyone aside because they are different or unpopular. Help us to see your face in those in need. When someone needs the help of a neighbour, may we be the one who steps forward and doesn't turn away. If we are feeling lost or alone, please give us the courage to share our feelings with someone who can help us.*

## The story
Who in the story has the children's sympathy? Is it just Mr Carmichael? Do any of the children feel sorry for Benjamin? Is it wrong to feel sorry for Benjamin when he caused so much trouble for the Headteacher? How do they feel the Headteacher would have been feeling when he finally returned to school?

## PSMC links
- Can the children remember a time when they have jumped to conclusions, thinking someone to be guilty of something before they had heard all sides of the story?
- Do they think teachers in their school – or their parents at home – are good at listening in such circumstances?
- Can they think of rules by which we should proceed when someone is accused of something and they deny it?

© Gary Nott and Brilliant Publications Limited
*This page may be photocopied for use by the purchasing institution only.*

Modern Christian Assembly Stories

# Mr Carmichael's Story

Benjamin had seen too much in his young life. His mother had a problem with drugs and alcohol. Benjamin didn't get enough to eat on some days and, some nights, he was cold. He had a series of 'uncles' – men who came and went. Some told him to make himself scarce whilst others were even more threatening. Benjamin's mother would hit him. Sometimes because she was mad, but at other times, because it was the easiest thing to do. Benjamin often played up. 'What was she to do?' his mother would ask.

When he was four, Benjamin was taken away from his mother and was sent to live with the Garmon family: Pete and Lucy. They had children of their own, Emily and Duncan. The house was warm and there was always plenty to eat. They were kinder than his mother but they could be strict. Benjamin didn't like it when they told him off. Most of the time, he didn't understand. What was he doing wrong? Benjamin went to school with the Garmon children – they were good children who behaved; Benjamin, said the teachers, did not. They said he was difficult. He wouldn't sit still and he wouldn't work. He preferred to wind up the boys and flick the girls' bottoms. He would punch and kick, when the other kids annoyed him.

When the lesson was in full swing, he could always be spotted – sitting on the floor, having time out for one reason or another. The teachers despaired. As he moved from Year 1 to Year 2, things got worse. Different people came in to work with him; to try and find out what made him tick. They suggested things that the teachers could try with him. Some worked for a while, but none ever lasted. Benjamin was unhappy; he didn't enjoy school. The Garmon family were finding him difficult. They said they couldn't take him places. They had looked after 'problem' children before, but no one quite like him.

Mr Carmichael was Benjamin's Headteacher. He was a kind man, he was nevertheless firm: he expected the children to behave and, when they didn't, he was disappointed. One day, Benjamin's teacher brought him to Mr Carmichael. The teacher was angry. Benjamin had hit another boy on the nose and he had made him bleed.

'I'll leave him with you!' the teacher spat and marched away.

Mr Carmichael looked at Benjamin. Why did the boy never stop pushing the adults with whom he worked? What was going on in his mind? Why did he have to make school so difficult?

Benjamin wasn't listening. He was rolling around on his chair. Mr Carmichael raised his voice, startling Benjamin. 'Sit outside, Benjamin,' he said, pointing in the direction of the open office door. 'You can lose 15 minutes of your play.'

---

When 15 minutes were up, Mr Carmichael came out of his office. Benjamin was sitting there. 'Off you go,' the Headteacher sighed. Benjamin slunk off, a scowl on his face.

The next day, Mr Carmichael's secretary came into his office looking troubled.

'You're not going to like this,' she said.
'What?' he replied.

I have Mr and Mrs Garmon outside, with Benjamin. 'They say you hit him.'

Mr Carmichael went cold. He thought back to yesterday, his mind began to race; he had seen Benjamin on his own, in his office – no one else there. It would be his word against the

Modern Christian Assembly Stories © Gary Nott and Brilliant Publications Limited

*This page may be photocopied for use by the purchasing institution only.*

# False accusations
## Mr Carmichael's Story

boy's.

He asked them to sit down.

'Benjamin said you hit him, Mr Carmichael.'

'I didn't,' he blurted out, almost tearful. He knew where this was going.

The police arrived at the school shortly afterwards.

They said Mr Carmichael would have to come to the station to be interviewed.

'Am I being arrested?' he asked. 'You are,' said the policeman, in a cold tone.

At the station, Mr Carmichael recounted his version of the previous day's events to the detective. He had raised his voice. Yes, okay, he had shouted. He had been frustrated; a point had needed to be made.

'And, you were angry, and so you hit him,' said the detective.

'No,' said Mr Carmichael firmly. 'I wouldn't, couldn't do that.'

A mark, the Headteacher suddenly thought. There would have been no mark.

'No,' said the policemen, 'but not all hits cause bruising or red marks. Sometimes, the person doing the hitting, can judge just how hard to hit.'

He was told he could go home.

At the time, Benjamin was somewhere, giving his evidence. Mr Carmichael would be contacted, they said, when the case moved on.

It was a wild and wet afternoon and, as he stood on the police station steps, he thought of his wife and children. How would he tell them?

The Chair of Governors phoned to say he was very sorry but that he would be suspended from school until the outcome of the investigation. He was to have no contact with anyone from St Cuthbert's.

He felt so alone.

His wife was good to him, at first. She knew that he wouldn't have been capable of such a thing. But she was angry. Angry with Benjamin. Then, angry with her husband, because he had been foolish enough to meet with Benjamin on his own. There was no one to back him up. The anger seemed some days to outweigh the love; she was sorry, but there it was.

The weeks dragged on. He felt unwell. He moped around the house all day, nothing to do except worry and ask himself why he had been on his own with the boy. The hearing date was set for 14th July: the eve of the summer holidays – a time when he would normally be looking forward to a break from school. Now all he could think of was how he wished he was there. How he had taken it for granted, just going in every day. He realised just how happy he had been.

Some parents wrote to him, saying that they didn't believe it; saying that he had their support and that he wasn't to worry, but he did. Others wrote to say, 'Don't come back, scum!' He had been judged by people who had no idea.

He dreaded the postman's rounds.

Then, with a week to go before the trial, he

© Gary Nott and Brilliant Publications Limited
*This page may be photocopied for use by the purchasing institution only.*

# Mr Carmichael's Story — False accusations

saw the detective at his door. His heart sank.

'We have some news for you, Mr Carmichael,' the detective began. 'Benjamin has told us that he got it wrong. You didn't hit him. He was angry with you for shouting at him. He's sorry. The charges will be dropped.'

Wrong?

Sorry?

It didn't seem real. Was it really over?

Weeks of waiting, weeks of worry, only to be told 'sorry.'

His wife hugged him. 'It's done with,' she whispered, 'over.' His children were happy. Their dad was going to be okay again.

Except he wasn't.

The doctor said it was only to be expected. The strain. Anyone would have crumpled.

And he did. Crumple. Broke. Snapped.

He went for long walks. Bought a dog. His wife would wait anxiously for him to come home. He took to reading the Bible. He shied away from people, even friends. Then one day in the Gospel, he read,

*The chief priests and the elders persuaded the crowd to ask Pilate to set Barabbas free and have Jesus put to death. But Pilate asked the crowd, 'Which one of these two do you want me to set free for you?'*

*'Barabbas', they answered.*

*'What then shall I do with Jesus called the Messiah?' Pilate asked them.*

*'Crucify him!' they all answered.*

*But Pilate asked, 'What crime has he committed?'*

*Then they started shouting at the tops of their voices: 'Crucify him!'*

*When Pilate saw that it was no use to go on, but that a riot might break out, he took some water, washed his hands in front of the crowd and said, 'I am not responsible for the death of this man! This is your doing!' (Matthew 27: 20–24)*

That night, for the first time, in a long time, he slept soundly. The next morning he got up early. It was time to return to school, he decided. But things were different. Though he was trying, he feared he might never be the same again.

Mr Carmichael insisted that Benjamin be allowed to return. He was a troubled boy who had seen too much in his life. 'He was damaged goods,' said some. But, Mr Carmichael wanted everyone to have as many fresh starts as they needed. After all, the Headteacher had his.

# Teacher's Notes
# Scarlett's Story

## Background
I read in the newspaper of how a school had left a pupil behind on a school journey. The Headteacher had to drive to collect her. Hard to believe but true! On many occasions, I have taken the children out on school trips and counting heads regularly is a big part of that, more so since I read of the colleague's misfortune in the newspaper. How embarrassing!

## General theme
As girls get older, they can be terribly mean to one another – more so than boys, in my experience. Putting others down seems to be one of the ways in which they assert their own individualism. Jealously is a big driver in such situations.

## What do Christians believe?
Bullying is wrong. We are asked to 'love another.' We are even called upon to 'love our enemies.' Does that mean that Christians think it right to let someone walk over you? No, it doesn't. It is always right to stand up to someone/or look to others to support you against someone. But, we must be open to the reasons why someone might choose to bully us and we are asked to pray for them. Never easy to do, but each week in Church, Christians pray for those that sin against them.

## Prayer
*Lord Jesus, you know that we don't always find it easy to forgive those who have been unkind to us. But you taught us to show forgiveness to those who have sinned against us, just as we ourselves are shown forgiveness. May we accept the apologies of others and be quick to apologise when we have fallen short of 'loving one another'.*

## The story
Belinda is jealous of Scarlett's relationship with Derek. She seeks to make Scarlett unhappy because of this. Bullies can be driven on by all sorts of motivation. Schools, just like the workplace, have bullies. This story has a timely resolution that is ironic: it is because she is focussed on Belinda that Scarlett spots she is missing. She then has a choice to make. Do the right thing and flag up Belinda's absence or keep quiet and exact some revenge. What would the children have done?

## PSMC links
- Has anyone been bullied? (Hard to answer.)
- Has anyone ever bullied someone else? (You probably won't get anyone admitting this.)
- What makes someone bully another? Do they enjoy it?

# Scarlett's Story

Year 6 had been looking forward to their class residential for weeks. They were off to a large house situated in the countryside. The visit was jam packed: a trip to a castle; an outing to a chocolate factory; an excursion to the theatre. Three days of fun and then there would be the evenings too, games and on the last night a disco. Scarlett, like the others was excited. She had had a tough time of late. Mum had been ill and Dad had lost his job. 'I'm not sure we'll be able to afford the trip,' Mum had confessed. But, Miss Jenkins, Scarlett's teacher had spoken up. The Governors of the school could help out in 'such circumstances'. Scarlett wasn't quite sure what she meant – such circumstances – it was grown-up speak – all she needed to know was that school would pay for her to go.

Her so-called friends had been mean to her of late. 'Your dad hasn't got a job,' Belinda had said. 'You're a waster now!'

Scarlett had tried to take no notice, but it wasn't easy to do. Belinda was popular: the other girls tended to follow her, do what she did, say what she said. So lately Scarlett had tended to hang round with the boys: Derek and Deon, and the rest. Derek was a good sport and she didn't mind playing football at break. Truth be told, she had always been a bit of a tomboy.

The week before the trip, there had been a meeting for parents. They had been told all the things that needed to be packed. There was a long list: pyjamas, spare pyjamas, uniform, spare uniform. There seemed to be a lot of spares needed; they were, after all, only going for three days but Miss Clarke said they had to be prepared for 'every eventuality' – more grown-up speak; Scarlett thought she was saying things could go wrong. Scarlett wasn't sure what could go wrong when there were teachers in charge. She could never have imagined what was to happen.

The morning of the departure arrived: 60 kids with suitcases and excited faces. The coach was a double-decker; Scarlett tagged along with the boys, sitting upstairs. The trip was three hours. Stephen Jenkins asked Mr Davies if he could have something from his lunch. 'Stephen,' said Mr Davies, 'it's half-past nine. We've only been on the road half an hour.'

'I know,' said Stephen, 'but I'm starving.'

'Put it away!' said Mr Davies, 'there'll be time enough for that later.'

When they arrived, there was the excitement of seeing with whom they'd be sharing. Scarlett realised that she couldn't be in the same room as Derek and the other boys. To her horror, she was put in the same room as Belinda. 'You won't know yourself,' Belinda said to her, 'the rooms are much bigger than what you're used to.' Scarlett walked towards the bathroom. Belinda blocked her way. Scarlett pushed past. When she came out Belinda was waiting for her, still blocking the way. She pushed her to one side and toppled into Stacey's arm.

'You touched her and you haven't washed your hands,' shrieked Belinda. 'Stacey's got Scarlett germs.'

With that Belinda took a tissue and began to rub Stacey's arm. Then she took the tissue and pushed it into Scarlett's face. Scarlett shrugged her off.

Scarlett stepped outside. She was upset. Far from home, she wanted to cry. Miss Clarke came by. 'Whatever's the matter darling?' she said kindly.

'Oh nothing, really,' she replied. 'Just missing home a bit.'

There was no way she was going to grass on Belinda – that would only make things worse.

Modern Christian Assembly Stories

36

© Gary Nott and Brilliant Publications Limited

*This page may be photocopied for use by the purchasing institution only.*

# Scarlett's Story — Bullying

She headed off for Derek's room. He was furious. 'Tell,' he said.

'No,' she insisted. 'Let's forget it. How 'bout some football?'

They stopped off for Deon and went outside for a kick about.

At mealtime, she sat with the boys. Belinda flashed her a look. Scarlett knew what it meant. There was more to come and her tummy sank. Was this what it was like to be bullied? Why did Belinda hate her so? What had she done? It wasn't her fault her dad had lost his job and what had that got to do with Belinda anyway?

That night, when they were sent to their rooms, Belinda started again. Scarlett ignored her. Maybe she could ask to move to another room. The only problem was Belinda would know she had got to her.

The next morning, they were heading for the chocolate factory. It was already hot and the forecast was one of scorching temperatures. The factory was small. It had an open workshop where the children could see chocolate being poured into moulds, making shapes like bunnies and eggs. It was fun and smelt heavenly. Back outside, it was boiling hot. Suddenly Jessie Jeapers' legs buckled and she fainted. Scarlett caught her, struggling with the heavy weight. Miss Clarke asked Scarlett to sit with her, while Jessie rested in the shade. Scarlett chatted to Jessie to make her feel better.

'Thanks Scarlett,' she said sheepishly. 'I'm sorry that I haven't stood up for you against Belinda; it's just that I'm frightened she'd turn on me, if I stood up for you.'

Belinda Sopworth. What a cow!

That afternoon, they went to the theatre. It was great fun. They had costumes for the children to dress up in and workshops where they got to take on the role of a character. She was put into a group with Deon, Sophie and Paula. Paula was shy and didn't want to act a part; don't worry, suggested Scarlett, you can stand by me and pretend to be my companion. They enjoyed themselves. Deon put on a wig and a strange accent: he was a real performer. Afterwards, Paula came up to Scarlett.

'Thanks for your help,' she said. 'I was embarrassed and you helped me. I am sorry I haven't stood up for you against Belinda. I should have.'

'Don't worry,' said Scarlett. 'It's not your fault that she's mean.' It wasn't, but that didn't make Paula feel any better. She felt flat – she hadn't done something and now it was too late; the damage was done.

They all clambered back onto the coach. They were late. They had stayed too long at the theatre, but the children had been enjoying it so. Mr Davies asked if everyone was on board. Yes, they chorused, and he told the driver to go. But they weren't all on board. Belinda was missing. Only Scarlett had noticed because she always had to know where Belinda was, so she could spot any trouble coming. Where was Belinda? Should Scarlett say something? No, she wouldn't. It wasn't down to her to look out for Belinda Sopworth. She settled back

© Gary Nott and Brilliant Publications Limited
*This page may be photocopied for use by the purchasing institution only.*

Modern Christian Assembly Stories

in her seat. But she couldn't relax. What had happened to Belinda? Where was she? Scarlett couldn't say nothing, she just couldn't.

'Mr Davies, where's Belinda?'

'Belinda?' said Mr Davies. 'Why she's here with us - isn't she?' Panic had crept into his voice. He quickly counted the children on the coach, 29, not 30. He had forgotten to count everyone when they had boarded as they had been in a hurry. He went white. Miss Clarke went red. Mr Davies hurried to the front of the bus. The driver muttered under his breath but indicated left. They turned round. Everyone was silent. They knew it was serious. People didn't get left behind on trips. Mr Davies would be in trouble, big trouble. Where was Belinda? Was she okay?

Mr Davies jumped off the coach when they pulled up at the theatre. He returned 10 minutes later with Belinda. She had been crying. She had gone to the toilet and when she'd come out, they'd gone. A simple accident. Miss Clarke looked worried: she was annoyed with Mr Davies, Scarlett could tell.

Belinda sat down at the front next to Miss Clarke. She didn't say anything.

Later that night, after dinner, and before the disco, Belinda came up to Scarlett. Scarlett groaned. Where was this going?

'I just want to say sorry,' she said, glancing down, not looking at Scarlett's face. 'Miss Clarke told me that it was you who spotted I was missing, who raised the alarm. Thank you. And I'm sorry to have been so mean to you. I will stop it. Right now!'

Scarlett was pleased. Pleased she had spoken out on the coach. Pleased that Belinda had said she would stop.

Later, Scarlett danced with Derek and he kissed her. 'You know why Belinda has been mean to you?' said Deon. 'She fancies Derek but he obviously prefers you.'

Scarlett sighed. Why hadn't she realised that?

Later, when they were back at school, Scarlett wrote down a piece from the Bible and passed it to Belinda. 'I read this and thought of you,' she said:

*You were like sheep that had lost their way, but now you have been brought back to follow the Shepherd and Keeper of your souls. (1 Peter 2:25)*

'My Mum,' said Scarlett, 'told me that it means it's never too late to say sorry and Jesus never gives up on us, no matter how many times we turn away from him.' Belinda smiled.

# Teacher's Notes
# Archie's Story

## Background
I once had a child take an inappropriate image of himself (not of his bottom!) and post the image on a chat room. I had to involve Social Care and his parents were mortified by their son's behaviour. It was very difficult to tell them that I had had to involve Social Care; they saw it as a reflection upon their parenting, when it wasn't, but it was a safeguarding issue. Children can sometimes disappoint us surprisingly by their actions; they don't always have the capacity to see the likely consequences of what they might do. We learn by our mistakes and we have had many more opportunities to do this than they.

## General theme
Sometimes we don't put enough thought into our actions and we can rue the consequences.

## What do Christians believe?
We all make mistakes. One of my favourite Psalms is "Your word is a lamp to guide me and a light for my path.' (Psalm 119:105) I think what that is saying to me is that I will try to act as the Lord has shown me – and if I then get it wrong, I will at least have done my best by Him. I have a little phrase that I use with the children: when they find themselves needing to make a choice in life, I encourage them to say, 'What would Jesus have done? What would Jesus have said?'

## Prayer
*Loving Father, we all fall short of your glory. We all make mistakes. Thank you that nothing we do can ever part us from your love, if we are truly sorry.*

## The story
Why did Archie post the inappropriate photo?
What were the consequences for him? His parents?

## PSMC links
- Talk about stranger danger.
- How can we stay safe on social media?

© Gary Nott and Brilliant Publications Limited
*This page may be photocopied for use by the purchasing institution only.*

# Archie's Story

It had started as a laugh. Henry had thought of it. A chat group, just for them. On their phones. Private. No outsiders. Secret.

At first they had exchanged messages about friends at school. Who liked whom; who fancied whom; who had fallen out with whom. Then James had posted a picture of himself with shades on – looking cool. One by one they posted photos of themselves in odd poses, trying to outdo one another. Morgan on a swing, standing on one leg; Candice on her Dad's motorbike, wearing his helmet; David kissing his dog – yuck!

What could Archie do? He couldn't think. He wanted to make them all laugh.

An idea came into his head. Once when he had been on holiday, a teenager on the beach had pulled his trunks down and flashed his bottom at some watching girls. Archie had laughed. Everyone had laughed. 'Mooning,' his dad said it was called. Archie went to his room. He had decided to moon. He angled the phone, and pulling his pants down snapped his bottom in the lens. He called up the group's names on the screen and typed, 'Get a load of this.' He hit the send key. He smiled, nervously. It was just a laugh, right? The others would surely see it as a bit of fun.

Beep. It was James texting. 'U r crazy,' the text read.

Seconds later …

Beep. It was Candice: 'LOL.'

Archie went downstairs to watch some TV. Later on, he was doing his homework when his phone beeped again. It was David. 'I could park my bike in that,' the message read. Archie wasn't sure what he meant. Then he got it. He laughed out loud. Out do that, if you can, he thought.

The next day, Archie was late for school. He rode into the playground just as his class were walking in. He quickly dismounted and taking his helmet off, pushed his bike into the cycle rack. It reminded him of what David had said the night before. He laughed.

Mrs Thompson had already started the register. He was just in time to call his name.

First lesson was maths. Jason was handing out the books. 'You're mad you are,' he whispered as he gave Archie his book. What did he mean?

Archie started to write the date down. As he sat listening to Mrs Thompson drone on and on about denominators and numerators he was suddenly aware of Sarah and Susie Jenkins giggling. They were looking at him. He couldn't see what they were laughing about. Did he have porridge on his face from breakfast? He wiped his hand across his face. No, it didn't feel like it.

Suddenly, Aaron burst out laughing. What was going on? 'Aaron,' said Mrs Thompson, 'perhaps you'd like to share the joke?'

'No, sorry, Miss,' he said, but you could see he was having trouble controlling himself. When Mrs Thompson turned back to the board, Archie could see he was looking at something in his hand. It was a phone. Aaron pushed it across the table, in Simon's direction. Simon picked it up and started to smile. He looked at Archie. What was the joke?

Mrs Thompson turned back to the class. 'Okay,' she said. 'Something's going on. What exactly?'

'Ask Archie Miss,' said Aaron.

'Well, Archie. What is it?' said Mrs Thompson. Archie just sat there. He didn't know what was going on. He was beginning to wish he hadn't been late. He wasn't in on the joke.

At break time, the class erupted onto the

*Modern Christian Assembly Stories*

© Gary Nott and Brilliant Publications Limited

*This page may be photocopied for use by the purchasing institution only.*

playground; some were holding their sides, unable to speak – others were whooping out loud.

'What is it?' Archie asked Candice.

'It's your photo,' she replied. 'Someone from the group has spread it around and now everyone has seen it.'

Archie went cold.

It had been just for the group.

No one else.

All the girls had seen it? He didn't mind when it had just been Candice and Ellie; but, now all the others too. He groaned. Archie was suddenly mad. Who would have shared the picture? It wasn't on.

Mrs Thompson had come out into the playground. She was making for him. Was she still annoyed with him from the lesson?

'Archie, a word,' she said. 'Mr Davies and I want to speak with you, young man.' He followed her to Mr Davies' office.

Mr Davies was usually friendly to Archie, but he sat looking stern behind his desk.

In front of him sat a phone. All at once, Archie knew what was coming. The room suddenly seemed smaller, crowding in on him. His stomach fell.

Mr Davies didn't say much. What was there to say? Why had Archie done it? For a joke. Mr Davies wasn't laughing. Nor would Archie's parents be, the Headteacher felt sure.

'Do you realise how silly you've been?'

'Yes.'

'The photo could just be passed on from phone to phone. Had you thought about that?'

'No.' Archie looked at the floor. He wanted it to open up and swallow him.

'This is serious,' Mr Davies said. 'Very serious.'

Archie sat in afternoon lessons, but he wasn't listening. What had seemed like a joke had gone wrong. Just his luck. What would Mum and Dad say? Dad had laughed on holiday, when the teenager had done it. Archie wasn't so sure that he would be laughing now.

Mum and Dad sat him down. Mum talked about how embarrassed she was. Dad said he had been an idiot. Chat rooms, he said, were dangerous places. Mr Davies had said he was obliged to share it with Social Services. Archie wasn't sure who they were, but it sounded like more trouble. Mum and Dad said someone would be coming round, to check that he was safe; that he wasn't living in a family that did the wrong thing.

The woman from Social Services was young. She seemed nice enough.

What kinds of things did he watch on the television?

Where did he go on the Internet?

Did he know what to do if something rude appeared on the screen? Something aimed at grown-ups?

Archie wasn't sure what she meant exactly.

He tried to look as though he did. Mum and Dad looked worried.

Had he heard of stranger danger? What might have happened if his photo had been forwarded to a stranger?

'Something bad,' he offered, quietly.

'Exactly,' she said.

She wanted him to promise that he would be more sensible in future.

He promised.

That night Archie prayed. It had been some time since he had last done that. He wondered if Jesus would forgive him. Mum thought not, at least not for a while, she had said. He opened his Bible and started to read.

Archie closed the Bible and shut his eyes. Life could be tough sometimes. He thought he would be forgiven and he thought too that Mum was wrong: he wouldn't have to wait for Jesus to forgive him. God wasn't like that. No, if he was truly sorry, Archie wouldn't have to wait. His God didn't make people wait. But, he was prepared to admit that Mum's 'forgiveness' might take just that little bit longer.

# Teacher's Notes
# Mrs Groves' Story

## Background
Death can be difficult to deal with in a school. I say 'can be,' because some children appear to take it in their stride, very matter of fact. Routine seems important. Children seem to function best with death when their set routines continue. In my time in schools, I have seen parents, staff and children pass on. It's always worse when it's a child: nothing can prepare you for the sight of a small coffin. However, when I was first a teacher, my Headteacher died at a young age. It hit the community hard, but even then I was struck by the pupils' resilience: many were absolutely confident that she was now with the Lord. The strength of their faith made me re-examine my own.

## General theme
How do we deal with death when we are young? Is it harder for an adult than a child? If so, why?

## What do Christians believe?
All life begins and ends with Christ. Our Parish Priest uses the following analogy when speaking at funerals of people who have died before their time: he says that they have gone on ahead in the journey that we are all making. I find this a comforting thought and I have seen it visibly lift others.

## Prayer
*Father God, your son, Jesus, gave his life so that we might have eternal life. Comfort those who have lost a loved one. May happy memories give them strength through the most difficult of times.*

## The story
Mrs Groves thought she had a struggle to make the school better. However, a much bigger challenge was to lie ahead, the battle with cancer. She achieved the former, but lost the latter. Sometimes we can become engrossed in a particular task, in this case rebuilding a school; but ultimately none of it might matter. It is how we have treated others in life that counts – whether we have a high-powered job or a much simpler life.

## PSMC links
- How do the children react to the story? How does it make them feel?
- Time is said to be a great healer – do they have experience of this? (You may be surprised at how direct children can be when talking about death.)

# Mrs Groves' Story

When she had been appointed to St Cuthbert's, Mrs Groves had been told that she had a battle on her hands. The inspection report was terrible. The children were badly behaved, the teachers down in the dumps. On her first morning, she had to break up a fight on the playground – between two parents! Later, walking down the corridor, she was nearly bowled over by a gaggle of girls. 'Let's walk, shall we?' she warned. Surprised, the girls slowed down. No one had ever asked them to walk like they meant it.

She walked into assembly and was greeted with a noisy welcome. Some children didn't stop chatting and one hidden voice at the back even booed!

'Listen,' she said in a strong, confident voice, 'I want to know, are you happy at this school? – Do you enjoying being here? Being in a school,' she continued over the rabble, 'where the teachers don't enjoy teaching? Where children misbehave? Where there is bullying? It can be different. You are worth more than that.' The children went quiet; the teachers looked up. They were listening. She had got their attention. Who was this small, feisty woman? Was she really going to change things?

At break time, she made her way to the art room. Some Year 6 boys were hanging round, kicking a ball, being difficult.

'Teachers don't come round this part of the school,' said Darren Jenkins.

'They do now,' she said. 'You're Darren, aren't you?' Well, Darren, you may well be my first permanent exclusion, she thought to herself, recalling what she had been told about him.

At the end of her first day, tired and drained, she had made her way to her car. Someone had written with their finger in the dust on the bonnet: 'Go home!'

The second day was tougher still. But Mrs Groves wasn't about to give up. She was made of sterner stuff.

The first thing she wanted to do was help the teachers to make lessons more interesting. She bought them lots of new resources and gave training on how they could best be used. Each classroom was fitted with the latest technology: an interactive whiteboard and a visualiser. The children were all entrusted with i-Pads. She insisted that children put their hands up in class, rather than call out. They had to move about the school quietly and call the teachers Sir or Miss. Lovely manners, she said, were important.

And she tackled the teachers too. She only wanted the best ones at her school. There was to be no place at St Cuthbert's for teachers who were only so-so. Those who didn't want to work her way, left. They were replaced by new and enthusiastic staff who brought a breath of fresh air to the classroom.

Bit by bit, Mrs Groves was changing minds. Children were making better progress in their lessons. They were beginning to realise that they could do things, that they could get things right. Teachers and children were beginning to enjoy themselves.

Darren Jenkins was eventually excluded. Everyone knew that this was now Mrs Groves' school.

By Christmas, St Cuthbert's was a different place. In a new uniform, children were beginning to take pride in their school. For the first time, parents were happy and wanted to support the teachers in helping the children to learn.

The school had a buzz about it. Everyone who visited said it had changed – it was

# Death | Mrs Groves' Story

unrecognisable. Margaret Groves had done well.

She had been in the Hall, hanging decorations on the Christmas tree when she had first noticed it. She scratched the inside of her neck absent-mindedly when she felt it: a small blob, no bigger than a pea. That's odd, she thought, funny place for a spot.

But the pea-like blob didn't go away as spots do. It hung around. It was then that she began to feel tired. She had always been tired, of course – running a school was a draining job. But no, of late, she was more tired than usual; and then she didn't feel like eating. She lost some weight.

'You're probably run down,' said her husband, one morning. 'You've been working too hard. Make an appointment to see Dr Jamieson.'

Whilst she was there, she mentioned the spot, which was more of a lump now, to the doctor. He wanted to do some tests. 'Routine,' he said.

Mrs Groves had her second appointment with the doctor. It was a Tuesday. She remembered the day of the week because she had had to ask Mrs David to take her after-school class.

She didn't hear much of what he said. She caught the words, 'I'm very sorry …' and 'cancer' – of course, she heard that. She stumbled back to the car not knowing what to think. She had always been a fighter. But this. How did you fight it?

She threw herself further into her work. The Year 6 children were getting ready for their SATs; Year 4 children were preparing an Easter production. It was a busy time. Her husband was, of course, worried about her. She told no one at school except Mrs Jacobs, the Deputy Head. She hadn't known what to say. What was there to be said?

She had her first dose of chemotherapy during the Easter holidays. It was awful. She felt so sick afterwards. But, she soon got used to the routine. Then, all her hair fell out and she had to wear a wig. No one said anything. 'Had they noticed?' she wondered.

The specialist doctor was very kind. 'Don't look up,' he said. 'Keep your head down and plough on. Let's not focus upon tomorrow, worry only about today. One day at a time, let's take it slowly.'

With her visits to the hospital for treatment now more frequent, the staff had to be told. They were kind; they sent her flowers and cards. The children and parents were left to guess what might be wrong for she wasn't in school for long periods.

The chemotherapy finally ended. It had been a long haul.

Then they waited.

The news wasn't good. The cancer had spread.

Her best option was a bone marrow transplant, they said. It sounded scary. They found a donor. She was in hospital waiting. 'It could work,' the doctors said. There was a definite chance. Hope.

# Mrs Groves' Story — Death

One summer's afternoon, when the children were getting ready for sports day and the end of term leavers' concert, Mrs Groves died. It was a peaceful death – she just slipped away.

———————

The children had to be told, of course. How to break it to them? They knew something had been wrong, of course. They had heard their parents talking. The funeral was a big affair. All wore bright colours, her last request. What can we do to show how much we cared for her, asked the children. 'By making St Cuthbert's an even better place to be,' said her husband. 'For her, because she believed in you! She still does!'

So the children of the school set about trying to do worthwhile things in her memory. Then one day Mrs Jacobs, the new Headteacher of St Cuthbert's, read the following passage from the Bible in assembly:

*For God loved the world so much that he gave his only Son so that everyone who believes in him may not die but have eternal life. (John 3:16)*

The children smiled. Mrs Groves was with them – she would always be with them.

# Teacher's Notes
# Billy's Story

## Background
We can all feel embarrassed from time to time. Some people are able to laugh it off, whereas others feel themselves dying on the inside. Many children are embarrassed when they go swimming with school. As a child, I was overweight and would dread swimming lessons for fear of someone passing comment about my size – especially when there were girls about. This story is intended to make children laugh. Not in an unkind way, but as an acknowledgement that what might be embarrassing for someone else can genuinely tickle our funny bones – try as we might not to laugh. It is easy to put yourself in Billy's shoes because we have all been there – although not necessarily in the swimming pool with no trunks on.

## General theme
How should we react to other people's moments of embarrassment? Is there a difference between laughing at someone and laughing with them?

## What do Christians believe?
Jesus could have felt embarrassed on many an occasion because he often did what was unexpected. He sat down with tax collectors and other people in society to whom he was expected to give a wide berth. He wasn't afraid of people laughing at him. He rode into Jerusalem on a donkey and allowed others to claim that he was a poor imitation of a king. He let them laugh; he wasn't bothered by their ridicule. He expected it.

## Prayer
*Lord Jesus, draw close to each one of us during the difficult times we experience. It can sometimes feel like the world is a very cruel place and that we are alone. Help us to remember that we are never alone. May we always think about the feelings of others and treat them as we would want to be treated ourselves.*

## The story
What do the children think of Billy? Was he foolish or brave to get out of the pool when he had lost his trunks? If this were to happen to one of their classmates, would they have laughed or tried to help?

## PSMC links
- Is it okay to laugh at other's misfortunes? Is it ever okay, or always wrong?
- What's the best way to react when something embarrassing happens to you? Can the children recall an embarrassing episode? Are they prepared to share? Did it seem worse at the time or is it still cringe-worthy?
- Is there a pressure to join in with the crowd and laugh rather than come to the person's rescue? Have they ever felt that pressure?

# Billy's Story

He had wanted to wear goggles but Mum thought the pool wouldn't permit them. 'Health and safety,' said Miss Rodgers, his teacher. 'I don't think you'll be allowed, but we can ask.'

'What could be dangerous about a pair of goggles?' he had asked Mum.

'All pools have their rules,' she had said. Year 5 were going swimming; they had been looking forward to it for weeks. They were to go on a coach to the town pool three miles away. Billy was already a strong swimmer. Dad had taught him when they were on holiday in Tenerife. On the Saturday they had arrived there, he hadn't been able to swim a stroke, but by the end of the fortnight, he was splashing about confidently.

Miss Rodgers was not going to be teaching them. They would have the pool's swimming instructor, Mrs Belbin. She was strict, said the kids who regularly swam at the pool in the evenings; she had a loud, booming voice. Billy hoped she would be friendlier than she sounded.

The lessons were to be on Thursdays, in the morning. This would mean they would get out of maths – even better. The day of the first lesson finally arrived. Billy bagged a place on the bus next to Marshall. En route, they chatted about swimming. Marshall could swim a length in a minute, Billy, a width in 10 seconds. 'That makes me faster than you,' said Marshall. Billy wasn't so sure, but he didn't want to argue. He liked Marshall.

Billy had a pair of brand new trunks. His old ones had been too tight. Mum said that the new ones 'are on the big side but you will grow into them.' They were Nike, blue with yellow stripes. They looked cool. Baggy, but cool.

The boys piled into the changing room. Sam Lawrence and Joe Elliott were flicking each other with their towels. Sydney Davis had brought his dad's deodorant and was busy spraying it around. It made Billy cough and Marshall sneeze.

The pool was a new one. It glistened in the sunlight that streamed through large windows. A tall lady in a tracksuit stood at one end.

'This,' said Miss Rodgers, 'is Mrs Belbin. She is going to teach you how to swim.' The children stood around, feeling self-conscious in their swimsuits. Billy was worried one of the kids would say something about his trunks, which he was struggling to keep pulled up – they really were too big for him.

They had to get in the water, one by one and swim to the other side. If Mrs Belbin then called your name you had to go and sit at the deep end. She would be teaching you. Another teacher, Mr Forsett stepped forward; he was to take the strugglers in the shallow end. Billy held his breath. Would he be good enough to be chosen? Johnny went first. There was an awful lot of splashing. He wasn't picked. He looked embarrassed. Next, it was Sally's turn. There was less splashing. Her name was called out and she made her way down the side of the pool like a prize cat and took her seat. A series of children then swam; some chosen, some not. Billy was second to last He pushed off and swam as fast as he could. He hit the other side at full pelt with his arms outstretched. He heard Mrs Belbin shout his name. He was pleased.

They were told to climb down the steps into the pool and swim a length. One by one they set off. Billy was enjoying himself. This was far better than maths. Mrs Belbin boomed out instructions: 'keep your head down, less splashing, cut into the water with your hands,

© Gary Nott and Brilliant Publications Limited
*This page may be photocopied for use by the purchasing institution only.*

Modern Christian Assembly Stories

**Embarrassment/Humour** — **Billy's Story**

and kick those legs!'

It was hard work. After 20 minutes or so, they got out for a rest. Billy struggled to get his breath back. Mrs Belbin certainly believed in working them hard. Miss Rodgers was sitting poolside; she waved, the children waved back. This was fun!

Next Mrs Belbin got them to stand in a neat line along the poolside. They were to jump in when they felt ready and then swim to the other end. There was no rush, they were to take their time – only jump when they felt ready. The children braced themselves.

Billy jumped in and, after a few seconds, came to the surface.

What was that bobbing on the surface in front of him? He rubbed the water from his eyes. To his horror, he recognised the blue and yellow stripes and the Nike logo. It was his trunks. They must have come off when he jumped in. He felt down in the water; he could feel his bum. He was naked. His heart sank. He stopped to look at Mrs Belbin who was shouting at him to swim to the end, to keep up with the others. He twisted round but the trunks had floated to the other side where a pool attendant was fishing them out of the water. The attendant was scratching his head looking puzzled. He then walked towards the lifeguard. Next he turned on his heels and swiftly went through a door. He had disappeared with Billy's trunks! Billy swam to the other end. He splashed his arms about on the surface in an attempt to stop the other kids from seeing his 'bits' through the water. He tried to catch Mrs Belbin's attention. But she just boomed out to keep moving – everyone was to 'keep moving'. He stayed where he was treading water. The kids had swum to the other end; they were not watching him. Instead, they were doing their best to keep up with Mrs Belbin's instructions. She spied him, still at the other end. 'Come on,' she boomed, 'swim.' There was nothing else to do. He thrust off from the side. He swam for all he was worth. He was conscious that his bottom was up on the surface of the water. Would the others see it? No, he had got to the other end and no one was laughing.

'Okay,' said Mrs Belbin, 'well done, everyone out.'

'Mrs Belbin!' he shouted but she had turned to walk towards the changing rooms. There was nothing for it, he would have to get out. He couldn't stay in the water. He swam to the steps with the others and climbed up. There was a shriek of laughter.

Penelope Carter was laughing, 'Look,' she cried, 'Billy hasn't got any trunks on.'

He tried to get to the top of the steps as fast as he could but there were others in front of him. Once on the side, he placed his hands over his privates and ran for the changing room door. The class had collapsed into shouts of laughter, pointing and shrieking. Mrs Belbin appeared to see what all the fuss was about and caught sight of Billy's white bottom disappearing fast into the changing room.

'Billy Wilson!' she thundered. But he was behind the door now, and he was most definitely not coming back out. The other boys couldn't stop laughing, wouldn't stop laughing.

'The girls have seen your bits,' they shouted.

'No, they haven't,' he said, shouting back, louder, 'I covered them up.'

'Not when you had to hold on to the rail by the steps,' laughed Jonathan Taylor, 'we all saw then.' They were in stitches. Billy was red faced; he felt hot and clammy. He pulled his pants on and got dressed, slowly for he was in no hurry to go outside. The girls would be waiting. How could he face them? And there was Mrs Belbin, what would she say?

He stepped outside with the others. The girls were giggling. Mrs Belbin was waiting for him. 'These are yours, I believe,' she said, holding his trunks in one hand. 'Yes,' he mumbled, 'sorry.' What else was there to say?

# Billy's Story

## Embarrassment/Humour

When he got in that night, Mum asked him how the swimming had gone. Had he been allowed to wear his goggles? Billy thought for a while before answering.

'Googles, no,' he said. He didn't tell Mum that he hadn't worn his trunks the whole while, either – he thought it best to keep quiet about that.

# Teacher's Notes
# Aaron's Story

## Background
We can all put people on a pedestal; however, when one is young there is an even greater chance that someone will make a particular impression on us – indeed, we talk of certain youngsters being at an 'impressionable age'. The inspiration for this story comes from the time I spied my favourite teacher smoking in the staffroom. I was shocked. I guess I was ten at the time. Teachers didn't smoke, at least I hadn't thought this particular teacher would. In my eyes, she was perfect. I never felt quite the same way about her again. I look back at the episode now and laugh – poor woman, she didn't deserve my disappointment.

## General theme
We all have heroes. We admire them from afar often; we imagine them to be ideal. Rarely do we ever get to know them, and our illusions remain intact. However, occasionally we become infatuated with someone we know and this can be a recipe for disaster. No one is perfect and we are perhaps unfair to them if we expect them to live up to our perceptions of them.

## What do Christians believe?
Christians believe that it is wrong to 'worship' anyone other than God. We shouldn't focus upon one another in that way, building one another up into some ideal to which we cannot hope to match. Our thoughts are better spent focusing upon Jesus Christ, who can alone fulfil our every need.

## Prayer
*Father God, we thank you for all those believers through time, and those we know now, who are good role models for us. May we look to their dedication and their strong faith to give us hope and encouragement for our own lives.*

## The story
How do the children react to the story? Do they think it was reasonable of Aaron to expect Miss Parker not to smoke? Are there things that teachers are expected not to do? If so, why, and is it fair to think of them in such a way?

## PSMC links
- Do the children have a hero? Have they ever met them? If so, did their hero live up to their expectations or were they disappointed with what they found?
- Why do we look up to other people? Is it wrong to do so?
- Can the children suggest some unlikely heroes?

Modern Christian Assembly Stories
© Gary Nott and Brilliant Publications Limited
*This page may be photocopied for use by the purchasing institution only.*

# Aaron's Story

Miss Parker was fantastic. At least, Aaron thought so. She was his favourite teacher; no one else had even come close. Last year, he had the dreaded Mrs Sherman, who gave you only a few seconds to answer your times tables and who kept you in at playtime if you were chatty. It had been a long year. But now, in Year 4, with Miss Parker, things couldn't be better. She was kind and pretty; she gave you time to answer questions and was quick to tell you where you were doing well. Aaron couldn't help but think she had a soft spot for him. She would ask him to take the register to the Office and he always seemed to be chosen to give out the books at the start of lessons.

On a wet Friday in November, when the children had been cooped up inside all day, Miss Parker announced that she had some news – important news. The Mayor had announced that a selection of children in the city's schools were to be treated to a tour in an open-top bus, as a reward for working so hard. Miss Parker announced with a beam that St Peter's had been chosen and out of all the classes at the school, theirs was the one going to go on the trip. The children were excited, very excited.

'An open-top bus,' said Deon, 'no roof, we will travel round like free spirits.' Nobody knew what Deon meant exactly, neither did he for it was something his granddad used to say – his Mum said Granddad was a child of the 60s but Deon didn't know what that meant either.

'Yes,' enthused Miss Parker, 'the buses are specially made without a roof so we can sit on the top deck and see everything. We'll have a spectacular view of the city. And what's more we are going at night – when the city's famous buildings will be lit up.' 'Wow,' thought Aaron, 'a real treat.'

'We will have to wrap up warm,' continued Miss Parker. 'Now here's the permission slip to take home to your parents. I want it in by next Friday,' she said – not that the children heard, they were all busy chatting about what they might see from the open-top bus.

The day of the trip arrived. The children were to go home after school and arrive at the bus station in the middle of the city for 7.00 pm. The day was one of excitement. Aaron had agreed to sit next to James. They planned to take it in turns sitting next to the window. 'Imagine,' said James, 'no roof.'

When Aaron arrived at the bus station, it was pandemonium. There had to be at least 200 children, all wrapped up against the cold. The adults were trying to move the children into neat lines ready to wait for the buses. Aaron's class was the second to last. The queue in front of them seemed to go on for miles. Suddenly from the middle of the chatter came an almighty shout of excitement. The first bus had arrived. Aaron strained to look. It was sleek red with an open top. Children and their adults began to board the bus and the queue moved forward a little. Then the second bus arrived, and the third and fourth. The buzz grew. Aaron had forgotten the coldness of the night. Miss Parker was at the head of the line.

Finally, it was their turn. The bus turned the corner and came into sight. But something was wrong. This wasn't an open-top bus, but an ordinary one; like the one Aaron got with his mum to go shopping on a Saturday. A tall man wearing a cap stepped forward to say that he was very sorry but they had run out of open-top buses. Their tour would have to be on a normal bus – one with a roof!

Miss Parker looked like she was going to cry.

## Putting people on a pedestal

### Aaron's Story

Her bottom lip was wobbling, just like Aaron's baby sister Annie's did. At that moment, Aaron forgot his own disappointment and felt sorry for Miss Parker. She had been so excited when she had announced to the class that they had been chosen, and now in the bitter, dark, cold night, she was left undone. Aaron approached her.

'Never mind, Miss Parker,' he said. 'We can still see all the sights and we won't be so cold.' Miss Parker sniffed into her tissue.

'Yes,' she said, brightening, 'let's make the most of our treat! Everyone on board.' There were a few moans and grumbles but they were quickly forgotten as the children clambered up to the top deck.

The tour was magical. The lights of the buildings shone out and the children noticed things that they had never seen before. James and Aaron chatted away and there were squeals of delight when they saw the Cathedral spire, lit beautifully against the dark night. As for the illuminated football stadium, Aaron thought that he had never seen anything so special.

After an hour of 'oohs' and 'aahs' the bus drew back to the station. Mums and dads were waiting on the kerbside, anxiously looking out for their child. They were pleased to see the smiling faces as the children clattered down the stairs and spilt out on to the pavement, thanking the driver as they scrambled for the door.

'Cheers, mate,' said James, cheekily. The driver smiled – he'd been young once!

Aaron found his mum through the crowd and she bundled him up in the warmth of her coat. How was it?'

'Great,' said Aaron.

'Quick, let's get you home.' They started towards the car but then Aaron said, 'Wait, I didn't thank Miss Parker, Mum. There she goes.' Miss Parker had just turned a corner.

'Be quick,' said Mum, Aaron dashed after Miss Parker. He hurried round the corner and saw her standing with her back to him. Aaron went to speak but something he saw stopped him. In the dark night, he saw something alight. What was it? Aaron realised. It was a cigarette. Miss Parker was smoking.

Aaron was shocked.

He stepped backwards and made his way back to Mum.

They got in the car. Aaron was quiet, all the way home. 'Are you okay?' Mum asked.

'Hmm,' mumbled Aaron, half-heartedly. Mum thought he must be tired. It was late and well past his bedtime.

Aaron didn't find it easy to drop off to sleep even though he was tired. He was disappointed. Disappointed with Miss Parker. Aaron's parents didn't smoke, and he had heard them saying it was 'a dirty habit'. And Miss Parker was a teacher. Teachers didn't do things like that, did they?

The next day, Miss Parker asked Aaron to give out the books at the start of the maths lesson. He was finding it difficult. Things didn't seem the same. He had thought she was so special and now things seemed spoilt.

That night, over tea, Mum said to him, 'Okay Aaron, what's the matter? You're not being yourself.'

Reluctantly, Aaron told her about the night before – what he had seen, and then he waited for Mum to speak. She was always so sensible. 'Well,' she said, 'smoking isn't illegal, Aaron. Miss Parker can smoke if she wants to.'

'But, you always said smoking was a dirty habit,' said Aaron.

'True,' said Mum, 'but that's just my opinion. Not everyone would agree. Miss Parker is still the same person you liked, for all the same reasons – she hasn't changed.' But Aaron thought she had. He was struggling.

The next day at school. Miss Parker asked to see Aaron at break time. 'Is there something wrong Aaron?' she said, 'you don't seem quite right.'

Aaron said nothing. He was embarrassed. He couldn't tell her what he had seen. 'The other night,' she said, 'I saw you. You caught me with a crafty cigarette, didn't you?' She smiled. 'I have been trying to give up, but I am finding it tough. Did I surprise you? Did you think teachers don't smoke, Aaron? Some do,' she said. 'I do.'

She smiled again. 'Off to play. Aaron, listen out for the story in RE this afternoon. See what it says to you.'

Aaron sat in his RE lesson and listened to the story. He wasn't sure what he was meant to see but he would try hard to understand what Miss Parker always called 'the message' behind the Gospel. This is what Aaron heard:

*Jesus said to them, 'All of you will run away and leave me, for the scripture says, "God will kill the shepherd, and the sheep will be scattered." But after I am raised to life, I will go to Galilee ahead of you.'*

*Peter answered, 'I will never leave you, even though all the rest do!' (Mark 26:31–33)*

Miss Parker read on. She told them how Jesus was taken away and arrested. Then she said:

*Peter was still down in the courtyard when one of the High Priest's servant girls came by. When she saw Peter warming himself, she looked straight at him and said, 'You, too, were with Jesus of Nazareth.'*

*But he denied it. 'I don't know ... I don't understand what you are talking about,' he answered, and went out ... (Mark 14:66–68)*

'Well?' said Miss Parker. 'What did Peter do?'

'He let Jesus down,' said Mirabelle.

'Yes he did,' said Miss Parker. 'The Bible doesn't tell us what Jesus would have said to Peter if he had seen him again that night.'

'No,' said John, 'but if he had seen him, I bet he would have forgiven him. He always forgave people.'

'Yes,' said Miss Parker. 'And we must do the same. When we feel someone had done something that we don't like, we must find it in our hearts to forgive them. Shutting the Bible, she caught Aaron's eye and smiled.

Aaron smiled back.

# Teacher's Notes
# Marley's Story

## Background
Starting nursery can be a time of huge difficulty for some children. Learning to rub along with adults who aren't family members can be a huge challenge for some little ones. It can take time to adjust. How such difficulties are handled can shape a child's school experience for years to come. Handled correctly, children can grow in confidence; good preparation for all the change that will inevitably come their way in the future.

## General theme
Change: why do some children (and adults) find it easier to deal with than others? What makes some people particularly vulnerable during such periods in their lives? (Low self-esteem?)

## What do Christians believe?
Change is never easy. It shakes us up. If we are not confident with who we are, we can feel particularly threatened. The teachings of Jesus ask us to focus ourselves on what is really important: our relationship with God. If that is right, we need not have fear of what life can throw at us, for the Lord will carry us when times are tough! (The 'Footprints Prayer' can be particularly moving.)

## Prayer
*Lord Jesus, your disciples were worried when you spoke of leaving them. But you promised to be with them always, through your Spirit. When our lives bring change, something new, or a fresh challenge, may we feel your love and strength supporting and guiding us. Help us to make good choices, guided always by your Spirit.*

## The story
How do you think Marley's mother must have felt when the people in church changed seats? Why was this behaviour particularly disappointing?

## PSMC links
- Have the children ever struggled with change? A new baby brother or sister? A new step-parent? A new teacher? Moving home?
- What happened in their case?

*Modern Christian Assembly Stories*

# Marley's Story

Marley was a complicated character. Since he had been born, he was the centre of his mum's attention. His dad had never lived at home; he was elsewhere. His mum had noticed by the time he was two, that Marley was different. He was prone to outbursts of temper, which were really trying – not just the usual tantrums that children of his age could throw, but sustained outbursts of temper that could be quite violent. He would hit her and spit; his temper seeming to choke the life from him and he would end up exhausted, spent.

She sought help. First, from her mother, who tried hard to help but who had no solution. Then the doctor, who said all children grow and change at different rates; this she found particularly unhelpful. What could she do to help him? She couldn't just wait around for things to get better. He couldn't just carry on, losing it. But, he did. In supermarkets, in the street, on the bus. Marley didn't seem to care that others would look, others would stare. He just carried on, snot running from his nose, cheeks red faced – a cry that cut across people's conversations.

People would comment, 'Just Look at him, talk about naughty!'

'Give him a slap! He needs a good hiding!' There were days when she could have cried and others when she did cry herself to sleep.

Marley's mum had her faith, a deep belief in Jesus. She would pray that Marley would settle down, change and be like the other children: give the love, affection and tenderness that he had inside him – must have inside him. She had tried taking him to church with her but people had tutted and raised their eyes to the ceiling. Then one week she had managed to coax him in, only for the family that they were seated by to get up and move to sit somewhere else. That had made her feel so low: that people could be so unkind in the house of God, where all were meant to be welcome. The priest had been furious when he was told, but Marley's mother had had enough. She would not take him back to church again.

Marley found new situations particularly tough. He would look for her to reassure him. 'It's okay,' she would say. 'There's nothing to worry about, trust me. Trust Mummy.' She would take him to the library for story time but he wouldn't sit. The sight of children gathered round made him tearful; he strained to get away.

Then the day came for Marley to start nursery. Marley's mum was worried. But Mrs Davies, who ran the nursery, said Marley belonged. It might take some time, but they would settle him in. The trick was not to expect too much, too soon. The first day, he didn't get past the front gate. He screamed and punched. He sat down on the path and wouldn't budge.

The second day was no better. Nor the next.

By Friday, his mum had managed to drag him to the door.

'Great,' said Mrs Davies. 'Next week, we'll tempt him in.'

But they didn't. And his mum felt like giving up.

'Next week, we'll come to you,' the staff said.

And, they did. And, after a while, and some coaxing from Mrs Davies, Marley spoke to them. He showed them his toys. All the while, keeping Mum firmly in his sights.

'Why don't you bring Cookie Monster with you to nursery tomorrow?' suggested Mrs Davies, as she knew this was Marley's favourite toy. 'You can show him everything that we have in the nursery and see what he thinks.'

© Gary Nott and Brilliant Publications Limited
*This page may be photocopied for use by the purchasing institution only.*

Modern Christian Assembly Stories

It worked. The next morning, with Cookie Monster in his hands, he walked into nursery and holding Mum's hand firmly, he walked around and saw what was on offer. He sat and had his snack away from the other children, who had gathered on the carpet. He stayed sitting on the edge for the story, but he listened.

The next few weeks, he came and sat, leaving his mum from time to time to join in, gradually becoming more confident. And then during one morning his mum said 'Goodbye,' and left. Mrs Davies held her breath. But Marley carried on playing with the sand, chatting to Christopher, whom he clearly liked.

Breakthrough!

---

The first outburst of temper came the following Tuesday morning. There was no warning. Marley just exploded.

It took both Mrs Davies and Miss Gunnell to hold onto him; to wait till the fight had gone out of him; to calm him down and sit him on a chair.

Marley's mum was apologetic. She had been worried that he would do that. What now?

'We carry on,' said Mrs Davies. 'We don't stop when we have come so far.'

The next time, was little over a week later. And, then it happened again one afternoon session. This time he hit a child. Mrs Davies was taken aback. She had never thought that he would hit another child. But, he had. And he was to do it again.

The nursery were not now sure that they could carry on. There had been complaints from other parents. The children were understandably wary of him. He played alone.

Marley's mum made her way to church and quietly prayed for a miracle.

Later that morning, Marley had been playing barefoot outside, in the sand, when he had flown into a rage. Screaming and kicking, he was picked up by Mrs Davies who carried him back inside. Then he bit her thumb. She winced.

'Calm down,' she said forcibly, and tightened her grip on him. He began to kick all the harder.

'What is it you want from me?' said Mrs Davies in desperation. 'What is it you want?'

'I just want you to hold me,' he spat.

She was taken aback by the request. She hadn't expected to hear that.

Striding to the quiet area she sat down and putting him on to her lap, hugged him. He hung on tight, wrapping his arms around her. She felt he would push all the air out of her, so tight became his grasp. The other children had become still and watched. Without a word, he pushed his head towards her and she instinctively kissed him on the forehead.

When Marley's mum came to collect him, no mention was made of the incident. But Mrs Davies smiled at her.

There were very few temper outbursts from that day on.

Encouraged by Marley's progress, one Sunday morning his mum took him back to church. He sat beautifully. This is what they heard:

*Once Jesus was in a town where there was a man who was suffering from a dreaded skin disease. When he saw Jesus, he threw himself down and begged him, 'Sir, if you want to, you can make me clean!'*

*Jesus stretched out his hand and touched him. 'I do want to,' he answered. 'Be clean!' At once the disease left the man.* (Luke 5:12–13)

Marley carried on attending St John's Nursery. Marley's mum thanked God, for she had received her miracle.

# Teacher's Notes
# Daniel's Story

## Background
I had a black colleague whose son won a ballet scholarship to an independent performing arts school. He could dance ballet. He was bullied at the school; his face didn't fit, quite literally.

## General theme
Why do some people use skin colour as a way of putting others down? Daniel manages to defeat one set of prejudices (boys don't dance), only to encounter another (boys who do dance aren't black). He has to pick himself up and struggle on.

## What do Christians believe?
The Bible has many stories of people who encountered setback after setback: Moses, Job and Saul are all good examples. The children could find out each one's story. My personal favourite is the story of Paul, who when obeying the Lord to go to a specific place and preach, was captured, beaten and thrown into stocks. What was his response? Did he give up? No, he began to sing the Lord's praises! Christians believe that we should use setbacks as stepping stones –'setups' – I once heard them called: they can lead us forward to greater glories, if we have the right frame of mind.

## Prayer
*Lord Jesus, during your life on earth, you were mocked, ridiculed and cast out. There is nothing that we will experience in life that we can't deal with together. When we are going through difficult times, when we have been treated badly, are lonely, upset or lost, remind us that your love will never leave us, your friendship will support us and your Spirit will strengthen us.*

## The story
Why did the boys in Daniel's first school think dance wasn't for boys? Are all kinds of dance included in this or are some forms acceptable? Why the difference? Can the children think of any famous dancers who are men? Why do the children in Daniel's new school focus upon his colour?

## PSMC links
- Have the children met racial prejudice in their own lives? What happened?
- Is racism the worst kind of bullying?

© Gary Nott and Brilliant Publications Limited
*This page may be photocopied for use by the purchasing institution only.*

# Daniel's Story

Daniel had always wanted to dance. There was a rhythm in him, a beat that he could not ignore. He heard it in his head when he slept and awoke with his feet ready to move. He liked all kinds of dance and whenever he got the chance he would show off his talent to Mum; he liked nothing more than to dance around the living room but he was less confident in front of others. He worried about what they would think. The boys in his class lived and breathed football. They joked about it, they played it and sometimes they argued about it. Daniel went along with it. He was frightened to be different; he didn't want to stand out. He wanted people to like him. And, they did – he was one of the lads.

Then, Mr Jenkins, their teacher, broke his leg. He had been playing football, of all things. Mr Davies, the Headteacher, wrote to the parents to say that Mr Jenkins would be absent for some time. A substitute teacher would be taking over, Miss Lucy.

Miss Lucy made an immediate impression. She was young and always ready with a beaming smile and had an infectious laugh. Everyone seemed to like her and, importantly, the class behaved well for her. Mr Jenkins would have been pleased. On Wednesday afternoon, the children had PE, their favourite subject. They either went outside for team games or stayed in the Hall and did gym. After lunch, the children came in happy and ready for what the afternoon might bring.

'Listen everyone,' said Miss Lucy, talking loudly to get their attention, 'please change for indoor PE.' The boys grumbled a little, they had wanted to get stuck into their team games. The girls were overjoyed – gymnastics!

'Okay, find a space,' said Miss Lucy. 'Let's warm up our bodies.' They did. Then they sat down again, obediently, ready for the lesson. Miss Lucy then did something unexpected. She asked them to find a space and, putting on a CD, asked them to close their eyes and listen to the music. Daniel's feet began to twitch.

'Now, I want you to stand and *mooooove* to the music,' she said. Move, or rather *mooooove* to the music – what did she mean? Nathaniel, who could be difficult, began to laugh. Sally joined in, soon half the class were giggling. Miss Lucy stopped the music.

'Hasn't Mr Jenkins ever done dance with you?' she asked. Daniel's mind was working overtime: dance, in school, could they?

'Listen,' pleaded Miss Lucy, 'I want you to be serious. Listen to the music and stay sitting. Then stand and begin to move, but only if you feel comfortable. If you don't,' she said, conscious that Sally was still giggling, 'just sit still and keep your eyes closed.'

Miss Lucy started the music again. She looked a little hesitant. She didn't want the class to be difficult. The music started. It was a fast rhythm punctuated with drums. Ellie Mae jumped up and began to move in time to the music. Miss Lucy, herself joined in and soon a group of the girls were moving about – some keeping time, others not. The boys sat and watched. One or too laughed, one or two sat staring. Daniel stood up.

'Come on,' he said, 'let's join in.' None of the boys stirred. At that moment, Daniel knew that he had to grasp the opportunity Miss Lucy was giving him. He began to move, and as the beat took hold, his body convulsed in an explosion of shape and movement. The girls stopped dancing, one by one. Miss Lucy stopped dancing. Daniel wasn't aware that they had, for he was lost in his own world: performing, just as he did at home, where his mum would be

# Daniel's Story

his appreciative audience. The music came to an end. Miss Lucy started to clap and the girls joined in. The boys sat still, looking awkward.

'Wow!' said Miss Lucy, 'Daniel, you're a natural. Really, what talent!' Daniel suddenly felt all self-conscious, naked; he felt as if he'd been transported momentarily to some other place.

After school that day, Miss Lucy asked to see Daniel's mum. She repeated that Daniel had a 'natural talent', whatever that meant, and that she felt sure he belonged in a school that specialised in dance; there were 'scholarships' for children these days, so Mum needn't worry about paying. She said she would speak to Mr Davies.

Mum wasn't sure. It would mean Daniel travelling some distance, for the dance school was on the other side of town. Daniel was young. Was he old enough to make such a journey? She couldn't go with him every day.

But Daniel ached for the chance. He had felt the experience of dancing in school and now to go somewhere where they were allowed to dance every day seemed unreal.

Miss Lucy was as good as her word. She sorted out what teachers call 'paperwork' and the day came when Daniel had his audition. It was to be at his school, St Swithun's. The examiners, Miss Lucy said, 'wanted to see Daniel in an environment that he knew' (more 'teacher speak').

After the audition, Daniel felt exhausted and elated all at the same time. The examiners huddled together and spoke with Miss Lucy. Their decision would be sent out in the post in the days to come, they said. The days to come, thought Daniel, when was that exactly? He needed to know.

'You were wonderful Daniel,' said Miss Lucy. It was the first time that she had called him that.

The boys in his class were edgy with him. 'Dancing,' scoffed Nathaniel. 'It's for girls – when are you going to start wearing dresses?' Daniel felt foolish – embarrassed. Mum was angry when he told her.

'You are to take no notice Daniel Ellison,' she said. 'That makes me so angry,' she added, spitting feathers.

The letter dropped onto the doormat on Friday morning. Daniel took it into the kitchen. Mum was there. He couldn't bear to open it. He had got his hopes up, but what if Miss Lucy was wrong, and he couldn't dance? He opened the letter. He had been accepted. His world was about to change, and he knew it.

_____

The girls had been supportive. 'Well done,' said Mirabelle.

'Great news,' chimed Danielle.

'You're gay!' barked Nathaniel. Daniel said nothing. He was going to a place where everyone danced. He would be happy there.

That first day, Mum was to go with him. The dance school was 30 minutes away on two buses and Daniel had to get to know the way. He had his bag neatly packed: dance pumps, t-shirts and shorts, all new and folded.

Daniel walked into his first class, feeling nervous. The classroom was a dance studio, with a sleek floor and strips of spotlights suspended from the ceiling. There was lively bustle in the air as the other students were arriving. No one spoke to Daniel. Daniel looked on in amazement. For every girl, there was a boy. It was hard to get your head around. All these boys – he felt at home – no – he didn't actually – something still wasn't right. He couldn't put his finger on it but he felt different.

The teacher called the class to attention. He ran through some steps and then asked the class to copy. Daniel quickly showed that he was in the right place; he flew through the air with poise and rhythm.

At break, still no one spoke to him.

It was odd.

# Racism

## Daniel's Story

The teacher came over; he was friendly; 'nice to have you here Daniel,' he said. 'I have been praying that you would walk through our door. No, seriously,' he went on, seeing Daniel's look of surprise. 'Literally, at church each week.'

Daniel didn't know what to make of it. It was odd. There were plenty of boys, why did the teacher want him there so badly.

In the afternoon, some girls spoke to Daniel; they seemed nice enough. The boys, however, kept their distance. There was something wrong, and he didn't get it. The children all had lockers to keep their things in and as he closed his that night, Daniel reflected on what had been a strange day. Dance, yes. Boys, yes. Friends, no!

The next morning, Daniel travelled on his own.

He went into the locker room and at first didn't realise what he was looking at. Then he realised what it was. Hanging from his locker door was a banana and a photo of a monkey. There was a note that read 'Go back to where you belong, you're the wrong colour.'

All at once, Daniel realised what he had felt yesterday had been real. He didn't fit in. His was the only black face at the school. Everyone else was white.

Daniel's stomach felt heavy.

He had felt hurt by the boys in his old school because they laughed at him wanting to dance. Now in this school, where there were lots of boys who danced, he still felt like an outsider … .

He could have cried.

Mr Spencer came in.

'That's not on,' he said, noticing the locker. 'I will speak to them about this.'

'No,' said Daniel. 'Please don't. I'm used to people saying things. It's just a different way for them to do it. In my last school, there were plenty of black faces. I may not have met this before but I am used to not fitting in.'

'Look,' said Mr Spencer, 'read this.' He handed Daniel a well-thumbed Bible. 'Look at page 84,' he said, with an encouraging smile. Daniel sat down on the bench and read:

*Jesus looked at his disciples and said,*
*Happy are the poor,*
*The Kingdom of God is yours.*
*Happy are you who are hungry now*
*You will be filled.*
*Happy are those who cry now*
*You will laugh.*

*Happy are you when people hate you, reject you, insult you … Be glad when that happens, and dance for joy, because a great reward is kept for you in heaven.*
(Luke 6:20–23)

'Dance for joy!' repeated Daniel, out loud.

He opened his locker and took out his kit. He took down the banana, picture and note and threw them in the bin.

He strode confidently into the dance studio. Dance for joy, he thought.

# Teacher's Notes
# Mr Jenkins' Story

## Background
We all lead busy lives. More and more things occupy our minds and time for what is really important to us – family, friends, God – gets squeezed. In my own life, I try to find time for my family, my job, my God, my friends and writing – in that order! Some would say I have my priorities wrong. On reflection, so would I.

## General theme
What is truly important? Do we pay lip service to things that we profess to hold dear? Is that society's fault for making us feel that we have to serve so many masters or should we be more assertive, taking control of our own destinies?

## What do Christians believe?
Nothing should be above our devotion to God. He should come first in all situations. How many of us can say that he does, with true conviction? Why do so many of us fail in this regard when in our heart of hearts we know what is true and good.

## Prayer
*Father God, as we listen to stories from the Bible, we hear so many times of people who have doubted you, disappointed you and turned away from you. But you always have mercy on those who come back, with a faithful heart. Forgive us when we forget you. Forgive us when we seem too busy for you. May we remember that everything good in our lives comes from you and always be thankful.*

## The story
In how many ways does Mr Jenkins let people down?
What is most important to him?
Does this change? Why?

## PSMC links
- How do we prioritise what is important to us?
- Do we ever get it wrong?
- What stops us from being the people we want to be?

# Mr Jenkins' Story

Mr Jenkins was feeling harassed. There were never enough hours to get everything done.

It was the day of the school church service and there was still a lot do. It wasn't easy being a Headteacher. Anyone who said it was, really didn't know what they were talking about.

'Mr Jenkins,' said a voice.' I've got my costume. But I'm not sure that it works.'

'Don't just barge in, Joshua,' he said. 'Close the door again and knock this time.' Joshua stepped outside and closed the door shut.

At that moment the phone rang. Mr Jenkins picked up the receiver. 'Hello,' he said. 'Hello. Who?' It was Mrs Watson, the borough inspector.

'Oh, hello, Mrs Watson, yes of course I have time for you. I always have time for you,' he said, sitting up to attention. Mrs Watson was an important person who needed to be courted.

Knock. It was Joshua, waiting patiently outside.

'No,' said Mr Jenkins, 'of course, it would be lovely to see you, so glad you can join us. Two o'clock at St Boniface's Church. Park in the car park opposite.'

Knock. Knock!

'The children have indeed worked very hard.' So have I, he thought – if only you knew. 'The theme?' she asked.

'Making time for Jesus,' he replied.

Suddenly, the door burst open. 'Did you say to come in?' said Joshua.

Mr Jenkins groaned.

Having despatched Joshua off to find Mrs Davies to sort out his costume, Mr Jenkins strode across to the children and parents waiting outside that morning. He opened the padlock and pulled the gates back. The children swarmed in, some shouting a cheery 'Hello'.

Mrs Fraser, Danny Fraser's mum, and a demanding parent if ever there was one, made a beeline for Mr Jenkins.

'Mr Jenkins,' she said, 'I've had some bad news. My father, you'll remember he's been ill, was diagnosed with Parkinson's Disease yesterday.'

'Oh dear,' said Mr Jenkins. 'I need someone to talk to,' continued Mrs Fraser. 'Could I come and see you later this morning for a chat.'

'Not this morning, no,' replied Mr Jenkins. There was trained sympathy in his face. 'We have the church service to rehearse. I'm sorry. Maybe tomorrow? Phone and ask Mrs Butcher to fit you in.' Mrs Fraser looked disappointed. She moved away, slowly. 'Really!' thought Mr Jenkins, 'I'd like to help but we have a service to prepare. We're getting ready for Jesus!'

Walking back into his office he spied Mrs Butcher, his secretary. She looked like she had been crying. Mr Jenkins knew she was having a difficult time as of late. Her husband had been made redundant and there was no sign of other employment. Mr Jenkins stopped in his tracks and retraced his steps, quietly, so Mrs Butcher wouldn't hear him. He would have no time to spend with her this morning. He was already late for his first class of the day. Rehearsals to follow, had the children learnt their lines? He had certainly asked them to, told them to: at home, no time in school – never was.

Mr Jenkins strode into class 5D. It was RE. He'd had no time to prepare. He seldom did these days. What could he do with them to fill the time? 'Do we have to do the Bible again?' asked Jimmy Wade. 'It's boring.' Mr Jenkins looked carefully at Jimmy. He really did lack respect. He made fun of everything and everyone. Mr Jenkins went to speak to him, but then thought better of it. There would be

*Modern Christian Assembly Stories*

© Gary Nott and Brilliant Publications Limited

*This page may be photocopied for use by the purchasing institution only.*

# Mr Jenkins' Story — Making time for Jesus

time to sort young Jimmy out later; at least, he had no time to do it now. He would have to let his comment go. He set the class to their task while he set about adding the finishing touches to some props that were needed for the service. To think, Mrs Watson was going to be there; he would need to impress.

He looked up. Sally and Christa were standing in front of him. 'Can we talk with you, Mr Jenkins?' said the girls. 'Laura is annoying us, and won't be friends.'

'Not now girls,' said Mr Jenkins. 'Tomorrow. Come and see me tomorrow; we can talk about it then.'

Back in his office, Mr Jenkins pulled his post in front of him. There were a number of letters from the local education authority and a flier that caught his eye; it was an appeal for money for the starving in Third World countries. They were looking for schools to get involved with their charity. There was a number to phone.

The letter said it was urgent. Mr Jenkins hesitated, but then quickly put the letter in the bin. They had supported a charity that term; there really was no time to help another. There was a knock at the door. It was Susie.

'I'm not too sure how to pronounce some of the words in what I'm reading this afternoon. Could you help me?' she said.

'Not now, Susie, find Mr Philips. I've just got time to check on the dining hall. It has been particularly noisy in there today.'

Mr Jenkins strode into the Hall, biting his way into his cheese and pickle sandwich, en route.

Two o'clock came. The parents and children gathered in the church. It was noisy. Mr Jenkins got everyone's attention, well almost everyone's.

'They had gathered,' he said, spying Mrs Watson out of the corner of his eye, 'to hear about being ready for Jesus.'

© Gary Nott and Brilliant Publications Limited
*This page may be photocopied for use by the purchasing institution only.*

Modern Christian Assembly Stories

Susie stood up and started to speak. But, something was wrong. She was stumbling on particular words – Nazareth, disciples and temptation; she clearly hadn't prepared. Mr Jenkins' attention was pulled away by some commotion. He spied Jimmy Wade, who was being disruptive – not listening to the readings, trying to chat to the person behind him. Mr Jenkins glanced towards the back of the church. To one side of the seated adults, sat Mrs Fraser, Danny's mum. She looked tired and drawn, as if she hadn't slept. He hadn't noticed that when speaking to her this morning. And, to her left was Mrs Butcher, his secretary, red eyed – she had clearly been crying, again.

His gaze came back to the front and there in the middle of the front line of the choir stood Sally and Christa. They were arguing with Laura.

Mr Jenkins went flat. His shoulders sagged.

In the front row sat Mrs Watson, the borough adviser. She looked stony faced.

Mr Jenkins looked back at the children at the front of the church. There stood Joshua, who was having a costume malfunction. His shepherd's cloak had slipped to the floor revealing his pants and vest. Jimmy Wade laughed out loud.

Trina stepped up to the reading from the Gospel. She read:

> *As Jesus and his disciples went on their way, he came to a village where a woman named Martha welcomed him in her home. She had a sister named Mary, who sat down at the feet of the Lord and listened to his teaching. Martha was upset about all the work she had to do, so she came and said: 'Lord, don't you care that my sister has left me to do all the hard work myself? Tell her to come and help me!'*
>
> *The Lord answered her, 'Martha, Martha! You are worried and troubled over so many things but just one is needed. Mary has chosen the right thing, and it will not be taken away from her.'*
> *(Luke 10:38–41)*

Mr Jenkins sat with his eyes closed. Hot and bothered, he wanted to shut the world out. But a nagging thought pushed its way in. He had been a little like Martha. Where in his day had he found time for Jesus? He hadn't found it in not preparing for 5D, nor in not taking time to chastise Jimmy Wade; nor in not talking with Mrs Butcher or Mrs Fraser. He hadn't found time when not listening to Christa and Sally. He hadn't found time for Susie; or poor Joshua, who now stood looking embarrassed in the front of everyone.

Mrs Watson stopped to talk to him after the service.

'Nice idea,' she said, 'but it strikes me that you need to find time for Jesus throughout the day, not just at 2.00 pm in the church.'

Much later, Mr Jenkins flopped into his office chair. The children and staff had gone home. He had had a bad day. But, somehow, he thought he had learnt something. And, stooping down to the bin he took out the appeal for aid in the Third World. He smoothed out the creases.

It was never too late, he thought, to make time for Jesus.

## Teacher's Notes
# Cameron, James, Jasmine and Derek's Story

## Background
Lots of people have secret fears! I don't like heights and I foolishly once got into a cable car. All I wanted to do was get to the floor, where I felt less vulnerable. Children have all sorts of fears: flying, the dark, ghosts, dentists, wasps, the list goes on. I once taught a child who was frightened of the rain!

## General theme
Anyone can be vulnerable to a seemingly irrational fear. Some people are open about their fears whereas others prefer to keep it a secret.

## What do Christians believe?
Christians believe that with God by their side, there is no fear that they cannot overcome. Christ had to overcome his own fears: he was on a path that would lead to his death. He looked to His Father to help him stay calm.

## Prayer
*Loving Father, life is full of challenges that need to be faced. Thank you that we are never alone in this.*

## The story
Mr Jefferson knows that he doesn't like heights but still steps into the pod. Why?
What will the children be thinking when they see their Headteacher act in this way?

## PSMC links
- Are the children frightened of anything? Are they prepared to share?
- What would they do if they were frightened of something?

# Cameron, James, Jasmine and Derek's Story

The children of Class 6R had been enjoying reading *The London Eye Mystery* by Siobhan Dowd. They were delighted when Mrs Jenkins announced that she would be taking the class to visit the Eye, the huge wheel ride that stood on the banks of the Thames.

In the novel, a friend of some children seemingly disappears: they see him get onto the Eye, into one of the large white pods, but he doesn't come back to earth when the wheel has completed its turn. The children in the class laughed. Would this happen to them? They were excited.

Mrs Jenkins had asked Mr Jefferson, the headteacher, to accompany them. Cameron and Derek made plans: they would go on the same pod and sit together on the coach. Jasmine saw Mr Jefferson in the corridor,

'Are you pleased to be coming Sir?' she asked. Mr Jefferson smiled hesitantly. He was and he wasn't. He liked going places with the children. But he had a secret: he wasn't good with heights and wasn't sure how he would cope with the London Eye. Still, it was too late now – it had been agreed – he was going. Mrs Jenkins was depending upon him.

The day of the visit dawned bright and clear: a great day for seeing London from the viewpoint of the Eye. Mr Jefferson pushed the sausage round his breakfast plate; he didn't feel hungry. The thought of the trip into the sky loomed large over him. What had he let himself in for?

The children arrived at school early. The coach was already there. Cameron and

## Cameron, James, Jasmine and Derek's Story

Derek clambered on board; Derek had ham sandwiches for his lunch; Cameron had cheese (his favourite). Jasmine was sitting in front of them. She was enjoying chatting loudly to James who was two rows in front.

'Jasmine,' called out Mrs Jenkins, 'I can hear you from here!'

'Sorry, Miss,' came the reply. But seconds later, Jasmine's volume had been turned back up! It always was.

The coach travelled on. The children 'oohed' and 'aahed' as they made their way into London; the sights came thick and fast. Mr Jefferson tried to take his mind off his discomfort.

'Are you okay, David?' asked Mrs Jenkins.

'Fine,' replied the Headteacher, 'just a slight headache.'

'Take these,' said his colleague, pressing some headache tablets into his palm. Mr Jefferson swigged them back.

The coach turned a corner and the Eye came into view. It was enormous, much taller than the children had imagined. Mr Jefferson swallowed hard; his heart had started to beat just a bit quicker, he thought.

Mrs Jenkins asked the children to quieten down. She told them that they were to walk carefully in pairs and not to cross the roads until an adult told them to. The class clambered off and walked in a crocodile to the Eye. Mr Jefferson made a point of looking down.

'Look sir,' said Cameron tugging on his arm, 'it's enormous.'

'Yes,' replied the Headteacher, focusing on the boy's face. 'Isn't it?'

There was a long queue. Mrs Jenkins went to speak to one of the supervisors, who opened a separate empty lane and the children went to line up. The excitement was mounting. The children were to go in to pods in groups of 12, each with an adult. Mr Jefferson had Cameron, Derek, Jasmine and James in his group and some others. The children waited patiently.

One by one the pods floated round; they skimmed the platform where the children were standing, moving slowly. The children stepped on as the pod came level with where they were standing. Mr Jefferson's group's pod arrived and they stepped on with their tour guide.

The guide introduced herself to the children and the Headteacher. Her name was Ellie. She would be telling them about what they were going to see. The children looked out of the glass sides of the pod. They were low down and the pod was moving slowly, almost gracefully. Mr Jefferson stared out of the glass. He was enjoying the view – maybe this wasn't going to be so bad after all; the thing was going at practically a snail's pace. But as the pod began to lift, Mr Jefferson absent-mindedly glanced upwards and caught sight of the top of the Eye; it was further up than even he had imagined. His stomach lurched. A shot of panic sped through his veins. This was not a good idea; he had known it but had ignored his better sense.

The guide was prattling on. 'The River Thames is one of the cleanest rivers in the world. If you fill a glass with it, it will appear cloudy but that is only because it sits on a clay base. It is, in fact, very clean water.'

Mr Jefferson was struggling to listen. The children were walking from one side of the pod to the other, drinking in all that they surveyed. The pod was rising imperceptibly upwards.

The guide continued. 'In the summer,' she said, 'dolphins have been known to swim up the Thames and have been seen from the pod.'

Mr Jefferson was now sitting down, staring at the floor. His gaze was fixed. He was feeling quite unwell.

Jasmine spotted him, sitting down. 'Come on Sir,' she shouted excitedly, 'you're missing everything.' She looked at her Headteacher. His hands were white, gripping the bench that sat in the centre of the pod.

'In a minute,' he answered.

Derek looked up, he had forgotten the

Headteacher in all the excitement. Mr Jefferson was sliding to the floor. What was going on? 'Sir,' he asked, 'are you okay?'

'I need to get to the floor,' Mr Jefferson whispered, looking white. 'Tell me,' mouthed the Headteacher, 'are we at the top yet?'

Derek looked up. 'No,' he replied, 'we're not even quarter of the way up yet,' he observed. The boy motioned to Cameron to come over. The two boys looked at their Headteacher. Jasmine and James were with the guide, looking at something she was pointing out in the distance; they hadn't noticed what was happening at the bench.

'Look,' said Mr Jefferson, 'I'm no good with heights, I'm afraid.' The two boys looked at him.

'Is he going to be sick?' wondered Cameron, out loud. Jasmine turned to look around the pod and saw what was happening. She hurried over and stood listening to what the two boys were saying.

'I can't breathe,' said the Headteacher. 'My chest feels tight.'

In the background, they could still hear the guide. If you look to the left, you will see the Shard, London's tallest building. Suddenly the guide realised that she was talking to just the one child. Where was everyone else? She glanced round and saw the Headteacher sitting on the floor. 'Why whatever's the matter?' she asked.

'Heights,' said Jasmine. ' Sir isn't good with them.'

'A bag,' said Cameron. 'He needs to breathe into a bag. It will help. My Auntie had to do that once. It's called a panic attack!'

James took the sandwiches out of the carrier bag that he was carrying and handed it to the Headteacher, who began to breathe into it. The children looked at him. Was he starting to look a little better? Yes, they thought so.

'Keep breathing into the bag,' urged Cameron. 'We've passed the top now, we're on our way back down.' Gradually, the pod descended. 'You can look up now,' said Cameron; we can see the ground easily. Mr Jefferson heaved himself back onto the bench and dared to look out. The pod was just 20 metres or so from the ground. He sighed with relief.

'Listen children,' he said, 'I feel a little foolish. Do you think we could keep this a secret?'

'Of course,' said Cameron. 'I remember when I wet myself on a school trip. The teacher, Miss Canon, said it would be our little secret. It made me feel better, less silly.' Mr Jefferson, smiled weakly. They were good children.

The pod slid to the ground and Mr Jefferson and the children exited.

Mrs Jenkins was waiting for them at the bottom. She smiled when she saw them.

'How was it?' she asked.

'Great,' said Jasmine. 'We saw lots of interesting things. Some things took Mr Jefferson's breath away,' she added, winking at the Headteacher, who grinned.

# Teacher's Notes
# Henry's Story

## Background
The facts about the spread of domestic violence make for grim reading. More and more of our young children are exposed to it. I once taught a child whose father had held his mother out of the window by her feet. The child had seen it all. How do you then come to school with peace of mind, let alone feeling ready to learn?

## General theme
Children often have to leave the marital home when relationships break down. On the way to a different life, they sometimes have to stay in a hostel; this can be a very unsettling time in their lives. The after affects can be felt for some time; even surfacing in adulthood in a variety of ways.

## What do Christians believe?
Love and fear do not coexist. 'Love is patient; love is kind.' (1 Corinthians 13:4)

In the past, some churches believed that the wife should grin and bear it; the relationship should be worked at; the wife should put up with it! The modern church takes a different view, thankfully. No one should live a life of fear.

## Prayer
*Dear Father, thank you for our families. Thank you for the people who love us and keep us safe. We pray for those people who don't have a safe and happy home life, for whatever reason. We thank you for the people whose job it is to support and care for them.*

## The story
How does Eddie feel about his Dad at the end of the story? Why might he be torn between his parents?

## PSMC links
- Why is violence never the answer?

# Henry's Story

Henry couldn't read. Letters on the page jumped about. 'Dyslexia,' his mum said; he didn't know what she meant. All he knew was that school was difficult – frightening, even. He would be shown how to read a word, but couldn't remember it the next day. It was like his memory was busted. The teachers didn't understand him.

'Why can't you remember?' they would say. 'We've done this.' They thought he was lazy, and he just wanted to muck about. He did, but only because he couldn't read. What was he to do? He couldn't just sit there and be the kid who didn't get it. He had to distract the others' attention from the fact that he was struggling. Each day was more difficult – every day he had to play the fool. Then there were days when he just panicked; panicked because he knew he would be asked to read aloud. He would insist on playing around and 'the usuals' would laugh and he would get told to stand by the side – resulting in no reading for him! Deep inside, he hated himself for disappointing yet another teacher but he couldn't read – what did they expect him to do?

Life at home was difficult too. They had stopped going to church – at one time, they had always been there. Instead, Mum and Dad rowed all the time. They argued about money and Henry too – his behaviour at school, his levels. Nan said Mum and Dad would be better off apart. Henry worried. He wasn't sure what she meant exactly. But he guessed they would be what he had heard his teacher call 'a split family'. Dad would live somewhere, Mum elsewhere. But how about him? Maybe he would go to Nan's? She always had time for him. She knew about the reading; she said he was bright, not stupid, that one day the penny would drop and he'd be away. Henry liked the sound of that. 'Be away!' It sounded like flying! Freewheeling! To be able to read what anyone put in front of you. Be clever, like the kids on the top table in class – they were cool.

Then it happened. Mum and Dad had been out for the night, drinking. Nan was babysitting. She had tucked him in, read him a story. He had awoken with a start. The clock shone out into his room: 00.31. Mum and Dad were at it again. Loud voices, each one trying to drown the other out. Mum sounded tired; Dad, angry. Henry slowly got up. He crept downstairs and approached the living room door. The voices were louder there. Mum was screeching, Dad barking. It was like a cat and dog, going hammer and tongs. Dad seemed to be winning. Henry opened the door and then saw it. Dad let go of a punch. Mum fell back towards the sofa, blood oozing from her mouth.

Henry burst into tears. He wanted them to see him, to stop. All he could do was sob. He had tried to say 'Stop it! Leave her alone!' but the words wouldn't come. All he had were tears. Mum came running to him and bundled him up in her arms. Dad was shouting that he was sorry, that he hadn't meant to.

It was too late. He had done it; he had hit Mum – he made her bleed.

Mum got into bed with him and pulled the duvet up high. 'It will be all right,' she whispered. He had stopped crying now. Dad was downstairs. Henry had a headache; his brain thumped. He couldn't sleep. He closed his eyes, but the room swam. Mum felt warm against him. In that moment, he knew he loved her. He hated Dad. What a pig!

The next day, Nan picked him up from school, said he was going to stay the night with her because Mum and Dad had a lot to talk about. The next day, it was Mum there – she

*Modern Christian Assembly Stories*

© Gary Nott and Brilliant Publications Limited

*This page may be photocopied for use by the purchasing institution only.*

# Henry's Story — Family breakdown

said he wasn't to ask questions, but they would be living somewhere new, just for a while – until she got them sorted. What did that mean? Mum said the place they were staying was a hostel. Just the one room, tired and bare. Next door lived a family of three; to the other side, one of five.

'It could be worse,' said Mum. She told him that she loved him. She seemed to be doing that a lot. Said it would work out.

'Where is Dad?' he asked. But he already knew the answer. Dad was long gone – 'a million miles away.'

'We'll be safe here,' said Mum, 'he can't find us.' Did this mean he would never see Dad again? He tried hard to remember the good times – the trips to the zoo, his birthday parties, Christmas – but all the while he was back standing in the doorway, seeing the punch – hearing it, feeling it. His head hurt; he felt winded.

What would Nan think? She was Dad's mum. She would take Dad's side, surely? It was natural. Would she still love Henry? He wasn't sure.

He went to school with the other kids at the hostel. They were sat at the back. 'You won't be here long,' said the teaching assistant who was asked to work with them. Henry kept his head down. He didn't want to go to school. He was frightened he would be caught out – made to read, which he couldn't, still couldn't ... .

Then one day, Henry just stopped going to school. Took a different turn. Hung around a newsagents until lunchtime, then caught a bus to town. He walked the streets, looking in shop windows, all the time trying to guess what the time might be. He was hungry. That night, he hurried his tea down. The next day, he didn't bother with school, nor the next.

Before he could be found out, Mum announced they would be moving away. They had a bright new home. A flat in another town. 'Where was Nan now?' he thought. 'And Dad?'

The flat was okay, small, but private. Mum set about cleaning it as soon as they arrived. Then they went shopping in town for some things to make it pretty. With the shopping finished, she treated him to a McDonald's. Sitting there with her in the flat, he felt better. Better than he had felt for a long time: cleaner, safer – calmer. It was, as she said, just the two of them now.

The next day she took him to school. He wasn't sure if he would stay. He'd see. He knew where the bus stop was so he could escape if he needed to.

Then he met her – his new teacher. She smelt nice, spoke softly. 'Let's see what you can do,' she said, 'and where we can help you to improve.' She was patient and made him feel like he was alone with her in the room. She said that he would get better at reading and, taking a bag, she placed some words inside. 'Try to memorise these,' she said, with a smile. 'But if you can't, don't worry; we'll get there eventually, together.'

Together – it sounded good.

She was everything that he hoped a teacher would be. He couldn't get enough of her. And, bit by bit, he inched forward. One day, Mum took him back to church. He went out with the other kids to hear the Gospel. This is what he heard:

*A teacher of the Law came up and tried to trap Jesus. 'Teacher,' he asked, 'what must I do to earn eternal life?' Jesus answered him. 'What do the scriptures say? How do you interpret them?'*

*The man answered, 'Love the Lord your God with all your heart and with all your soul and with all your strength and with all your mind; and love your neighbour as you love yourself.'*

*'You are right,' Jesus replied; 'do this, and you will live.'* (Luke 10:25–28)

Life had been difficult these past few months. Despite himself, Henry sometimes missed Dad, and Nan. But with her, his new teacher, there was something to look forward to. There were other kids too. Kids who didn't expect him to play the fool. Kids whom he could trust – who didn't judge him - and who came round to his flat for egg and chips, his favourite. Mum was pleased to see them. He was beginning to make progress. And Mum was happier – happier than he had seen her for a long time. They were going to church again. Henry was feeling much better. He thought about the words of the Gospel that he had heard: 'Do this, and you will live.'

Henry still couldn't read well. But he had begun to think that one day he would. That one day things would sort themselves out, just as they had for Mum – whom he loved, that much he did know.

Then one day a postcard plopped onto the mat. He read, 'I Miss You So Much, Love Dad.' Henry didn't know what to think: Dad missed him. He had read it. Yes, read it.

He wanted to talk it over: with Mum; and her, his teacher; and Jesus, of course.

He would.

# Teacher's Notes
# Mr Peters' Story

## Background
Across the country, Year 6 children in many schools have a very tough time in their last year in primary school. Once, it was perhaps the highlight of their time in that phase of their education. Now it is driven by preparation for SATs – end of year government-regulated exams. The curriculum is often narrowed with subjects like art, history and geography being replaced by extra maths and English lessons. No one resents this more than the teachers, who are under enormous pressure for the children to do well. We are all marching to someone else's beat: that of central government. Some teachers – and children – do crack under the pressure; thankfully very few break.

## General themes
When is it right to stand up for yourself and say enough is enough?

## What do Christians believe?
Christians believe there are always two sides to a story. The important thing to do is sit down with a person and ask them why they are acting in the way that they are. It is always good to talk. If we pray for a solution to our problem, God will answer our call.

## Prayer
*Loving Lord, draw close to us when we are lonely and feeling that no one is on our side. Help us to remember that we are never truly alone, as you are constantly with us, guiding us and comforting us and surrounding us with your love.*

## The story
Mr Peters means well but he has lost his perspective. Ultimately, it makes him ill. His replacement is not cut from the same cloth: he is not worried by end of year results because he probably thinks he won't be around by then. The headteacher in the story is reasonable: she listens to the children's complaints but remembers there is a person with feelings at the centre of it, Mr Peters.

## PSMC links
- How useful is a petition when things are going wrong? How does it make the person on the receiving end feel?
- Is there a better way to raise concerns when you are worried about something?
- Petitions can strike fear into the person on the receiving end. Is a petition a form of bullying?

© Gary Nott and Brilliant Publications Limited
*This page may be photocopied for use by the purchasing institution only.*

Modern Christian Assembly Stories

# Mr Peters' Story

SATs! It was all Mr Peters seemed to think about. 'This will help to get you ready for your SATs. Don't forget, you will need to know this for your tests. When you take your SATs, you will most certainly need to remember this.'

The mums and dads had not been slow to catch on – 'This year is the most important year that you've had,' they said. 'It's time to knuckle down.' 'Let's put your studies firSt' Class 6P were fed up. Every day seemed to be full of English and maths; history and geography had disappeared off the timetable. PE had been cut from two to one lesson a week – and if it rained, it was replaced with yet more maths. Then there were after-school catch-up sessions. On Wednesdays they had 'triple English'.

'It's not fair,' complained Jacob to his mum. 'This isn't what school is meant to be about. Mrs Howlett says school days are meant to be the best days of your life – well these aren't, I can tell you.'

The strain was showing too on Mr Peters. He had become snappy. The children were less confident around him. He looked tired and didn't smile; not even when they tried to have a joke. Then one Monday morning, he suddenly wasn't there. They had a string of substitute teachers and at the end of the week they took home a letter to their parents. It said that Mr Peters was suffering from exhaustion – that he would not be back that term. Mrs Howlett said that their thoughts and prayers were with him and that they wished him a speedy recovery.

The children were flat. They had been fond of Mr Peters at the start of term; before he had gone turbo, as Richard Williams called it. Thinking back Jacob could see what Richard meant. Mr Peters had thought of nothing but next May's exams; it had been unhealthy.

The following Monday they arrived in class to find a new teacher standing before them. He introduced himself as Mr Tompkins. He would be with them till Christmas he said. He started off by asking them to sit in a circle and then he said he wanted them to think about all the things that they enjoyed about school. There was an awkward silence.

'The end of the day,' said Billy Carmichael. The children laughed – even Mr Tompkins laughed. Seeing him smile, the children began to relax; there was something different about him.

'Let's make a list of all the things you used to enjoy about school,' he said.

'Science,' said Zoe, 'planning investigations and seeing what happened.'

'Great!' said Mr Tompkins, 'what else?'

'History and geography,' said Liam. We used to do projects like the Vikings and the Street Where we Live!'

'Okay,' said Mr Tompkins, 'we're cooking on gas now!' The children weren't sure what he meant but they sensed that he was pleased. He was still smiling.

Over the next few weeks, Mr Tompkins reinvented school. He took the children out of the classroom: they went on discovery walks, where they were encouraged to paint and draw what they saw. They had science days where they could spend all day investigating, 'How strong is an ant?' or 'Why do my dad's feet smell?' They studied the Tudors: finding out what made Henry VIII tick; why Elizabeth I had been such a great queen. They were encouraged to question and reflect.

But, surprisingly, the bits the children enjoyed the best were maths and English lessons. There were fewer of them now, but they spent their time reading Shakespeare and poetry in English; and in maths, the lessons were filled with problem solving that was fun and challenging.

As they approached Christmas, Mr Tompkins began to read them the story of Scrooge by Charles Dickens; the children hung on the teacher's every word. He would finish each day by taking out his guitar and they would sing songs. School was suddenly fun and relaxed again, and they loved it. They left for their Christmas holidays happy. Mr Tompkins hadn't mentioned SATs once, realised Jacob: did this mean that they wouldn't be taking them anymore? He put it out of his mind. Why worry? He was only ten, leave that to the grown-ups!

The children were keen to see Mr Tompkins on their return after Christmas; they had missed him. But when they arrived in class, they found Mr Peters standing at the board. He had lost weight. Yes, he was definitely thinner. He looked worried. Not a good look for someone returning from being off sick. He was quiet that first day. The class were subdued. They were missing Mr Tompkins. Mr Peters wasn't a good swap – not good at all.

The next morning, he called them together and said that he had been looking at their books. He didn't like what he had seen. The SATs were now only a term away; there was much to be done. They had stood still whilst he had been away and it was time to make up for lost ground. SATs were suddenly back and it didn't feel good.

It was Jamie who first said the word. It was break time on the second Friday of Mr Peter's return. 'Petition.' Some of them had heard the word before, others hadn't. Most didn't know what it meant. It was a way of protesting, said Jamie. Grown-ups would write a letter of complaint and then invite people to sign it.

'My Mum signed one once,' he said, 'against the use of animals in testing make-up and deodorants.'

'Cruel,' said Harper. The others nodded.

'But what are we protesting about?' asked Alice.

'Isn't it obvious,' said Jamie. 'Mr Peters.' There was silence. Nobody wanted to say what they were all thinking: could they? Did children protest against their teachers?

'Wouldn't it be unkind?' asked Dominic,' I mean, he's been unwell.'

'My Mum says he still looks in a bad way,' added Jasmine.

'Mine too,' chipped in Dean.

'Unwell or not, he's the one being mean. All we're doing now is getting ready for the ruddy tests,' said Jamie. 'It's boring.'

No one said anything. What was there to say? Jamie was right. Since Mr Peters had returned to school, they had done nothing but maths and English, test paper after test paper, wall-to-wall revision.

'Why don't we set up a Facebook page where we sound off about how unfair it is – that could be our petition; people can become "friends" and agree with what we are saying.'

'No,' said Jamie, 'you have to be 13 to set up a Facebook account.'

'My Mum will let me set one up,' said Jasmine, 'so long as I don't tell her what it is for.'

It was agreed.

Later that week, they set the page up: it was called 'Down with SATs. Bring back Mr Tompkins!' Within a week, nearly all the class were members and some children from other years had even joined too.

On Monday morning, Mrs Howlett called Jasmine and the others into her office. 'It is time,' she said, 'to stop this.' She had seen the Facebook page; a parent had showed her. It was very unkind to Mr Peters, who was only trying to do his best for them. Besides, children under 13 weren't allowed to have Facebook accounts; she had reported it that morning and the page would be deleted by the end of the day.

# Getting things out of proportion

## Mr Peters' Story

The children stood in front of her desk looking sullen. Grown-ups – they got to call all the shots.

'Have you,' she asked, 'thought of talking to Mr Peters, telling him about how you are feeling?' They looked at their feet. No, they hadn't thought of that. Things had just sort of happened. They had got carried away. They were angry. Mr Tompkins hadn't taught them like that. Why should Mr Peters?

'I think the best thing we can do now is to sit down with Mr Peters and see what he says,' the Headteacher proposed.

Mr Peters was in listening mode. He didn't snap. Mrs Howlett looked pleased.

'Okay,' he said, 'I've listened to you. Now I want you to listen to me. The SATs are important. We can't just ignore them, but perhaps I haven't been going about things in the best way. It matters to me how you do in your tests – we do have to spend some time practising for them. But, we need to make time for some other stuff too. I see that now. I get it. We'll make time for a bit of everything, if you promise to take revision seriously.'

It was a deal.

That afternoon, they spent the whole time doing RE, a subject that the children loved. There was lots of thinking and talking time. The Gospel reading they studied was a parable; Mr Peters said he had chosen it specially:

*At that time the Kingdom of heaven will be like this. Once there were ten girls who took their oil lamps and went out to meet the bridegroom. Five of them were foolish, and the others were wise. The foolish ones took their lamps but did not take any extra oil with them, while the wise ones took containers full of oil for their lamps. The bridegroom was late in coming, so the girls began to nod and fall asleep.*

*It was already midnight when the cry rang out, 'Here is the bridegroom! Come and meet him!' The ten girls woke up and trimmed their lamps. Then the foolish ones said to the wise ones, 'Let us have some of your oil, because our lamps are going out.' 'No, indeed,' the wise ones answered, 'there is not enough for you and for us. Go to the shop and buy some for yourselves.' So the foolish girls went off to buy some oil; and while they were gone, the bridegroom arrived. The five girls who were ready went in with him to the wedding feast, and the door was closed.*

*Later the other women arrived. 'Sir, sir! Let us in!' they cried out. 'Certainly not! I don't know you,' the bridegroom answered.*

*And Jesus concluded, 'Be on your guard, then, because you do not know the day or the hour.'* (Matthew 25:1–13)

Mr Peters closed the Bible shut. 'It is important,' he declared, 'to always be ready.'

Class 6P did well in their SATs. They were, after all, well prepared. Mr Peters was pleased. So too, were the children.

# Teacher's Notes
# Conrad's Story

## Background
The hero of this story is an unlikely one. His friends would not have expected him to step forward in a crisis.

Bimpton, the zoo in this story, is a fictitious place. However, I have taken children to a nearby zoo on many occasions. One morning, the local headlines were dominated by the fact that the wolves at the zoo had escaped from their enclosure when visitors had been in the park. This got me thinking. The risk assessments we had carried out did not cater for escaped animals!

## General themes
People like to pigeon hole us, put us into a category or type – it often suits them to do so. However, we are all authors of our own life stories and, as such, we each have the capacity to surprise.

## What do Christians believe?
Jesus taught us not to think of others in a way that limited or defined them. He was always prepared to give others a fresh start, look at them with different eyes. The tale of Zacchaeus, the tax collector, makes this point very well. The crowds saw him in one way but Jesus saw past that – to the person he might be.

## Prayer
*Forgiving Father, we are sorry for the times we have judged other people, without trying to find out what they are really like. Help us to follow the example set by Jesus, by accepting and not judging.*

## The story
How would the children have reacted in Conrad's shoes?
Can they think of any other instances when something unexpected has happened? Where were they? What did they learn from the situation?

## PSMC links
- How do we label people in our own lives? How do people act if people characterise them in a particular way? How is this unhelpful?

© Gary Nott and Brilliant Publications Limited
*This page may be photocopied for use by the purchasing institution only.*

# Conrad's Story

Bimpton Zoo was one of the finest in the country, Europe even. The class had been excited when Mr Porter had announced that they would be visiting Bimpton as part of their work on habitats and camouflage. Conrad was as enthusiastic as the other children: 'I've always wanted to go,' he said at morning break. 'But Mum has never fancied it. She says she doesn't like smelly animals.'

'I can't wait,' chipped in Annie.

'Zoos,' sniffed Peter Preston, 'they're just prisons for animals. Boring, or what?'

'Turn it in,' said Jamie. 'You'll enjoy yourself when you get there.'

'Not me,' insisted Peter, 'to think – we could have gone to the aircraft museum.' The other children sighed. Peter could be difficult. He never seemed happy unless he was moaning.

The day of the trip dawned bright and sunny and there was a buzz of excitement as Mr Porter called the register.

Have you got your lunch, Jamie?' asked Conrad, for the second time that morning. 'Mine is cheese sandwiches, with crisps and a chocolate roll.' Conrad liked to talk about food. It was his favourite topic of conversation.

He was a tubby boy who ate too much and got teased by the other children from time to time. 'Who ate all the pies?' they would shout, quickly followed by, 'Conrad did!' Then they would burst out laughing. They never seemed to tire of the joke. Conrad would laugh too in order to show that it didn't bother him. It did, of course, but he wasn't going to let on. They all saw him as something of a lardy boy, no good at sport and always the last to get picked when they were choosing teams.

'You'll grow out of it,' Mum would say. 'It's just puppy fat.' Conrad wasn't so sure. But there it was. 'If they weren't calling you tubby,' Mum said, 'they would be calling someone else something far worse. Remember, you're doing that kid a favour.' Conrad didn't quite get what she meant. But he would smile, to reassure Mum he was okay. He didn't want her to worry. But, she did – all the time – he was her baby.

The coach let out a huge sigh and pulled away from the school gates. The driver looked as if he had driven too many school parties. 'I want no mess,' he announced over the microphone, sounding tense. 'Behave yourselves, this is my coach', he added with a snarl. Mr Porter frowned.

'Sir, how far is it to go?' called out Aaron. 'Given that we only left 20 minutes ago, quite some distance,' replied Mr Porter, looking bemused.

They pulled into the zoo just after 11 o'clock. The early morning sunshine had disappeared, to be replaced by dark clouds and, as they sat on the coach receiving last minute instructions, the rain began to fall. The children groaned.

'Now come on,' sang Miss Dangerfield. 'It's not what we wanted, but we can sit here in the dry or we can go explore the zoo.'

The children thought that they would rather sit in the dry, thank-you-very-much, but Mr Porter and Miss Dangerfield were suddenly up, urging them off the coach; and, with moans and groans, they filed off. They were put into groups and assigned to an adult helper. They were each allocated a different starting point and made their way off into the zoo. The rain stopped. The sun came back out.

Conrad's group started with the rhinos, which were mating. Miss Dangerfield, his group's leader, looked embarrassed; she shifted from one foot to the other. 'It's nothing that we haven't seen on Animal Planet,' said Candice. 'Really, Miss. Don't let it worry you.'

# Conrad's Story

The giraffes were tall and elegant. There were three. Their long tongues were blue and sticky. The children enjoyed feeding them with the branches that the keepers passed to them.

It was time for the children's own lunch. They came round the corner and they spied a picnic area in front of a tiny café. The chairs were vacant – perfect. They sat down with a plop, for it was hungry work, visiting a zoo. Conrad was hungry, as per usual. They opened their bags and a variety of packed lunches appeared.

'Did I tell you I have cheese sandwiches?'

'Yes Conrad,' they chorused. The children were happy to sit munching. Miss Dangerfield asked them what they had liked best. The rhinos, they said with one voice. Miss Dangerfield blushed.

After a while, they finished their food. It was time to move on: the elephants and tigers were waiting. They picked up their things and made off.

'Miss,' said Conrad, stopping, 'I've left my water bottle behind.'

'Hurry and get it Conrad, we'll just be up there.'

Conrad returned to the picnic spot and his eyes quickly scanned the seats for the bottle, for he didn't want to be left behind. It was there, just behind the parasol. He picked it up and turning on his heels, made his way back round the corner. What he saw made him stop dead in his tracks. A wolf stood in the middle of the path.

Conrad knew it was a wolf as soon as he saw it; it was too big for a dog and besides, he knew dogs weren't allowed in the zoo. Wolves were, but he had expected to see them behind bars. He knew Bimpton had a pack; he remembered reading about them on the website. This was terribly wrong. A wolf wouldn't be outside its enclosure. The wolf suddenly moved, stooped down and looked in his direction. He froze. He didn't know what else to do. It was that or run, and he wasn't a fast runner. Then he saw it, a second wolf, then a third. The place seemed to be teeming with them.

With a start, the creatures turned and ran off, towards the giraffes.

Conrad didn't need any encouragement, he ran back to the café and pulled the door tight behind him. He stood motionless, his back to the door. The girl behind the counter looked at him. What was this boy up to? He looked white.

'A wolf,' he said. 'I just saw a wolf.'

'Really?' she said, 'and what do you want, a medal? We have lots of animals – it's a zoo! You need to get out more,' she said, laughing at her own joke.

'No,' he gasped. 'On the path, out of its cage. With his mates.'

She looked astonished. And then pushing straight past him, she shoved her face up against the glass of the door. 'I can't see them," she blurted out.

'They ran off,' he said, almost shouting now. 'Towards the giraffes.'

© Gary Nott and Brilliant Publications Limited
*This page may be photocopied for use by the purchasing institution only.*

The girl picked up her walkie-talkie and spoke into it. She asked for the main desk.

'I've got a boy here who says he's seen a wolf out in the park.' Her voice trembled.

'Stay put,' came the reply. 'Don't move.'

They waited for what seemed like an age. The walkie-talkie burst into life. 'We have escaped animals,' it said. 'Take shelter and stay put. A team of marksmen are on the way.'

'Here,' said the girl, 'have one of these, for the shock.' She offered him a chocolate ice cream. He took it. He wasn't sure that it would be any good for shock – weren't you meant to drink tea? At least that's what his mum always did when there was bother.

It seemed like an age. They had both stayed crouched on the floor, behind a chiller-cabinet that they had managed to push up against the door.

They both heard it. A shot rang out. Then, another.

More waiting. More ice cream. It seemed to help – Conrad always felt better when he ate.

The clock showed 4 o'clock. Three hours had passed since he had rushed into the café.

The walkie-talkie crackled. 'This is the Head Keeper speaking. The danger has cleared. It is safe to come out.' They weren't sure what to do.

What if they were wrong? What if the wolves were still out? What if other animals were now out of their pens?

'I suppose we can't stay here forever,' said Conrad. But, just then Miss Dangerfield and the children flew at the door.

'Conrad!' she shouted through the glass, 'we were so worried about you.' He could see that Candice and Mary Jo had been crying. They looked dreadful.

When they had got back to the entrance, the café girl could be seen pointing Conrad out to a group of police and keepers. 'That's him,' she was busy insisting, whilst tugging at the arm of a policeman.

'Well done, young man,' said a policeman, approaching Conrad. He looked important, like he was in charge. 'You raised the alarm and without that, it might have been grim.'

Grim, Conrad thought, that didn't sound good, not good at all.

As they made their way out of the exit they had to fight their way through police and reporters; there was even a television crew. The zoo staff looked strained, hot and bothered; some had faces that were red, blotched – had they been crying too?

The driver ushered them back on board. He reported that no one knew what had happened exactly. The wolves had got out – five, maybe six. Two had been shot dead, the others recaptured. No one was saying how it had happened. Everyone on the bus cheered when they saw Conrad; word had spread that it had been he who had raised the alarm. He looked embarrassed but Mr Porter and Miss Dangerfield were having none of it.

'Three cheers for Conrad,' they cried. He felt like a hero. The kids were looking at him – suddenly he wasn't fat Conrad anymore – he felt like somebody – someone important.

As they pulled back home into Peters Avenue, there was a loud cry as parents saw their children returned safe and sound. There had never been a school trip like it!

Conrad knew where he wanted to be that evening. He told Mum he wanted to go to church; he had some thanks to give. He knew he had been scared; he could still taste the ice cream – he had never known 'scared' like it.

When he got into bed that night, Mum was wanting to read to him.

Last thing before he fell asleep, he thought of Peter Preston. He couldn't help but chuckle. 'Zoos,' Peter had said, 'were boring.' He wondered where Peter was now and what he would be saying.

# Teacher's Notes
# Eddie's Story

## Background
I have worked with children whose mothers would come drunk to the school gate at home time. Anyone can be vulnerable to the comforts of alcohol: the harder life is, the more some people seek to escape and, for some, alcohol is an easily accessible route to feeling better, in the short term, at any rate.

## General themes
Family breakdown can come in all shapes and sizes. Sometimes other parts of life begin to break down following a marriage collapse. Some children are exposed to these things very early in their lives and we would prefer this not to be the case.

## What do Christians believe?
Christians realise that human beings are frail. We are all susceptible to the pressures of modern-day life and different people attempt to cope in different ways. The Christian viewpoint is to understand where someone is coming from – what has led them down a certain path – to meet them with compassion in their hour of need.

## Prayer
*Compassionate Lord, you did not turn away from anyone who had been cast aside, whatever they had done. Please be with those who are finding life very difficult at the moment. Help them to feel your love and strength in their time of need.*

## The story
How does Billy cope with his mum's drinking? Why does Billy's mum drink? What effect does alcohol have on their lives?

## PSMC links
- Should alcohol always be avoided?
- How about other substance abuse – cigarettes, drugs. Do the older children have a viewpoint? (They will!)

© Gary Nott and Brilliant Publications Limited
*This page may be photocopied for use by the purchasing institution only.*

# Eddie's Story

The windscreen wipers thudded left, then right. The rain kept on falling. They had crawled in traffic, these past five miles. Eddie was tired of the morning school run. Ever since Mum had got her new job, they had had to leave home at 7.30, with Eddie having to go to breakfast club before school started. It was not how he wanted to begin his day. He hated breakfast club. The toast was always cold, the milk warm. As he looked through the windscreen, he clocked the traffic. The car in front had a dead brake light. Eddie fixed upon it. A van cut in the space between them. Eddie stared at its bumper. His gaze lifted upwards and he caught sight of a caption emblazoned on the van's rear window: *How's my driving? Phone 0800 1354 6489.*

Hmm, he thought. How about if Mum had one of those stickers across her front: *How's my parenting? Phone 0800 1354 6489.* She had been odd lately. She said she needed to work the hours – they needed the money. She had been up and down. Happy one moment, laughing and joking; down the next, miserable and irritable. Eddie hadn't known how to take her. Since Dad had left, she was not the same. Why should he be at breakfast club? Other kids' mums walked them to school an hour later, after breakfast at home, in the kitchen, snug and warm.

Later, Eddie sat in assembly. Mr Peters was delivering his usual Monday assembly. A list of moans and groans: litter in the playground; running in the corridors; graffiti on the walls. Eddie's imagination began to run as he sat daydreaming. What if Mr Peters had a sign on his forehead: *How's my headteaching? Phone 0800 1354 6489.* Eddie chuckled at the thought.

Later that day, he let himself in at home. Mum wouldn't be home before dark. Eddie did his homework and settled down in front of the television. He was bored. Re-runs of Ben 10 were all that was on. Where was his DS? He hadn't seen it for days. He searched his bedroom. It wasn't there. Maybe it was in Mum's room? He remembered he had been lying on her bed, playing it at the weekend.

He glanced around. No.

Under the bed? No.

Absent-mindedly, Billy pulled out the drawer in the base of the bed.

Bottles.

Two empty wine bottles and a half full bottle of clear stuff – was it water? No, the label said vodka.

Odd. Why would there be bottles here? Mum usually kept alcohol, 'booze' as his Uncle David called it, in the garage.

He went downstairs. Lost in thought.

When Mum came in. She went straight for the fridge and poured a large glass of wine. Billy hadn't noticed before but now, thinking about it, she did that each night. She hadn't used to do that – not when Dad was at home.

Billy stayed up a while longer and then went to bed. He woke up with a start. He had been dreaming. He looked at his alarm clock. 1:24 the red digits cried out. He heard the television downstairs. Getting up, he pulled on his dressing gown and went down the stairs. Mum was asleep on the sofa; on the table stood two bottles of wine, both empty.

Billy went back to bed. He was worried.

A picture was beginning to slot into place: Dad leaving, the bottles under the bed, Mum being up and down – one minute happy – the next sad, the rush to the fridge to pour a glass of wine as soon as she got in.

# Eddie's Story

## Alcohol abuse/Desperation

Eddie knew adults drank alcohol. He had seen them do it, at parties, weddings and Christmas; Dad had liked to have a beer when watching the footie. The stuff often made people loud, sometimes sad, sometimes bad tempered.

Eddie hadn't thought about it before. But could you actually drink too much? Was it bad for you? He thought so because Mum hadn't liked Dad to drink too much.

---

The next day at school, Eddie was miles away.

He was only ten but his life was full of worry. Was it meant to be like this? The other kids sensed that something was wrong. Billy said nothing. He didn't want them to know about Mum. It was a secret.

---

The weeks passed. The routine was unchanged: school run, Mum at work, then drinking as soon as she got in. Now that he was looking for it, Eddie noticed that Mum was never without a glass of something in her hand – wine to begin the evening, and then her favourite, vodka, as the evening wore on.

Then one day Mum was unwell and unable to go to work. When Eddie asked what was wrong, she snapped at him. 'I'm just feeling poorly – everyone does from time-to-time – get over it.'

David's mum came and picked him up. 'Is Mum okay?' she whispered on the way to school. 'She doesn't seem herself lately.' Eddie wanted to tell her about the booze. But he couldn't – he didn't want to let Mum down by sharing her secret.

The next day, Mum went into work but she looked ill, tired and drawn. When she got in, she poured herself a large glass of wine.

One Tuesday afternoon, John Loader got himself into bother at school. He was being rough, hitting Michael over the head with a sponge ball. Billy stood watching. Miss Simpkins, his teacher exploded. She was so angry. 'And, what about you Eddie, you stood there doing nothing.'

Eddie burst into tears. Everyone stopped to look. Miss Simpkins rushed over. 'I'm sorry Eddie. I didn't mean to upset you like this. Why, whatever's wrong? There is no need to cry, is there?'

But she had upset him. Standing there, doing nothing. Was that what Eddie was doing with Mum? Miss Simpkins had hit a nerve.

Eddie thought back to the day when he had seen the sign on the van: *How's my driving? Phone 0800 1234 7648*. He wished there was a number that he could phone called: '*My Mum's Drinking. Phone 0800 3422 1276*'. Then, he remembered an assembly when someone had come and spoken about a helpline for kids in bother.

He searched for it on his i-Phone and found a number.

He dialled.

'Hello,' said a voice, 'this is Cynthia. How can I help?'

---

Eddie felt better afterwards. There was no quick fix. The lady suggested that he should speak to someone at school, someone he could trust. He didn't want to.

---

Christmas came and went. Mum drank, and then some.

One evening, she fell over – she just crumpled down on the floor in a heap of giggles. Eddie had to help her to bed. He felt awkward seeing her in her underwear. She was making no sense. Booze, it was horrible stuff. Eddie was never going to drink.

The months dragged by. Secondary school was coming and the Year 6 trip to Rochester.

## Alcohol abuse/Desperation — Eddie's Story

He should have been excited. But all the time his mind was heavy. Then, one afternoon Billy came home to find Mum in bed. She looked yellow and when he helped her up he noticed that her tummy was swollen.

'Phone the doctor, Eddie,' she said.

The drive to the hospital was awful. The ambulance steered its way through traffic, the siren clearing the way.

---

Uncle Chris came. 'How long has Mum been drinking, Eddie?' he asked.

'Ages,' said Eddie quietly. 'Since Dad left I guess,' he added.

Billy went for a walk. He didn't like the hospital. It smelt funny. People looked unhappy, worried. He saw a sign that said Chapel. He went inside. It was a tiny church. There was a stained glass window and flowers. There were Bibles. Billy opened one; the page fell open and he began to read:

*Early the next morning he (Jesus) went back to the Temple. All the people gathered round him, and he sat down and began to teach them. The teachers of the Law and the Pharisees brought in a woman who had done wrong and they made her stand before them all. 'Teacher,' they said to Jesus, 'this woman was caught doing something wrong. In our Law Moses commanded that such a woman be stoned to death. Now, what do you say?' They said this to trap Jesus, so that they could accuse him. But he bent over and wrote on the ground with his finger.*

*As they stood there asking him questions, he straightened himself up and said to them, 'Whichever of you has committed no sin may throw the first stone at her.' Then he bent over again and wrote on the ground. When they heard this, they all left, one by one, the older ones first. Jesus was left alone with the woman still standing there. He straightened himself up and said to her, 'Where are they? Is there no one left to condemn you?'*

*'No one, sir,' she answered.*

*'Well then,' Jesus said. 'I do not condemn you either.' (John 8:2–11 – adapted)*

Somehow, it made Eddie feel better. He couldn't say why. There were some cards and leaflets at the back of the Chapel and he stood there for a few minutes reading them.

---

The doctors said Mum would be okay, but she wasn't to drink another drop. Uncle Chris said if she did, that would be it, 'Curtains.' Eddie didn't want to ask what he meant. Deep down, he knew.

'I love you Eddie,' said Mum. 'I'm sorry.' She began to cry.

'Don't Mum,' he said. 'I feel better now the secret's out. Here's a card I found in the Chapel.' It said simply: *Want to give up drinking? Phone 0800 4567 3458.*

'We'll make the call,' said Eddie, sounding grown-up. And they did.

# Teacher's Notes
# Mr Johnson's Story

## Background
In my time in teaching, I have had instances when children have alleged that they are being hit by their parents. Never nice to hear; upon investigation on some occasions, it has proved to be true. At other times, the child 'appears' to have made the thing up. I work now in a school that has a number of Black African children: the number of allegations that I have to deal with has risen. I don't believe that this means all Black African parents living in the UK use corporal punishment but, in my experience, a minority do. In my view, they don't do this because they love their children any less, but because they feel it is the right way forward – they were treated like this by their parents and so the cycle continues … .

## General themes
Is it right for parents to chastise their children through the use of corporal punishment?

## What do Christians believe?
Almost without exception, the Black African parents who have told me that they hit their children are 'God fearing' people.

The Old Testament is full of stories where punishment is physical. But it was written a long time ago when many peoples' attitudes were different. It is 'of its time'. Jesus talks only of love. 'Love one another,' he says. Some parents discipline their children through hitting them because to them that is part of 'loving' them; they seek to correct inappropriate behaviour. It is a difficult one!

## Prayer
*Father God, you gave us free will and the ability to make choices for ourselves. We thank you for this. Help us to turn to you when we have a decision to make. May we keep the example of Jesus in mind whenever we have choices to decide upon.*

## The story
Involving Social Care is never easy to do. Why would Mr Johnson find it difficult?
Why did the squeeze of the hand mean so much to the Headteacher?

## PSMC links
- Is it ever right to smack children? Is it legal? (Yes, but you cannot leave a mark or smack a vulnerable part of the body.) Do the children have a view?

# Mr Johnson's Story

Mr Johnson opened the card. Retirement – it seemed unreal. He sat surrounded by presents – some big, some small. Had he had really been teaching for 30 years? Now it was almost finished, over. He didn't know how he felt exactly. Not as he thought he would feel – that was for sure. No relief, no joy. Instead, a deep sadness that his adventures were coming to an end.

And what an adventure it had been.

Schools had changed. His school had changed. At one time the mums and dads were quick to ask how they might best help their children. Nowadays, it was a different story. They would come in angrily to see him, asking why the teachers had done what they had done, why they had said what they had said. They were quick to take sides – always their child's. Mr Johnson despaired. Why couldn't mums and dads see that the teachers were just trying to do their best?

But the children were still great. There were one or two who pushed the boundaries, tested his staff but, for the most part, the children were kind and supportive of one another.

And here he was on his last day in charge. What would it bring?

The phone rang. It was his secretary. 'Look, we wanted you to have a quiet day but there's been some trouble and it involves Benjamin, Joshua and Emmanuel – you know what their parents are like. Would you talk with the boys?'

'Well,' he said, looking at the three lads. 'How can I help?'

'It's my phone, Sir. It went missing yesterday,' reported Joshua, 'at the end of the day.'

'Missing? From where?'

'The classroom, Sir. I put it in my bag, like we're told to do,' Joshua replied. 'During the lunch break, Benjamin said he was going to take it. Emmanuel said so.'

'But I didn't,' said Benjamin. 'I was just joking.'

'Joking?' said Mr Johnson, looking perplexed. 'Why would you joke about such a thing? Did you take the phone, Benjamin?' asked Mr Johnson.

'No Sir,' pleaded Benjamin. 'Honest. Please believe me.'

Mr Johnson looked at the small boy in front of him. Was he lying? It seemed too big a coincidence. He must have taken the phone, surely.

'I'll have to contact your parents, Benjamin. This is a serious matter. Joshua's parents will be expecting me to do something.'

'Please Sir,' he said, 'don't. They'll beat me.' He began to cry.

'Step outside please, Joshua and Emmanuel.'

Mr Johnson asked Miss Williams (the Deputy head) to join them. She shut the door firmly. 'When you say beat, what do you mean?' she asked Joshua.

'I mean with a belt. It's an African thing. All Africans do it. Please don't speak to them.'

Mr Johnson frowned. He didn't agree with what he was hearing; it was nonsense. He knew plenty of loving African families who would not dream of hitting their children.

What was he to do?

The phone had been taken. He needed to do something about that. But then there was what Benjamin had said about being beaten. That was far more worrying. Could it be true? Or was the boy making it up to get out of the phone business? The Headteacher couldn't be sure.

He would speak to Benjamin's parents firSt Miss Williams went to telephone them. The

*Modern Christian Assembly Stories*

© Gary Nott and Brilliant Publications Limited

*This page may be photocopied for use by the purchasing institution only.*

boys were sent back to class.

Later that day, Benjamin's parents walked into Mr Johnson's office.

He explained about the missing phone. 'Benjamin wouldn't have taken it. He's not that sort of boy,' his father said, indignant that Mr Johnson could be suggesting their son was a thief.

'I didn't say he took it,' said Mr Johnson, 'only that he had said he intended to take it and then the phone went missing.'

'Our son wouldn't take something that didn't belong to him.'

Mr Johnson sighed. How many times had he heard that?

'None of us can be sure what our children do when we are not around,' he said, gently.

'Listen,' he added, 'there's something else. Benjamin has told us that you hit him with a belt.'

'Yes we do,' replied the father looking Mr Johnson directly in the eye.

'Well, I have to tell you,' said Mr Johnson, 'that this is unacceptable and I am duty bound to report it.'

'Report it if you must,' said Benjamin's mother. 'We will always punish our son as we, his parents, see fit. We are good, God-fearing people.'

Later, Mr Johnson sent for Benjamin.

'Listen,' he said. 'I have spoken with your parents. I have told them that they are not allowed to beat you with a belt. It is against the law. Not all Africans do this, Benjamin. It is wrong to say they do. But I have reported the matter this afternoon to some people who can help you.'

'Help?' said Benjamin. 'Who?'

'They are called social workers,' said Mr Johnson and their job is to help families when things go wrong. You do not need to be frightened. They will be there tonight when you get in from school and will want to talk to you and Mum and Dad. They may bring a policeman.'

'They'll beat me!' blurted out Benjamin, 'for telling,' and with that the boy buried his head in his hands.

'No, they won't,' said Mr Johnson. But he had to admit he wasn't sure. He was worried. Had he made things worse for the small boy standing in front of him? He had had to do something.

Later that evening, in his bedroom, Emmanuel pulled out a box from under his bed. In it was a shiny phone. When he had heard Benjamin joke that he would take it, he had had the idea to steal it himself. Suspicion was bound to fall on Benjamin, not him. He would have the phone and no one would be any the wiser.

Elsewhere, Mr Johnson was sitting in his office. He felt flat. His last day had turned into something he wouldn't want to remember.

Then an idea came to him. He logged on to the computer system and found Joshua's mobile number. He punched the numbers into the phone. After a short while, it was Emmanuel who answered … .

Mr Johnson decided that he would call into Benjamin's house on the way home. Having said goodbye to his staff one final time he headed for the boy's street. He sat in the car outside; it was raining. The lights were on in the house.

He dashed across the road and rang on the bell.

Benjamin's dad answered. 'You'd better come in,' he said.

He called for Benjamin.

'We have talked things through and made Benjamin a promise that we won't hit him anymore.'

Mr Johnston smiled. 'The phone,' he said, 'another boy had it.'

'We told you our son was no thief,' said Benjamin's' father.

'You did,' said Mr Johnson.

# Child protection — Mr Johnson's Story

He stood up to go. Benjamin stepped forward and squeezed his hand. All at once, Mr Johnston caught his breath sharply. It was a lovely way to finish 30 years of teaching. A squeeze of the hand – no child had ever done that before. He had had to wait for the very last moment as a Headteacher for the bit that would mean the most to him. He could enjoy his retirement and he would always remember his final day.

# Teacher's Notes
# Matthew's Story

## Background
One morning, a colleague handed me a copy of the local newspaper and said there was an article inside which would interest me. I soon found it. It was written by an ex-pupil, now a young man. It was entitled, 'Glass half-full?' It told Matthew's story. I couldn't remember if I had been the Headteacher to tell him to think of life like a glass half-full, but (perhaps rather vainly) I hoped I had. Matthew wasn't expected to live into his teens but as I write he is still going strong into his twenties. He is an inspiration to all whom he meets.

## General themes
It is perhaps too easy to focus upon what we can't do, rather than what we can. As able-bodied people, we take for granted many functions that are out of the grasp of disabled people – whatever form that disability may take, whether it be physical, mental or both.

## What do Christians believe?
Christians believe that all life is sacred. God creates all life and some lives are harder to live than others. I remember watching the Paralympics and hearing one contestant say, 'I wouldn't wish my disability away; it makes me the person I am – a winner!' What a humbling thought and one that might surprise the children.

## Prayer
*Lord Jesus, help us to use the talents you have given us wisely. Thank you for those people who use their talents and good qualities to change the lives of others.*

## The story
Have the children ever felt on the outside of an invitation? What is it like not to feel included?
Have they met any people who have a disability? What did it feel like to be around them? How do handicapped athletes represent the thousands of unsung heroes who go about their business every day: those for whom getting out of bed in the morning or on to the bus is a titanic struggle?

## PSMC links
- Have the children ever felt awkward or embarrassed when confronted with someone's disability? Is it understandable to feel like that?
- Is that how disabled people would want us to feel?
- How might we reach out to the disabled in our community?

# Matthew's Story

Matthew was full of life, which was surprising for he faced a number of challenges that most children do not. For a start, he couldn't walk. He had to be lifted in and out of his wheelchair. He needed help with the toilet and feeding himself. This would have proved embarrassing to many children, but Matthew took it on the chin. He couldn't lift his head for long periods without someone helping to keep it up; it just became too heavy for his neck. The technical name for his condition was Spinal Muscular Atrophy Type 2. It was a long phrase and Matthew wouldn't learn to say it until he was much older. When he was five, his parents took him to see a specialist. The doctor outlined all the things he would never be able to do. Matthew's mother grew angry. She didn't want to hear about that; she wanted to focus upon the things that Matthew would be able to do, not the things he would find impossible. His parents were determined that he would go to a normal school, which he did. The kids there accepted him and liked him for what he was: warm and kind, with a quick sense of humour. He had an adult to help him, who pushed his wheelchair; lifted his head up when he felt tired; and helped him to put pen to paper. The others kids didn't mention Matthew's disability – it was not something they focussed on – he was just Matthew. They liked to play chase with him; he would scoot after them in his wheelchair – it was fun. Occasionally they would have races, and it wasn't unusual for his wheelchair to go up in the air, on just the two wheels. Matthew kept this from Mum!

The next year, Matthew's parents took him back to see the specialist doctor. This time, there was no talk of what Mathew couldn't do – only what he could. His mother gave up her job and his Dad put his promotion on hold. They didn't think they would have Matthew for long. The doctors said they should prepare for the worst. It was a horrible phrase but they knew what it meant: their son was a gift from God and they were determined to make the most of every day that they had with him. His mother had her faith and she would pray. Not for a miracle, for she knew that it wouldn't happen; Matthew's frail body would never be able to do the things other children took for granted – walk, jump, run and swim – the strength in his muscles simply wasn't there. No, she prayed that Matthew would be happy in himself, that he would enjoy the small things in life; that people would be kind to him.

One day, a child in his infant class made fun of his thin arms. Why were they like that? he asked. So tiny, they looked like they might break. The other children were furious. How dare someone talk to their friend like that! They shooed the troublemaker away for he should be ashamed of himself. Matthew felt warm inside because his friends cared about him – it was good to know.

The following year, when he was eight he went back to see the doctors.

'You're still here,' one joked with him. His parents held their breath. Would Matthew see the funny side? Of course he would.

'Yes, doc,' he laughed, 'I'm still here and what's more, I'll see you next year too.'

The next two years flew by. Matthew's friends grew taller and bigger. Matthew remained wedded to his wheelchair. Then one day, in assembly, a coach came to speak from a nearby outdoor adventure centre. He gave a presentation of what the children could expect to do, if they were to persuade their parents to send them along during the forthcoming school break. Matthew sat to one side, in his

*Modern Christian Assembly Stories*

© Gary Nott and Brilliant Publications Limited

*This page may be photocopied for use by the purchasing institution only.*

# Matthew's Story — Disability

wheelchair. He felt awkward. Now in Year 6, he sensed that everyone belonged 'to a club' to which he was not invited. At break time, the children couldn't stop talking about the fun things that they had seen on offer: raft building, abseiling, canoeing and rock climbing. Matthew felt down. Though it might sound silly, for most of the time, his disability (significant though it was) went unnoticed. However, today he felt as if he was different. Apart. Not a member of the same school to which his friends belonged; to which he had always felt like he belonged. He didn't welcome the feeling. His helper asked him what the matter was.

'Nothing,' he replied but she knew this wasn't true. After break, the Headteacher, Mr Talbot asked to see Matthew. Matthew was nervous. Mr Talbot was an intimidating presence. He ruled the school with a rod of iron. True, Matthew had seen his gentler side (on occasions) but nevertheless, to be summoned to his office was a little scary.

'Hi Matthew,' he said, as the boy's wheelchair was wheeled into his office. He looked at Matthew's carer. 'Can you give us a minute?' he enquired. 'I'd like to have a chat, just the two of us.' Matthew's carer slid out of the room.

'How's tricks?' asked Mr Talbot.

'Hmm,' said Matthew, 'okay, I guess.'

'Mrs Dukes seems to think that you were a bit down after this morning's presentation,' said the Headteacher.

'Yes, a bit,' admitted Matthew. 'It made me feel awkward, different – knowing that I will never be able to do those kinds of things.'

Mr Talbot sat back in his chair, looking serious, concerned. 'Give me a minute,' he said, and disappeared out of the office. Matthew was confused. Now he was sitting on his own in the Headteacher's office. It felt so weird. It was the first time that he could remember being there on his own. Mr Talbot reappeared, holding a glass of water. He rested it on his desk.

'Tell me what you see,' he said to Matthew.

Matthew looked surprised. What was Mr

© Gary Nott and Brilliant Publications Limited
*This page may be photocopied for use by the purchasing institution only.*

Modern Christian Assembly Stories

Talbot up to? 'A glass of water,' he offered, his voice tentative. 'Yes, a glass of water,' agreed the Headteacher. 'But, describe it.'

Matthew looked at the glass. What exactly was it that the Headteacher wanted him to say. 'It's half empty,' he observed.

'Hmm,' said Mr Talbot, 'but is it?' He called Mrs Dukes, who had been sitting patiently outside, back into the room. 'We're describing what we see,' he said to the carer, with a broad wink. 'Tell me, what do you see, Mrs Dukes?'

'That's easy,' she laughed, 'a glass that's half full.' Matthew looked again at the glass. Was it half-full or half-empty? Were they the same thing? Mr Talbot was nodding, and he took a deep sigh before talking again.

'Matthew,' he said, 'to some people, they will always be looking at a glass that is half-empty. They are the kind of people in life who will think about what they haven't got, not what they have; the things that are going against them, rather than the things that are going for them; the chances that don't come their way, rather than the opportunities that do. And then there are the other people in life,' he continued. 'To them, the glass will always appear half-full: they will count their blessings; think of the things that are working for them, not the things that aren't; the gifts that they have, rather than the things they can't do. So my question to you Matthew is this: what kind of a person are you going to be? One whose glass is half-full, or one whose glass is half-empty?'

Matthew left the office that day with a small seed planted in his brain. He realised that there were many things he couldn't do; that was obvious; he didn't need to be told that. But there were many things he could manage: he could make people smile and laugh; he could cheer people up; he could talk; he could do all sorts of things with numbers and written words.

The following year, he went back to the hospital for his annual check-up.

'There's something different about you Matthew,' observed the doctor. 'And I don't mean the obvious. I can see that since I saw you last, the strength in your arms has grown weaker; the muscles in your neck are less strong, so you can't hold your head up for as long; however, I don't mean any of that. You seem all together more radiant. You were beaming as you came into my office today. What's happened?'

'Well, Doctor, I'll explain,' said Matthew, 'tell me, do you have a glass of water?'

Matthew went on to visit the doctor each year and at the time of writing this story, he is still visiting the doctor each year. He is now 26 years old. He can't go out in the cold winter months for fear of catching a chill that may prove serious to him. Like all of us, he has difficult days – but, perhaps his are just a little more difficult. Most recently, when a friend of his was upset, the only thing he wanted to do – to give her a hug – he could not. But he is an accomplished young man. He writes on disability issues for his local newspaper and of course his mum and dad love him to bits and are very proud of his attitude to life. Matthew's glass is half-full. What about yours?

# Teacher's Notes
# Karnel's Story

## Background
I have worked with many families for whom attendance at school for their children is an issue. They seemingly don't worry about the odd day missed here or there and, before they know it, the amount of absence has racked up. Bad habits once established can be difficult to break. Sometimes, families need others to suggest practical strategies in order to move forward – they themselves can't see a way out of their difficulties.

## General themes
It's a slippery slope. So much that we encounter as children and adults, starts slowly and can build. As an adult I think of gaining weight or owing money: before you know it the pounds have crept on or the debts amassed. Children won't have experienced these dilemmas but, nevertheless, may have realised that small problems can grow into larger ones quite quickly. I once heard a life coach describe people's battles with weight gain as akin to becoming further and further from the shore: before you knew it, the swim back to the beach looked like an overwhelming challenge. It is at this point that we all do well to remember that even the longest journey starts with one small step. Nothing is insurmountable if we put our hearts into it.

## What do Christians believe?
The Bible contains many examples of people whose situations seemed too difficult to bear or whose problems seemed insurmountable but demonstrated firm faith. The woman who had been ill for 12 years (Matthew 9: 20–26); the boy who is brought to Jesus by his father for healing (Mark 9:14–29); the widow who had lost her only son (Luke 7: 11–17). As Jesus told his followers: 'Everything is possible for the person who has faith.' (Mark 9:23)

Isaiah tells how God promises never to abandon those who turn to him in need: 'Do not be afraid – I will save you. I have called you by your name – you are mine. When you pass through deep waters I will be with you; your troubles will not overwhelm you.' (Isaiah 43:1–2)

## Prayer
*Loving Father, may we always remember to always turn to you, in the good times and the bad. We are never alone as you are always by our side.*

## The story
Can the children pinpoint a moment in the story when the problems began? How did Karnel and his mum react when they realised the problems were getting out of hand? What would the children have done differently?

## PSMC links
- Have the children ever experienced a problem that seemed to gather size like a snowball rolling in the snow? What did they do?

© Gary Nott and Brilliant Publications Limited
*This page may be photocopied for use by the purchasing institution only.*

# Karnel's Story

Karnel was unwell. His mum phoned the school to say he had a cold, with a nasty cough. He sat on the sofa and cuddled up to his mum where they had fun watching Disney movies on DVD. He drank lemonade and ate crisps. The next day he was still too unwell to go in. And, the next. On the following day, he was feeling better and so he returned. But he'd enjoyed being off with Mum, he'd had fun. When he thought back, weeks later, that had been the start of things.

There was only the two of them. It had always been like that, the two of them, on their own.

'Nice to see you back, Karnel,' said his teacher, on his return. 'A cold wasn't it?'

'And a cough,' said Karnel.

Then the baby came. Things changed. He didn't want to go to school. Mum would be at home with the baby, just the two of them – he felt like he was missing out. Though he tried to stop himself, he couldn't help but feel jealous.

'I don't feel well,' he said.

'Where does it hurt?' asked Mum, anxious.

'My tummy,' he replied.

'Okay,' Mum said, 'have the day on the sofa.' They cuddled up.

The next day he went back to school. 'Feeling better?' asked his teacher. 'What was it this time, tummy upset?'

'Yes,' said Karnel, quietly.

Then he woke up not wanting to go to school again. 'Is there something wrong?' asked Mum. 'Is someone being unkind to you?'

'Yes,' said Karnel. 'The other kids are mean to me.' They weren't, but he didn't want to go in. He lied.

'Well, just today,' said Mum. Secretly, she would be pleased to have the company. It was lonely being at home with just the baby. No one to talk back to her; they cuddled up on the sofa, drank lemonade, ate crisps and watched DVDs.

It became a habit.

He often wouldn't go to school on Mondays; or Fridays – they would start their weekend early.

He began to fall behind in his work. That made him want to go even less.

Mum was called into school.

'We're worried about Karnel,' said Miss Prince. 'He seems to be missing so much school.'

Karnel sat by Mum looking sheepish. Miss Prince was looking at him. He felt guilty. He wished she would look at Mum, not him.

'He's had a run of being poorly,' said Mum. 'What am I to do? If I send him in, you'll only send him home again. You don't want the other kids getting it too, do you?'

Miss Davies didn't look happy.

Karnel attended school every day in a row for the next two weeks but it was a struggle. He had gotten used to his days off.

He had another day off, a Tuesday. There was nothing wrong with him. He just wanted to be with Mollie and Mum, to sit on the sofa; drink lemonade, eat crisps. Things began to slip again. Then one day Mum sent him out for chips at lunchtime. He had to run past school so he wouldn't be seen. He glanced across: was that Mr Tompkins the Headteacher at the window? Had he seen him? Karnel felt a buzz. It was a feeling of excitement. Had he gotten away with it?

'I have to go out to town, Karnel, you'll have to come with me,' said Mum one day when he should have been in school. There was nothing wrong with him, but Mum enjoyed having him around. She worried what the school would say but she pushed it out of her mind. They were

*Modern Christian Assembly Stories*

© Gary Nott and Brilliant Publications Limited

*This page may be photocopied for use by the purchasing institution only.*

happy at home together.

Karnel liked the visit to town. Something else to do on their days off, he thought. Mum took him for a cake and a drink.

Then one morning, when out, they were approached by two women in the street. They said they were from the council. They were called attendance officers. They said Karnel looked well so why wasn't he in school? Karnel hid behind Mum's coat. He was scared. What would they do? Karnel was to go into school the very next day, they said. Mum would be hearing from them they added.

Then a letter came.

It was from somebody called an Education Welfare Officer. The letter explained that it was Mum's job to make sure Karnel was attending school regularly. It said he had missed too much school of late. There was to be a meeting.

Mum looked worried.

The day of the meeting arrived. Miss Prince was there. Mum was there, as was the Education Welfare lady. She looked stern. She didn't smile. Did Mum know that she could be fined for poor attendance? She could have to go to court.

'Karnel,' said the lady, 'had begun to slip behind in his studies.'

Then Karnel's auntie was taken ill. Mum said that they would have to go and stay with her in the next town. They made their way there by train. Auntie was in hospital. She had two children, Billy and Chloe. Karnel liked them because they were fun. Karnel went to the hospital each day with Mum. Auntie Gill would have to have an operation. After three long weeks she was ready to come home, exhausted. Bit by bit, Mum got her back on her feet.

After a month, Karnel and Mum could make their way home. It was a long train journey and by the time they got in they were tired. There were a lot of letters waiting on the doorstep. Mum made a cup of tea and began to open them. She stopped at the third one, holding it in her hand. Then she burst into tears. It was from the Education Welfare Officer. She was being asked to attend another meeting at the school. Karnel had missed another four weeks at school. People weren't happy.

That night Mum and Karnel sat down together. It was time, Mum said, for a heart to heart. They had made some mistakes. What had started out as the odd day here and there off school had added up. They had got into a routine: Karnel missing school, them just spending time together. Karnel had liked school once. Why, wondered Mum, had things changed? Karnel explained he was scared that he was missing out, what with the baby at home. And Mum admitted she was to blame too. She was lonely. She wanted a partner, but she had no one. Karnel had become the man of the house when he should have just been her son. Did he understand? He thought so – kind of. Mum said she'd enjoyed having him at home. She said that she had felt lonely without anyone to talk to all day. Mollie couldn't talk. It was no company.

'Let's make an appointment to see Miss Prince,' said Karnel.' Let's explain everything to her.' She would understand.

Miss Prince was dubious at first. She had heard it all before of course. They had said they would change, said that Karnel would become a good attendee. But something in their voices made her take them seriously. Everyone deserved a second chance, if not a third and fourth.

Karnel would go back to being a boy of eight. He would attend school each and every day. And, he did.

Weeks later the Educational Officer wrote to Mum again. This time it was to congratulate her on a job well done. Karnel had attended every day for the spring term and he was to receive an attendance certificate. It made him feel so proud. It was a new start, and he and Mum were determined to make the best of it.

# Teacher's Notes
# Scott's Story

## Background
Disability comes in all shapes and sizes. Physical disability is perhaps easier for people to spot and this enables them to react positively for the most part. However, when children have other kinds of disability – those that affect their mood or ability to communicate effectively – it can be much harder to deal with. I have worked with lots of children with such 'invisible' disabilities. I have found that often young children in school are able to recognise these differences seemingly intuitively and often don't feel awkward around the person with the disability – they may see them as 'different', it is true. Invariably though, they want to 'look after' class mates who come across differently. They can be fiercely protective of them.

## General themes
How do we deal with people whose brains are wired differently? Do we laugh and cross over to the other side of the road? Or do we embrace them and welcome them into our friendship groups?

## What do Christians believe?
There are many examples in the New Testament of how Jesus showed immense compassion to those in need and he taught his followers about never turning their faces away from the most vulnerable: 'I was hungry and you fed me, thirsty and you gave me a drink; I was a stranger and you received me into your homes.' (Matthew 25:35)

## Prayer
*Lord God, You made us in your image and you love each and every one of us the same. Help us to see the opportunities we have every day to show your unending love to the people we meet, through what we do and what we say. We ask forgiveness for the times when we have turned away from those people who needed us to offer them the hand of friendship.*

## The story
If the children had been in the story, would they have laughed at Scott? Or would they have been unnerved by him? Why did the different adults in the story react as they did?

## PSMC links
- What do we do if we see someone acting strangely – maybe wailing or laughing or rocking? Are we embarrassed and do we laugh or do we shy away? Which would be better? Which would cause the least hurt?

*Modern Christian Assembly Stories*

# Scott's Story

SATs mattered: SATs were serious. Scott was finding Year 6 tough. The other kids seemed fine, they weren't bothered. He wanted to talk to Mum about it, properly; but when he brought it up, she always said the same. 'Just do your best. That's all your dad and I can ask.' But, Scott was worried. What if he couldn't do his best? What if he mucked up – what then?

Scott could remember when it first started. Before then, he had been normal. It had been Oliver's birthday party. It was an outdoor event. They had to put on army uniforms and drag themselves round a junior assault course. He had enjoyed it: getting muddy, with commando paint daubed across his face. When he had got home he had showered. Later, sitting in front of the television, he saw that he had dirt still beneath his nails. He went to the bathroom and started to scrub.

Sitting down, he settled back to his television programme. He felt uncomfortable, edgy. He wanted to wash his hands again. Already? There was no need. But, he couldn't resist. He went to the bathroom. They looked clean, but felt dirty. He washed them.

The next day at school, he went to the bathroom to pee. He washed his hands. He was reminded of the previous evening. He dried his hands. They felt unclean. He washed them again.

Back in class he tried to settle back to work. He couldn't concentrate.

At lunchtime, he washed his hands again. Twice.

That evening, he locked himself in the bathroom. He poured the sink full of hot water and lathered the soap. It felt good washing: he relaxed. It was like having an itch that needed to be scratched. When he washed his hands, he felt good: better, relaxed.

'Are you in the bathroom again?' Mum shouted. 'You spend your life in there these days!' It was true these past few weeks had been a nightmare. Forever feeling like he had unclean hands. Feeling a sense of relief when he washed them. His hands were becoming red and sore. The skin was broken and had even begun to weep in places. Scott kept his hands in his pockets and tried to eat alone in his room. But, Mum soon spotted the soreness.

'Whatever's happening with your hands?' she said. She booked an appointment with Dr Davies.

'Hmm,' he said. 'I don't know if you are allergic to something – maybe it's something you've touched. Step outside Scott, and take a seat in the surgery while I have a quick chat with Mum.'

After what seemed like an age, Mum came out. She looked worried. When they got home, Mum and Dad sat him down.

'Scott,' they said. 'The doctor thinks there might be a simple explanation for the soreness of your hands. You are washing them too much. Let's try to wash them less. You really only need to wash them after going to the toilet and before meal times. Are you worried about anything?'

'Yes,' he blurted out, 'the SATs.'

'Just do your best,' they said, 'that's all you can do.'

Wash his hands less. That would be hard; they were dirty and needed to be cleaned. Scott still felt he simply had to wash them. He would try to cut down. He didn't like having sore hands. But, it wouldn't be easy.

The next day, Scott needed to pee at school. Mr Smith said he could go the bathroom but Scott hesitated outside. He didn't want to go in. The toilets always seemed filthy in school.

© Gary Nott and Brilliant Publications Limited
*This page may be photocopied for use by the purchasing institution only.*

**Modern Christian Assembly Stories**

Then, he would have to wash his hands. No, he would wait till he got home. Scott was busting by the time he got indoors. He stood over the toilet. It was such a relief. He washed his hands afterwards.

Gradually, Scott trained himself to wait until he got home to use the bathroom.

The work in class was tough. He tried to listen hard but some of the ideas that Mr Smith talked about were too difficult. One day, he asked to wash his hands in the sink.

'Why are they dirty?' asked Mr Smith, sounding surprised.

'I've got ink on them,' he lied. He felt better when washing his hands. Mr Smith asked to see Mum at the end of the day. She wouldn't tell Scott what it was about. 'Just things,' she said. 'Things. Nothing to worry about.' But Scott was worried. The SATs were getting closer.

The other kids had started to notice his hands. He told them he had eczema. Another lie. Scott felt worried most of the time, anxious, unable to settle – unable to concentrate.

Then it happened. He recognised the feeling during maths. He needed to poo. But he couldn't, not here, not at school, not in those toilets.

He asked to go to the bathroom.

He shut himself in the cubicle. He couldn't bring himself to sit on the toilet seat. It was unclean. He dropped his pants and pooed where he stood. He missed the toilet pan. He panicked afterwards.

In the afternoon, all the boys were called into the Hall. 'Someone,' said Mr Tubbs, 'has been quite disgusting in the toilets. The cleaners will refuse to clean it I'm sure. How could anyone have done such a thing?' He expected the culprit to own up or all the boys would miss afternoon break.

All the boys missed afternoon break. Scott felt ashamed. He asked to wash his hands. He felt nervous, panicky.

At the end of the day Mr Smith asked to see Mum. They met in Mr Morgan's office. They were some time.

Scott and Mum walked home without talking. Scott didn't want to know what they had spoken about. Mum looked worried and wanted to speak to Dad on her own as soon as he got in.

The next week, Mum said they were going to the other side of town to see a doctor who wanted to talk to him. 'What about?' demanded Scott. 'Wait till we get there,' she replied.

The doctor's surgery was white. There were people sitting outside waiting. Scott waited. His hands felt like they needed a wash. He wanted to clean them. He wanted to pee. He would wait.

'Scott Tompkins,' the receptionist said. 'Mr Stevens will see you now, Mrs Tompkins,' she said.

'Hello Scott,' said Mr Stevens as they entered his room. He seemed nice. He was trying to make Scott relax, he could tell. Scott liked him. He was friendlier than Doctor Davies. Less stern.

'So when did it start Scott?'

Scott said nothing.

'Come on,' he said, 'you can tell me.'

'When did what start?' he replied.

'This feeling that your hands were dirty. The need to wash them.'

Scott said nothing.

'Show me your hands, Scott.'

Scott held them out.

They were red raw – he hadn't noticed just how bad they had become.

'It started after Oliver's party,' he mumbled into his chest and began to cry, slowly at first, then uncontrollable sobs that shook his whole body. Mum put her arm on his shoulder.

'Tell me about only being able to use the toilet at home.'

Mr Stevens seemed to know everything. Scott was embarrassed. Ashamed.

But later, much later, he felt better for having talked to Mr Stevens.

---

Scott saw the doctor again the following week. Mum had been brilliant. She said he wasn't to worry, everything would be all right.

'Scott,' said the doctor, 'you aren't well – like someone might have a broken leg, you are having problems with your brain – it's not working quite as well as it should. You have something called OCD,' he said. 'We don't need to worry what the letters stand for – you can find out when you are older. It sometimes comes on when someone is worried about something. You've been worried about your SATs, Mum tells me. It's your brain's way of coping. It has given you something else to think about – something you can control.'

'Something,' said Mr Stevens, 'is telling you that you need to wash your hands when you don't. I want us to try something.' Like a conjuror, the doctor took out a bucket of a mud like mixture. 'I want you to put your hands inside,' he said. Scott felt sick. He couldn't.

'Go on,' encouraged the doctor. Slowly, Scott put his hands in the mixture. 'Now let's hold them there for a minute,' Mr Stevens urged.

Scott managed fourteen seconds. (The doctor told him afterwards.)

The next session, Scott held his hands in the mud for three minutes.

By the end of the month, he could do it for five.

In the weeks and months to come, Scott slowly got better. He needed to wash his hands less. When he felt the urge, he found something else to do – he had to take his mind off it, said Mr Stevens.

Someone came into the school each Thursday to talk to him. She was nice. She helped him to say how he was feeling. He was grateful.

One Wednesday in the classroom, after his SATs, Scott needed to use the toilets. He went out. He peed and washed his hands, just the once. He felt an enormous sense of pride as he walked back into 6H.

'Okay?' called out Mr Smith, with a smile on his face.

'Okay?' queried Danny. 'Why, what's wrong with you?'

'You'd never guess,' said Scott. 'But I'm getting better.'

# Teacher's Notes
# Ethan's Story

## Background
My concern about including this story was that colleagues might find it far fetched. However, it is in fact a true story: a sandwich in my son's former school found its way to the school newsletter in similar circumstances. Headteachers are under all sorts of pressures and the weekly newsletter is kind of an open window on their psyche. Some like to bemoan parents' lack of consideration for the school's neighbours when parking; others have different bones of contention. When I read the newsletter which contained the offending sandwich, it did make me chuckle. There but for the grace of God … .

## General themes
Children can occasionally be in awe of their headteacher. There can be a thin line between respect and fear.

## What do Christians believe?
Christians believe they are stewards of the world that God created, caring for everything and everyone in it. They have a duty to use resources responsibly, showing compassion and love to humankind and all the creatures who share this amazing planet. 'You have set the earth firmly on its foundations, and it will never be moved. You placed the ocean over it like a robe.' (Psalm 104:5–6)

## Prayer
*Creator God, We see examples of the beauty of nature every day, from the fiery sunrise to the glowing moon in the dark night skies. May we treat planet Earth with the respect it deserves, trying not to be wasteful. Help those who worry about not being able to feed their families. Thank you for those people who work to bring food and clean water to those in need.*

## The story
Did the headteacher have a point? Or was he overreacting? Did this story make the children laugh? Do they think Ethan was acting reasonably when he threw away the sandwich or should he have finished it?

## PSMC links
- There has been a big drive in schools in recent years to be ethical: to think about the planet, its limited resources and those who live in countries where there is not enough food to sustain the population.
- Can the children think of countries that need our help? How can we give it?
- Have any of the children heard of Fairtrade and the work that it does?

*Modern Christian Assembly Stories*

# Ethan's Story

Mr Templeton's reputation went before him. He shouted, and then some. He had been Headteacher of St Peter's Junior School for some considerable time; he had even been there when Clive, Ethan's far older brother had been to the school. 'He's a nutter,' said Clive, laughing.

Ethan's time at his infant school was coming to an end. In September, he would be transferring to the big school. Joshua, Ethan's best friend, was going to St John's instead. Joshua's mum didn't like the sound of Mr Templeton; she was 'voting with her feet,' she said. St John's had Miss Benedict, 'a sweetie,' said Joshua's mum.

'Am I moving too?' Ethan asked.

'No, don't be silly,' Mum had said. 'Mr Templeton's bark is worse than his bite.' Ethan didn't know what she meant exactly.

'He's an odd cookie,' she added, 'but he won't bother you. You're a good boy – you've nothing to worry about.' Even so, Ethan was apprehensive.

The summer holidays stretched out before them. There were to be adventures: a holiday in Majorca and a visit to see Nanny in the West Country. The weeks sped by. Ethan turned brown under the sun. At the back of his mind, he was thinking about his new headteacher. Would he shout at Ethan? He couldn't talk to Mum about it. She would say he was being silly and yes, he probably was.

The last week of the holiday was a mad dash. There was so much to buy. A new uniform and pens and stuff.

'What would you like in your lunch box?' said Mum as they made their way down the supermarket isles. Remember it has to be 'healthy' – it's a rule of the juniors – no chocolate or cake. Ethan sighed. The infants hadn't had such a silly rule. 'I bet the teachers eat chocolate at break time,' said Ethan, 'and cake. It's not fair.'

'Don't be difficult Ethan,' Mum scolded. 'When you are a grown-up you can eat what you want, but for now there are rules and all the children at St Peter's have to follow them. If you can't decide, then I'll choose later, I haven't got the time to stand and argue.'

The first day at school arrived. Ethan was nervous. So were his friends. Everything was different; it wasn't what they were used to. There were big kids too. In his last school, he had been one of the tallest; now here, he was amongst the smallest.

They met their new teacher, Miss Williams; she seemed nice enough. They were given a place to sit and she began to explain what would happen during the day. Ethan was sitting next to Michael. He knew him from the infants, but he hadn't been one of his close friends. He smiled at Michael. Miss Williams began to teach them. She went quickly. Ethan had to think hard to keep up. Then it was break time. He ran into the playground with Michael. The other Year 3 boys had started a game of football. Ethan and Michael joined in. After break, it was reading comprehension. Ethan was asked to read a paragraph out loud. He managed it. He felt better after that. He had read well and he was pleased with himself.

At noon, the bell rang for lunch. He tidied his things away and went to wash his hands with the others. Sitting down in the Hall, he opened his lunch box. A ham sandwich. He frowned. He didn't like ham, Mum knew that. Why had she given him that to eat? He ate his apple and cheese string. He quickly made his way over to the bin and, when he was sure no one was looking, tipped the sandwich away. He went out to play.

He didn't see Mr Templeton all day; however, in the afternoon he could hear him shouting in the corridor. Someone had done something wrong. He remembered what Mum had said, 'His bark is worse than his bite.' He was certainly barking. Would he then bite?

The next morning flew past. He sat down for lunch with Michael and Joe. Mum had said sorry for giving him ham the day before. She said she thought he would try it: 'New start,' she had said, 'new things.'

He looked in his sandwich box: Marmite – that was more like it. He started to tuck in. The boys were excited. It was PE that afternoon and they hoped they would be playing football. The Hall suddenly went quiet. A tall man marched in.

'Look out,' said Michael, 'it's Mr Templeton.' It was the first time Ethan had seen the Headteacher about whom he had heard so much. He was ever so tall with a shock of blond hair. He wore glasses. Ethan hadn't pictured him with glasses; tall, yes, glasses, no. He found himself staring at Mr Templeton who caught his gaze. Ethan looked down. He was in no hurry to get the man's attention.

'Quiet please,' he said in a strong loud voice. Not a shout, thought Ethan, but loud nevertheless. 'Yesterday,' he continued, 'someone put a whole uneaten ham sandwich in the bin. What a shocking waste of food. I am not happy. We expect children to eat their packed lunches here at St Peter's – not waste them.' Ethan went red. He wanted the table to swallow him up. He felt like everyone was looking at him. Did they know it had been him? Had someone seen? Surely not? Mr Templeton turned on his heels and strode out of the Hall.

'Crikey,' said Michael, 'I wouldn't want to be in that kid's shoes should old Temples find them!'

The boys went out to play football. Ethan was quiet. There was no way Mr Templeton could track him down, he told himself: he was safe, had to be. Should he tell Mum? No, better to keep quiet.

The afternoon flew by, but Ethan was still pleased to hear the bell at the end of the day.

At home, he relaxed. What a school! Joshua's mum had had the right idea sending him to St John's.

Ethan didn't sleep well that night. He dreamt of giant ham sandwiches.

The next day, he hoped that Mr Templeton wouldn't come into the lunch hall at dinner time. But, he did. He went round the tables looking into children's lunch boxes. 'He's looking for chocolate,' said Joe. Ethan looked inside his box. No chocolate. What a relief! Well done Mum, following the rules.

The week sped up and by Friday, the saga of the ham sandwich seemed forgotten. Janey was giving out the newsletters before home time. Ethan looked at his. To his horror, there in the middle of the first page was splashed a photo of a ham sandwich. Underneath was a caption, it read simply 'What a Waste!' Ethan read on. It described how a dinner lady had found the sandwich in the bin on Monday, untouched. It talked about the fact that there were children starving in the world; in this day and age, it said, it really was criminal that someone would waste food so blatantly. Ethan walked home without saying a word.

When he got in, Mum took the newsletter from his bag. In the kitchen, she stood reading it; her face blank then stern. Turning to look at him, she whispered, 'Tell me that isn't your ham sandwich.'

'Yes it is,' he mumbled. What else could he say?

Mum looked at him.

He looked at Mum.

Suddenly, they both exploded with laughter. It was so funny, they were in stitches. To think his ham sandwich had made the front page of the school newsletter. Ethan, all at once, felt better.

Later that night, Mum said, 'I don't know what makes that Mr Templeton tick but one thing's for sure, you are going to be okay at St Peter's. Your second week can't be as eventful as your first!'

That night, he read his Bible:

*There is no fear in love; perfect love casts out fear. So then, love has not been made perfect in anyone who is afraid, because fear has to do with punishment. (1 John 4:18)*

He didn't know what it meant exactly; he so often didn't when reading the Bible. He recognised the words love and fear. He had been frightened of Mr Templeton. But he knew that Mum loved him. Is that what it meant? Love was more important than fear; that love stops you feeling frightened? He thought it might do. He remembered how they had laughed about the picture of the sandwich. He loved his mum. That much, he knew.

Teacher's Notes
# Mrs Barley's Story

## Background
I can remember going to school after having had a hair cut as a child. I tended to feel conspicuous. I didn't like the attention and was always waiting for someone to say something derogatory. Children seem to notice everything and can be dreadfully unkind; sometimes without realising it. I began to wonder how an adult in school would cope with unwanted attention regarding their appearance.

## General themes
Are we all self-conscious about our appearance? Should we be? Isn't it what is on the inside that counts?

## What do Christians believe?
Christians try to follow the example set by Jesus to accept and love others. Yet, it is difficult not to judge, not to make assumptions about others from their appearance and to accept others for who they are. Jesus did not 'fit in'; he was derided, cast out and mocked. God's love is there to sustain those who believe in Him:

'I prayed to the Lord and he answered me; he freed me from all my fears. (Psalm 34:4) The Lord watches over those who obey him, those who trust in his constant love.' (Psalm 33:18)

## Prayer
*Loving Father, help us to love and accept all those we meet, for who they are, not who we want them to be. Help us to always extend the hand of friendship to new pupils in our classes, new members of clubs or groups we attend or to new neighbours. We all have times when we are self-conscious or worried about something or feel that we do not fit in. Please be our strength in times of need.*

## The story
There are some potentially humorous parts in the story – did the children laugh at any point? Did they feel awkward about finding bits of the story funny? If so, why? Did Mrs Barley need to be so worried – were her fears unfounded?

## PSMC links
- What other physical attributes can make people be self-conscious: weight, height, complexion?
- Have the children ever felt this way? How did they attempt to cope with their discomfort?
- Are people always unkind in this regard or have the children met with kindness in such circumstances?

# Mrs Barley's Story

Little Heath was a happy school. The children worked hard and the staff were jovial. Mr Stephens, the Headteacher, was pleasant enough and he worked hard, very hard. Sitting out in Reception was Mrs Barley, the school secretary. She was the face of Little Heath, its heartbeat: the first port of call for parents and teachers alike, for anyone who might be looking for someone or something. She had worked tirelessly at the school for over 20 years and was very firmly part of the furniture. Older now, she moved a little bit less quickly and forgot things from time to time but nevertheless the school community knew that she was indispensable. There was no question of that.

It had been a Monday morning, Mrs Barley was quite clear about that. She had woken late and whilst busying herself with make-up and clothes, she had suddenly noticed a clump of hair on the pillow lying at the head of the bed. She raised her fingers to her scalp and rooted about. Yes, there was a spot that felt different to the rest of her head. The hair must have fallen out from there. Odd, she thought. But before she could give the matter further thought, she was swept away by the demands of getting breakfast for her husband and grown-up son. At work that day, she was particularly busy and didn't give any more consideration to the morning's unusual and slightly unwelcome discovery.

The next morning, she woke earlier than usual, unable to sleep. She lay still on the pillow. She didn't want to get up, fearful that there might be another clump of hair today. Eventually, she could stand the suspense no longer and sat up and turned round to stare where her head at been resting. Relief! A clean pillow. She comforted herself with the thought that yesterday's clump must have been a one-off. School came and went and the next few days passed by. Busy, busy, busy – it was always the same story. So many people needing her time: a kind word here, a reminder to someone to do something there.

She had been looking forward to that weekend, for her daughter was visiting on Sunday with her young family. Grandchildren – they were the apple of Mrs Barley's eye. She practically jumped out of bed on Sunday morning, anxious for the day to start. Then she noticed it. More hair on her pillow, more than last time. She went to the bathroom and, positioning a hand mirror behind her head, looked at the reflection of her scalp in the bathroom mirror which she stood facing, horrified. There was no escaping the truth. Where there had been hair there was now a bald patch. She panicked. Why was her hair falling out? Would it all fall out? What would she do were that to happen? She combed the remaining hair down to conceal the bald patch and went downstairs. When her daughter visited that afternoon, she confided in her.

'You'll need to see the doctor,' she advised. 'He'll know what to do.' The next morning there was more hair on the pillow and she phoned the doctor and went to work late.

The doctor said that it happened. Occasionally, people lost their hair – it could be a sign of stress, worry or sometimes there was seemingly no explanation. For men, it was less of a problem. There were plenty of bald men, he chortled – quite unhelpfully.

Then realising his insensitivity, he put a serious look on his face and added that he realised it was more difficult for a woman. A woman's hair, he recalled his mother saying, was her crowning glory. It was a phrase with

© Gary Nott and Brilliant Publications Limited
*This page may be photocopied for use by the purchasing institution only.*

# Mrs Barley's Story — Pride

which Mrs Barley was familiar.

As she drove to school, Mrs Barley was worried. If she were to continue to lose her hair, it would only be a matter of time before the folk in school began to notice and then the children. Children could be cruel and Mrs Barley began to worry that they would point and stare. Mr Stephens was in a flap when she arrived, he couldn't find some paper or other. Where had she been? He had needed her. Taken aback by his irritability, and still preoccupied with her troubles, she burst into tears. Mr Stephens felt awful. This was Mrs Barley: she was unflappable. When the rest of the school was flustered, she was always so calm. He closed the door to his office and sat her down. What was it? Was she ill?

'Sort of,' she replied and then taking her courage in her hands, she told him about her hair falling out. Mr Stephens blushed. He wasn't sure what to say. He wasn't used to talking to a woman about such personal matters. He was a man's man.

He slipped next door and fetched Mrs David. What could she suggest? 'Have you considered a wig?' she asked. 'They make very good ones now.' Mrs Barley stopped crying. It was a thought, a possible way forward.

That weekend Mrs Barley went shopping for a wig with her daughter. They laughed when in the shop. It was either that or cry – the secretary felt the situation was so desperate.

'Do you fancy being a redhead?' joked her daughter. 'Or a blonde?'

'No, no,' said Mrs Barley. 'I want a wig the same colour as my own hair – what little I have left, that is. I don't want anyone to suspect that my hair isn't my own.'

Her daughter wasn't so sure. However, good the wig might be, she felt sure that the people at school would be able to tell that she was wearing a hair piece. Would the children laugh? Some could be so unkind. Having visited three shops without success, their spirits were sinking. Then in the fourth shop, they struck gold. A perfect match.

Back home, Mrs Barley wore her wig around the house over the weekend, to get used to the feel of it on her head.

Then Monday morning dawned. Mrs Barley felt self-conscious. Would people notice? Would they snigger? Point?

She sat behind her desk in Reception. She couldn't help but fiddle with the hair piece sitting on her head, positioning it, shaping it. She was suddenly approached by Mrs Duncombe, a difficult parent. She wanted to see Mr Stephens. Her son Deon had been picked on last Friday afternoon. She wanted something done about it.

Miss Simpkins, one of the younger teachers, sidled up and interrupted, would Mrs Barley be kind enough to photocopy some work she needed first thing that morning? The teacher seemed to be staring at her hair. Or was Mrs Barley imagining it? Mrs Duncombe, too.

Quickly, she rose to go and photocopy the bundle the teacher had deposited on the desk. Mrs Barley was then swept away with the business that was Little Heath. She quickly forgot about the fact that she was sitting in Reception in full view of everybody, wearing a wig.

Later that morning, she took tea in to Mr Stephens and dropped some papers on the floor. She bent down to pick them up and when she straightened up, Mr Stephens stood staring at her. 'Your hair,' he mumbled.

'Yes,' she said. 'I know. I'm wearing a wig.'

'No,' said Mr Stephens. 'I mean, it has slipped – the back is now at the front.' There was nothing for it. Both the secretary and Headteacher began to laugh.

'Oh dear,' said Mrs Barley, 'I must have bent down too quickly.' She walked to the mirror that hung on Mr Stephen's wall and straightened the wig. 'There,' she said, still laughing, 'I'll lean down more slowly next time.'

# Mrs Barley's Story — Pride

The day passed with a busy stream of traffic to her desk: children who had lost money; teachers wanting phone calls made; and parents with queries.

As she tidied her desk at the end of the day, Miss Simpkins was just leaving. She plonked her bags on the floor and looked at Mrs Barley. 'Your hair,' she said. Mrs Barley flushed red.

'Yes,' the secretary replied hesitantly.

'It looks lovely, I meant to say earlier. The new style really suits you.' With that the teacher picked her bags up and made her way out into the car park.

Mrs Barley sighed. It had been an eventful day. But she had survived. She was already looking forward to tomorrow – wig and all.

# Teacher's Notes
# Nadia's Story

## Background
I once had an ex-pupil who broke into school with a relative in order to steal money. It shocked the school community. The staff felt let down but at the same time desperately sorry for the girl involved.

## General themes
We are all vulnerable. In life, people exist who have to do things that we know are wrong.

## What do Christians believe?
Jesus never turned anyone away, especially those who were shunned by society or whose lifestyle choices were frowned upon. He ate with tax collectors and others who were deemed 'undesirable'. When Jesus went to the house of Zacchaeus, the tax collector, the crowd of people complained (Luke 19). Jesus showed us how to be loving and accepting of others, teaching that we must treat others as we wish to be treated ourselves.

## Prayer
*Merciful Father, thank you for the unending love that you give. Help us to always treat others with the same love that you show us. Forgive us when we judge other people; may we be loving and compassionate in all that we do.*

## The story
How do the children feel about Nadia? Do they think they would have felt strong enough to stand up against her mother's boyfriend? Do they have a view about Nadia's mother's part in the story?

## PSMC links
- It can be difficult when separated parents bring a new partner into the home. In this case, things are taken to an extreme. But the children may well have been in a situation where they were coerced into doing something that they knew was wrong. They may be prepared to share.

# Nadia's Story

Nadia was an unhappy girl. She didn't fit in, she said. The other girls in Year 6 didn't understand her - didn't get her. They always thought she was being difficult, when she wasn't. She just saw things differently to them.

Mum said she was highly strung. She wasn't sure what that meant exactly, which didn't help matters; just one more thing that somebody said that was to be worried about. Mrs Tomlinson invited her to a lunchtime friendship group. These must be the other kids who didn't fit in, thought Nadia.

She talked about wanting to kill herself. When he heard that, Mr Davis, the headteacher, asked to see her. Why, he asked, did she say things like that? Did she mean it? Where had she heard it? No, she didn't mean it, she said. It just seemed to pop out, when she got frustrated – when things seemed like they were crowding in on her. Lucy Jenkins labelled her a 'drama queen'. Nadia scowled when she heard what she had said.

Her dad had left when she was young. She couldn't really remember him; just that he shouted a lot and made Mum cry. Mum always seemed to have a new boyfriend. Nadia did not like any of them, but they never hung round long. Then Colin moved in; he was different. He smiled a lot and took an interest in Nadia. He didn't shout like Dad had and seemed to make Mum happy too. Life was a little sweeter.

The day arrived when the school photographer visited. Nadia hated having her photo taken. 'Do I have to?' she asked Mrs Jacobs, her teacher. 'I'm ugly,' she sighed, heavily.

'Don't be silly,' replied her teacher, 'you have a lovely smile. Let's try to do something with your hair.' Nadia's hair was limp and black; it was not her best feature. She pulled away from Mrs Jacobs who was wielding a hairbrush. Skulking off to the back of the classroom, she sat with her arms across her knees. She choked back the tears.

Everyone took their turn to have their photo taken. Nadia was out of the photographer's chair the minute she was in it. The Monday the photos arrived back in school, Nadia's heart sank. Mrs Jacobs handed the snaps out. Nadia's looked terrible; she looked like she had a squint and her hair looked decidedly greasy. She quickly stuffed it into her bag; she didn't want Lucy Jenkins to see it. On the way home, Lucy came running up. 'Show us your photo,' she teased. Other girls had gathered round.

'No,' barked Nadia. 'Leave me alone.' Lucy and the other girls ran off laughing. Nadia hurried the short distance home.

Colin was there when she got in. 'Good day?' he called through cheerfully.

'No,' snapped Nadia. 'I want to die.'

'Don't be silly, love,' said Colin. 'What's the matter this time?' Nadia stomped to her room – she didn't want to discuss it. She put her music on and lay crying on the bed. Life, her life, it was so difficult. She hated herself. Later, she went downstairs for something to eat. Mum and Colin were standing drinking coffee in the kitchen. Mum was looking at Nadia's photograph – she must have fished it out of Nadia's bag. 'It's lovely,' she cooed, 'they've caught your smile!'

'Don't be ridiculous,' Nadia spat.

She couldn't believe they were talking about the same photo. Colin took the photo proof and looked at the back. There were details of how to pay and order the snaps you wanted. He whistled.

'Have you seen these prices?' he said.

# Vulnerability

## Nadia's Story

'They're having a laugh!' Nadia made herself a sandwich and crept back to her room. Later she was watching EastEnders when Colin started to talk about school. Mum was in the kitchen, washing up.

'What happens when the photo money comes in from parents?' he asked, in a quiet, casual voice.

'What do you mean?' asked Nadia.

'Well, where does it go? The office?' he continued.

Nadia stopped to think.

'No,' she said, 'it sits in a cardboard box on each teacher's desk. The teachers wait till all the money is in before they send it to the office at the end of the week.'

Nadia went back to watching the television. She was confused. It was an odd question for Colin to ask. Why would he want to know about something so boring?

The next few days at school came and went. Before the children knew it, it was Thursday home time – just one more day before another weekend. Nadia had beans on toast for tea. Mum had returned her photo order with £25, enough for two photos – one for her and another for Gran.

Nadia went to bed after EastEnders and stayed up reading the latest Jacqueline Wilson before falling asleep. She awoke with a start. There was someone standing over her. It was Colin; she could tell by his breath. He placed his finger to his mouth.

'Shh,' he whispered. Not a word. You'll wake your mum. Quick out of bed and put these clothes on over your pyjamas.'

'Why?' she said. 'It's dark – the middle of the night', she added seeing the clock blink 2.00 am.

'I'll explain when we're downstairs.' He twisted her arm and it hurt. Nadia was all at once frightened. What was happening? She thought about calling out to Mum but when she opened her mouth to scream, no sound came. Before she knew it, she was being quietly bundled downstairs, half-dressed.

---

Once out onto the street, Colin pushed her hard against the bush. 'Don't breathe a word,' he menaced, 'or I'll hurt you. Do as you're told and you'll be back home before you know it. Now stay close to me.'

'Where are we going?' she asked.

'The school,' he replied and with that he frogmarched her down the road.

Nadia was confused. Why would they be going to school? What was there that Colin would want?

Once there, he threw her over the gate and then jumped it himself. 'We're going to collect in the photo money,' he chuckled, 'before the teachers send it down to the office tomorrow. You're going to be my eyes, to show me where the classrooms are. We'll set the alarm off but should have enough time to collect the cash before the Old Bill arrive.'

He pulled her against a wall and lifting his elbow, whacked the glass pane of a window in the bottom left-hand corner. The glass smashed and, taking a cosh from under his coat, he pushed the glass shards out from the wooden frame. Then Colin and Nadia were through the open space and into the corridor. Pulling her this way and that, making her show him where the classrooms were, he proceeded to force the door to each room and then, using a torch, located the box of photo money and pushed it down into a black sack.

After 30 minutes, they had finished and left the building the same way they had entered. Keeping to the shadows he pulled her back the short distance to the house and quietly let them both back in.

'Shh,' he said and then, twisting her arm, said she was to go quietly to her room. 'You'll not tell anyone about tonight. Or there'll be trouble for you and your mum, do you understand me?'

Nadia nodded. She was frightened and just wanted to get back to the safety of her room. She shut the door behind her and stood with her back to it. Her heart was thudding. What had just happened? It was like something off TV but it was real. She had just helped Colin to steal a great deal of money – there had been lots of envelopes, many containing cash. She suddenly realised that she was utterly exhausted. She cried herself to sleep.

She left for school the next morning before either Colin or Mum were up. Everything seemed normal, although she noted that where they had smashed the glass the night before, there was now a wooden board.

Mrs Jacobs said nothing. Clearly, Nadia guessed, the staff had decided that no one was to say anything, so as not to frighten the children. A break in, it wasn't nice. They may be keeping quiet but all the adults looked tense, she thought. Assembly was cancelled. Mr Davis was busy, they were told. At break time, the playground was buzzing. Children had noticed the boarded-up window and some had put two and two together.

'There's been a break in,' said Lucy Jenkins.

Nadia wanted the ground to open and swallow her up. She didn't know what to do. Should she keep quiet or own up? To whom could she talk?

After break, Mr Davis appeared at the classroom door with Miss Jeffries, the Deputy Head. 'Nadia,' he announced, 'we'd like a word.'

Once in his office, Nadia clocked two police officers who were sat drinking tea. 'We know all about it love,' one of the policeman said. 'Colin Baker was seen entering your house in the early hours with you and a bag. It didn't take us long to work out what had happened.'

'I want Mum,' blurted out Nadia.

'Did Mum know what Colin was up to Nadia?' asked the second officer softly.

'No, of course not. It was all him. Mum knew nothing. He made me help him, you have to believe me.'

The officers looked at Mr Davis. 'Is Nadia a girl who can be trusted?' one asked the Headteacher.

Mr Davis sighed. Nadia was difficult. But he had no reason to think her dishonest. He said as much. The policeman smiled. 'Colin Baker says it was your mum's idea and that you said you would help in return for money,' he said.

'It's not true,' said Nadia and she burst into tears.

Later that day Colin Baker admitted that Nadia and her mum had had nothing to do with the burglary. They were released to come home. The house had been turned into a crime scene so they had to spend the night at Gran's.

They cuddled up together in bed.

'You know Mum,' said Nadia. 'I used to think I didn't fit in and that my life was bad. But I realise now that life can be much, much worse. I am so relieved that they believed us. I feel lighter, all of a sudden – happy, even. And I'm going to try to be more cheerful about things moving forward. I'm going to try hard to fit in.'

Mum gave her a squeeze.

'You'll be fine Nadia,' she whispered. And kissed her daughter gently on the forehead.

# Teacher's Notes
# Father Liam's Story

## Background
As a practising Catholic and Headteacher of a faith school, I have seen the willingness of some parents to regularly attend worship when a school place is on the horizon, only to let their attendance at church relapse once the place is secured. This can be very disappointing for all concerned but is perhaps most so for the parish priest. Different priests have tried different ways to tackle the problem but there does not seem to be an easy solution: perhaps, in essence, it begs the more central question of why so many people of faith do not feel the Sunday service has something to offer them.

## General themes
Can you force someone to do something that is ultimately a very personal decision for them – whether it be to attend church, to vote or to give to charity?

## What do Christians believe?
Christians believe Jesus built the church upon Peter, the rock (Matthew 16: 18), and that He is present when believers come together: 'For where two or three come together in my name, I am there with them.' (Matthew 18:20). God is deserving of worship and thanksgiving and there are many examples in the Bible of believers delighting in praising His name, for example: 'Praise God with shouts of joy, all people! Sing to the glory of his name; offer him glorious praise!' (Psalm 66:1–2)

## Prayer
*Father, thank you for the opportunities we have to praise your name, in prayer and in songs. May we treasure the times when we come together to give thanks to you. We remember those people around the world who do not have the freedom to worship and are persecuted because of their belief in you. Please be with them as they live out Your Gospel message.*

## The story
Father Liam means well. But he sets out to make people do something – attend church regularly – that must perhaps ultimately be a voluntary action, not an obligation. People will only moan and groan if they are coerced into something they would rather not do and, in this case, it is the opposite effect of what the priest is seeking – it puts off those who genuinely want to spend time with him each Sunday in church.

## PSMC links
- Have the children ever felt pressurised into doing something that they would rather not? How did it feel? Can they give an example?
- If the story is being read in a church school, can anyone identify with it on a personal level?

# Father Liam's Story

Father Liam was feeling weary. He had been the parish priest at St Saviour's for over 20 years. Whilst he was used to everyone and everything in his parish, this brought its own problems. For truth be told, he was a little tired of his parishioners, and they were a little tired of him. He could be grouchy. He didn't mean to be, but there it was. On a Sunday afternoon, he would kick off his shoes and snooze after lunch; Mass done, sermon delivered, he could feel content that he had got through another week. Some weeks he felt like he was 'hanging on' – life was so demanding and he had less energy than he once had.

One particular Sunday, two rather unexpected things happened. Firstly, his snooze was interrupted by a ring on the door bell. It was just coming up to 4 o'clock. Vexed, he opened the door to find the Carmichael family standing on the steps to the presbytery. They were a faithful family, who attended Church every Sunday, rain or shine. They had a matter they wished to discuss with him. Which secondary school should they choose for their oldest boy, David – St Cedd's or St Barnabas'? He sighed. It was Sunday afternoon, his private time. There was nothing for it, he would have to invite them in. A little over an hour later they left, happy with the advice that the priest had been able to dispense. Father Liam settled back into his chair. The conversation with the Carmichaels had reminded him that there would be many more families than usual in Church over the next few weeks. It was September and it was therefore time to choose schools for the following year. To gain access to a church school, a family would need a letter from him, their parish priest, saying that they attended church each and every week.

For many, that meant they would only now start attending regularly. Who did they think they were fooling? He wouldn't have seen them for years (except perhaps at Christmas and Easter) and then for a few weeks that autumn they would turn up each week – anything to get into the local church school, which was always the best school around.

The phone rang. It was a former parishioner who now lived in the next town. He needed to see Father urgently. It would mean a short drive on the motorway. The priest clambered into his car. This Sunday was not at all going as he had planned. The parishioner comforted, Father Liam drove back, stopping in the motorway service area en route. He needed some chocolate. The service area was packed with people on their way to somewhere or other, paying for petrol and grabbing the goodies that were placed by the tills to tempt them.

The following Saturday, Father sat down in the Church Hall with the parents of the children who would be making their First Holy Communion the next spring. He talked to them about what a special time this was in their child's life. Taking the body and blood of our Lord at Mass was the most important part of a Christian's week. He could sense disengagement in their eyes, a familiarity that he didn't like. The Carmichaels were there, this time with their younger son, George.

Father looked around. He recognised the Carmichaels, of course, and a few others, but most of the families there were strangers to him. He didn't see them at Church each Sunday. Just as with the parents who were now choosing schools, he would see these parents just for a brief time – now that they wanted something from him.

He was suddenly reminded of his stop at

**Disappointment**             **Father Liam's Story**

the motorway service station: so many of his flock only seemed to pop into Church at certain times – when there was a school form needing to be signed; a First Holy Communion to be arranged; even a baptism to be booked or a marriage to be scheduled. Such people, he suddenly realised, were using his Church like it was a motorway service station – just dropping in the middle of a journey to somewhere else, when it suited them. When they had what they wanted, they would move on– until that was, they needed something again. He suddenly saw red.

Turning his attention back to the assembled First Holy Communion parents he announced boldly that this year, he would be doing something different. In addition to the Saturday morning class for the children, there would be a piece of homework that would have to be handed in by every child at Mass each Sunday for the next six months. There were sideways looks amongst the parishioners.

The parents of any child who didn't hand their homework in, he added, would be asked to leave the programme for that year and come back when they were ready for the commitment. He mumbled something about his church not being a service station and with that shuffled out of the hall. There were groans and grumbles: having to come to church every week for six months, Father Liam couldn't be serious. But he was and he wasn't finished there. In church that Sunday he announced he would only sign the school forms of parents who had attended church every week for a whole year and if you wanted your child to be baptised, you would need to have been coming for a similar amount of time.

Members of Father Liam's flock were most unhappy. Letters were written to the Bishop. But Father Liam would not give way; they were his new rules and people would have to live with them, he said. Everyone, he said, should attend Mass each week.

---

*Modern Christian Assembly Stories*         © Gary Nott and Brilliant Publications Limited
**114**         *This page may be photocopied for use by the purchasing institution only.*

# Father Liam's Story — Disappointment

The Carmichael family were troubled. They had always come to church each week. But suddenly church was full of people who didn't want to be there – who, they felt, had been forced to be there. It made the Carmichael family feel uncomfortable, uncertain. The church suddenly felt different. The assembled parishioners moaned and groaned – smiles were rare. With a heavy heart, the Carmichaels decided to stop worshipping at St Saviour's Church and instead to go to the nearby Corpus Christi Church.

Father Liam didn't notice their absence, at first. But one day, he bumped into the family at the local motorway service area. Recognizing them, he enquired as to why they had stopped coming to church; it was, he said, a disappointment to him for they had been such a faithful family.

Mr Carmichael spoke up. He told the priest that he hadn't wanted to be in a church with people who had been forced to be there. He wanted to sit next to brothers and sisters in faith who were choosing to be in church rather than somewhere else.

Father Liam was troubled. Maybe he had got things wrong. True, the numbers of families at church had risen, but at what price? He had lost the Carmichael family – a good faithful family – the kind, he realised, to whom the church should be a regular home. There would, he now realised, always be people who saw the church as a service station – somewhere to pop in to when you needed it – en route to somewhere else – but that was life. He couldn't hope to change people with rules. In doing so he would just end up making everyone unhappy.

That night Father Liam wrote a letter to the Bishop. In it, he asked for a new parish – a place to start afresh. A place where he would insist that the only people who were at church – week in week out – were those parishioners who actually wanted to be there. A few weeks later, he received a long letter from the Bishop. In it, he said, that whilst moving parishes might be a quick fix, how much more satisfying would it be to stay put and try to work differently with the people of St Saviour's. The Bishop made a good point. He would start tomorrow with a visit to the Carmichaels. Father Liam went to bed that night happier than he had been for quite some time. As he drifted off to sleep, the words of one his favourite hymns, played gently in his head: *'Freely, freely, you have received; freely, freely give … .'*

# Teacher's Notes
# Serena's Story

## Background
Diabetes is a serious condition. When one is diagnosed at an early age, it can be dispiriting. There is so much to learn about keeping oneself well and the discipline involved is not insignificant. I have worked with several children who have been diagnosed – the youngest at three. It brings pressure to bear upon the parents, who understandably question their misfortune, 'Why,' they ask, 'did it have to happen to us?' For schools comes the challenge of training staff to meet the needs of the youngster involved. This story centres on diabetes, but there is a huge range of medical conditions with which mainstream children now come to school.

## General themes
How do we manage the various medical conditions with which children can present? Children all want to feel 'normal' – to do the things that their classmates can do. The challenge for schools (and parents) is to manage the condition with the aim of ensuring as much of a sense of normality as possible.

## What do Christians believe?
A life lived in faith is not a protection from illness, sadness or despair; however Christians believe that God's love is there to support them through the ups and downs of life. As Paul wrote in his letter to the Romans: 'Who then can separate us from the love of Christ? Can trouble do it, or hardship or persecution or hunger or poverty or danger or death? ... there is nothing in all creation that will ever be able to separate us from the love of God, which is ours through Christ Jesus our Lord.' (Romans 8:35, 39)

## Prayer
*Loving God, thank you for doctors, nurses and all those who work with people who are unwell. We pray for everyone who is poorly at this time, at home or in hospital. Bring them strength and comfort in their time of need.*

## The story
Serena must feel bewildered. Her condition is life changing. It is in some senses a burden. She just wants to feel normal.

## PSMC links
- Do the children know anyone who has to live with a chronic medical condition?
- Do they know how they manage to cope? Have they ever asked them or would they feel uncomfortable in doing so?
- Do the children think it would be easier to cope as an adult or a child? Why?

# Serena's Story

Serena remembered when it started. It was the day of Josh's birthday party. She woke in the night to wee. Just the once, but it was unusual because she never did that. The next day Mum noticed that she was drinking more than usual. And it was true, she seemed thirsty all day. She drank a lot but the thirst didn't go away. That night she awoke having to wee again, this time twice. That month was awful. She lost weight and was irritable all the while. All the time needing to wee and drinking more and more frequently in order to quench a raging thirst.

Mum took her to see Dr Jacobs, who was kind and warm and who listened carefully to her description of her symptoms. 'I have an idea what might be the trouble,' he said. 'But we'll do some tests to see for sure. I need some blood,' he smiled gently, 'not much, just a prick.'

The doctor produced a tiny machine and pricked Serena's finger. He pressed her finger onto a strip of card, then placed the card into a slot and a number appeared on his machine. It blinked 25!

'Hmm, Serena, will you just pop outside for a second?' Dr Jacobs said. 'I want to talk to Mum.'

Mum reappeared in the waiting room and said they needed to pop to the hospital. 'It's nothing to worry about,' she said, seeing Serena's troubled face. 'We just need to see another doctor who can help more.'

They arrived at the casualty department and spoke to the nurse at the counter. There was a long queue of people waiting to see someone but Serena's name was called almost immediately. Her finger was pricked again and before she knew it, she was hooked up to a drip – a bag of fluid that was connected to her hand by a tube. The pain, where the tube went into her vein in her hand, was so horrible it brought tears to her eyes. Serena was scared.

A nice doctor appeared as if by magic. 'Serena,' he said. 'I want you to listen carefully. Your body needs something called insulin. All our bodies do. Your body hasn't got any and so we need to give it to you, which is what we are doing now. You'll soon start to feel better, I promise. I'll talk with Mum and then I'll explain anything you still need to know once you have had a chat with her.'

Serena lay in the bed. It was the first time she had been in a hospital bed. Then her dad appeared. She cried when she saw him. 'Dad,' she whispered, 'am I going to die?'

'Of course not my darling,' he said. He stroked her hair. It made her feel better. Mum reappeared after half an hour or so holding a booklet.

'Okay,' she said, as the nurse looked on reassuringly. 'Serena, you have been feeling unwell and now we can get things sorted. You have something called diabetes. It means that the sugar in your blood, which gets there from the food you eat, can't get to your muscles because your body is not making something called insulin. Insulin opens the doors and lets the sugar get to all the parts of your body that need it for energy.' It was a lot to take in.

'Was the sugar just floating about in her blood, with nowhere to go?' she wondered.

'Kind of,' the nurse said.

But the doctor added, 'we can give you insulin and everything will be okay.'

'You're going to have to stay in hospital for a few days,' said Mum, 'until we all learn what to do. I can stay here and sleep too. It will be fun, the two of us.'

Serena wasn't so sure. But she was tired and

© Gary Nott and Brilliant Publications Limited
*This page may be photocopied for use by the purchasing institution only.*

# Medical conditions — Serena's Story

just let the adults' words wash over her.

She smiled weakly. Mum looked worried, Dad too. She decided to put a brave face on things. She could, she thought, just cry and cry – but what did that ever achieve? Serena was very grown up for ten – more than even she realised.

Serena came home on Thursday, three days after being admitted to hospital. Routine, said Mum, was going to be our new best friend. There would be routines all day long. She said they would soon get used to things and they were going to be able to talk to Vicky, a specialist nurse, who had promised to be with them every step of the way.

Vicky was a brick. Kind and pretty, she spoke slowly and carefully. Serena, she said, was a big girl, a young lady, and if there was anything she wanted to know, all she needed to do was ask. The next few days were a blur. Serena remembered lots of pricking of her fingers and then Mum would shoot insulin into her thigh using a kind of pen with a tiny needle. It didn't really hurt; it was just a little uncomfortable. Mum would read the amount of sugar in her blood and then know how much insulin to give Serena. It was (as Mum said) all about routine. Serena was to have three sensible meals and no treats to eat – at least not to begin with – it would only complicate things. If there wasn't enough sugar in her blood, she could have an energy drink; which would put things right quickly.

Serena was away from school for four whole weeks. It seemed an age. But Vicky said it was important that Serena was stable before she returned to school, whatever that meant. Serena thought she got it. Then the time came for her to return. There was to be a meeting before she started back and everyone would be there: Miss Davies (her teacher), Vicky, Mum and Mrs Jacobs – the school's teacher for children with special needs. It was odd. Serena had been aware of Mrs Jacobs before her illness. She worked with Tommy and Claire, who were a little slow to take things on board. Did that mean she was now slow to understand things? She didn't think so but she couldn't be sure.

Miss Davies looked apprehensive. Mrs Jacobs explained that this was all new to them: they had never had a child with diabetes in school before. Mrs Jacobs wasn't sure they could cope. Vicky gently insisted that it was the school's job to cope. Mum looked anxious. 'I'm sorry,' said Serena. 'Sorry to be so much trouble.'

'No Serena,' said Miss Davies, 'you have nothing to apologise for. It's just that it's all new and we don't want to let you down or get things wrong.'

'Look,' said Vicky, 'we will all move forward together slowly.' She began to explain about the pricking and the pen, which Serena would use herself.

'Wow,' said Mrs Jacobs, 'you're going to do the injection.'

Modern Christian Assembly Stories

'Yes,' said Serena. Mum had taught her how. She was confident that they could do this.

Mum stayed in school for the first few days; shadowing the teachers, helping to reassure them that they were doing the right thing. Then she was just a phone call away. But Miss Davies stayed calm and grew in confidence. Serena did likewise.

At the start of playtime, Serena had to sit inside with Miss Davies and eat a snack. Miss Davies needed to be sure, she said, that the snack was eaten. And at lunchtime, Serena's blood needed to be tested and if there wasn't enough sugar in it, she would need a snack before her injection pen of insulin. But more often than not, it was fine and the pen could be used and then Serena got back to the school day. The only downside was that by the time she got through with the pricking and the insulin injection, everyone else had found where they were going to sit. Serena was always arriving late. It bothered her and she spoke to Vicky about it.

'Maybe we could stop things for you at a quarter to twelve so you can get all the diabetes stuff over with before it is time to sit down for lunch,' Miss Davis suggested. It worked and Serena was happier.

George Johnson, the terror of Year 6, upset Serena one morning by saying, 'You take drugs, you do!' But Serena's friends Chloe and Lucy were quick to her defence.

'Of course she does,' they said, 'she needs them to help her. There are such things as good drugs, you know.' They made George feel stupid. Serena squeezed their hands in gratitude.

After six months, Serena returned to the hospital with Mum and Dad and was surprised when the doctor presented her with a small certificate, which read simply: 'Well done, Serena, your condition lives with you, you don't live with it!' Serena stopped to think. Yes, she understood what the doctor wanted to convey to her. She wouldn't be beaten. Life was about getting on with things and Serena was determined to do just that.

# Teacher's Notes
# Mr Terry's Story

## Background
We all have our dreams and schools are places where such dreams are encouraged: as a banner boldly proclaimed in my school, 'You are the author of your own life story!' I once worked with a caretaker who dreamed of hitting the big time in the world of show business. What he didn't realise was that he was already appreciated by all of us in the school community for his sparkling sense of humour: he already had his audience, ready-made.

## General themes
Sometimes we can't see what is all around us. We are always looking ahead, striving for something more. Nothing wrong with that, as long as we take the time along the way to appreciate what we already have.

## What do Christians believe?
Christians believe that God has a plan for each and every one of us. He sends his Holy Spirit to guide our footsteps. The First Letter of John encourages believers not to become fixated on things that the world values, but to remain focussed on God: 'Do not love the world or anything that belongs to the world … . The world and everything in it that people desire is passing away; but those who do the will of God live for ever.' (1 John 2:15, 17)

## Prayer
*Heavenly Father, thank you for all the blessings you have given us. May we remember to be grateful for all that we have. Send your Holy Spirit to guide our footsteps and help us to keep our hearts and minds open to your plan for our lives.*

## The story
Mr Terry has, on the face of it, a rather boring job. But it is an important one. Without him, things wouldn't get done and the school would be a less safe and attractive place to be. He dreams of making people smile but doesn't realise just how fond the school already is of his jokes and sense of fun.

## PSMC links
- Do we show the people we love that we appreciate them?
- Can the children think of someone in school who does a fantastic job but never gets thanked? (There may be lots.)
- Moving forward, how might we show them that we care?

Modern Christian Assembly Stories

© Gary Nott and Brilliant Publications Limited

*This page may be photocopied for use by the purchasing institution only.*

# Mr Terry's Story

Mr Terry was busy clearing leaves in the playground. In these autumn months there were so many of them; it really was a thankless job but it had to be done. Wet leaves could be slippery and the children might fall at break time; he wouldn't want that. Mr Terry sighed as he lent on his broom, surveying the now tidy tarmac. Clear of leaves, the playground edges would be once again carpeted yellow and red tomorrow morning. It was so windy. He hurried out of his daydream: there was fox poo to wash away before the children thronged onto the playground at 10.30.

His job was not a glamorous one. Terry Knight, or Mr Terry as he was known to the children and staff of St Joseph's, had been the school caretaker for as long as people could remember; he was, they said, 'part of the furniture'. He was a bit of a character, was Mr Terry. He loved nothing more than to share a joke with staff and children alike – he was known to be a bit of a comedian!

But it went further than that. Deep down, he harboured a secret. He wanted to perform, on stage – in front of an audience – to make people laugh with his jokes. He watched the stars on television and dreamed of hitting the big time.

'That could be me,' he would say to his wife.

'Don't be silly, Terry,' she would say. 'You're a school caretaker. Your best friend is a broom,' and she would laugh like a drain. 'Listen to me,' she would say and – confident that she wasn't bothering to look at him – Terry would mouth her next words in silence, as she proclaimed, 'If there's a comedian in this house, it's your wife.'

One Tuesday morning, tucked away in his small cubbyhole of a room, he settled down to enjoy a cup of tea with the morning paper. He had five minutes before the Headteacher, Mr Steele would come seeking him out with a list of jobs as long as your arm. And then he saw it: an advert that boldly invited readers to come to local auditions for the popular TV programme, 'We've Got Talent'. Do you sing, dance or tell jokes? asked the advert. Mr Terry put down his cup of tea and sat bolt upright. Could he? Should he? Was this to be his chance?

He began to recite some of his favourite gags to himself. Despite what his wife said, the kids and staff always laughed at his one-liners. Could he take to the stage?

He scribbled the details of the audition down and set about the next job of the day: taking the rubbish out to the bins. His mind was racing; he felt hot, on edge. He threw the rubbish sacks into the bins as if he were Superman. He felt light, as if he were walking on air. The next morning he woke wanting it to be Saturday already. The next two days dragged by. He was fit to burst.

However, that weekend Mr Terry was feeling less confident when he joined the queue of wannabes that had turned out for the local auditions. Would he see anyone from school? He hoped not. He would feel embarrassed at having his ambition exposed to youngsters from the school.

He had brought his broom and overalls with him. He had decided to sell himself as the laughing caretaker – to play to his strengths. He knew about schools and what kids found funny. Standing in front of him in the queue were three bright eyed teenagers.

'What do you do old man?' one of them joked, 'sweep floors?' Terry blushed. He suddenly felt silly. His wife had been right – he was no comedian. He turned to make his way back down the queues but the gangways were packed – no one looked in the mood to budge.

© Gary Nott and Brilliant Publications Limited
*This page may be photocopied for use by the purchasing institution only.*

# Valuing what you have — Mr Terry's Story

He was trapped. Terry realised with dread that he would have to go through with it. He waited in line, his last shred of confidence draining – like a balloon losing air, he suddenly felt deflated.

'What's your name and act?' enquired a young girl holding a clipboard.

'Terry,' he mumbled. 'Mr Terry, the laughing caretaker.'

'Original,' she said, with a quick grin. 'You're next, break a leg!'

Terry's turn had come to enter the audition room. He stepped into the glare of bright spotlights shining down at him. He could just make out a table with three young people sat at it at the front of the stage. The judges. None of them was smiling.

'Name?' came a voice out of nowhere.

'Mr Terry.'

'Act?'

'Comedian.'

'You have two minutes.'

Terry took a gulp. His heart was pounding. He was sweating buckets.

'Aah, why did the pretty teacher fall in love with the school caretaker?'

There was a pregnant pause.

'Because he swept her off her feet,' blurted Terry without conviction.

Nothing. Silence. Terry couldn't see anything. The lights were so bright; they were hot too and he began to sweat more freely. He had planned to walk about the stage, sweeping as he told his jokes. But instead he stood rooted to the spot, hanging onto his broom as if his life depended upon it.

He tried another. 'Why did the pupil throw his watch out of the school window?'

Terry didn't wait for an answer.

'He wanted to see time fly. '

Still nothing.

'Do you sing?' came a voice.

'Sing?' echoed Terry. 'No, I'm afraid I don't sing.'

'Well keep following your dreams Terry, but don't give up on the day job or the broom.' The invisible researcher laughed at their own joke.

Terry couldn't wait to get off the stage. He felt foolish. He hurried down the side of the room and pushed the door, which led onto the street. He needed air. Lots of it. He felt as if his rib cage was caving in.

He sat down on a nearby bench. Stupid, stupid, stupid. He felt annoyed with himself.

'Mr Terry. How did you get on?' came a small voice, 'I saw you in the queue.'

Terry looked up. It was David Baker from Year 5. Terry groaned. His secret was out. 'Not too well, David. I don't think I'm through to the next round.'

'Neither am I,' said David, 'they didn't like my dancing.' With a sigh the small boy turned away and walked off at his mother's heels. 'See you back at school,' he shouted with a grin.

When Mr Terry got home, his wife was waiting for him.

'Where have you been with your broom and overalls?' she enquired.

'Work,' he lied. 'I had a few jobs to do before tomorrow.'

' Overtime, I hope,' she said, 'you'd better get paid for it, Terry Knight.'

Terry took a long bath. His hopes, which had built steadily over the last week and had been so high, now lay in disarray. He couldn't put them back together. He pushed himself down below the surface and rising, shook his head free of water.

The next Monday there were more leaves, more sacks of rubbish and yet more fox poo!

Mr Steele sought him out at lunchtime.

'What's the matter, Terry?' he said, 'you're not your cheerful self.'

'Nothing,' said Terry. 'Just one of those days.'

'Don't give me that,' said Mr Steele. 'There's something wrong, isn't there.' Terry took a deep breath and told the Headteacher about his

# Mr Terry's Story — Valuing what you have

failed audition – his 'audition disaster', as he put it.

The Headteacher smiled weakly. 'Look Terry, we all have dreams. I dreamt of playing for Arsenal. But very few people get to realise them. The thing to do is to count your blessings. Be grateful for what you have.'

'But what do I have?' said Terry, blinking back a tear. 'I'm just a caretaker.'

'Just?' said Mr Steele. 'I want you to come to the hall today at 2.45,' he added. 'Bring your overall and broom.'

Terry slunk away. Mr Steele was acting strangely. What did he have in mind? Was he wanting Terry to sweep the hall this afternoon? He had already done that this morning. At 2.45 Terry walked into the school hall and was met by thunderous applause. The whole school sat assembled in front of him.

'Now,' said Mr Steele emerging from the shadows, 'tell us some jokes. Make us laugh.'

Terry looked up at the smiling faces in front of him. He recognised the faces looking back at him. He cared for these children day in and day out and he suddenly realised that they cared about him. Taking his broom firmly in his hand, he said:

> There are two muffins in an oven.
>
> One muffin turns to the other muffin and says, "Boy, it's hot in here."
>
> The other muffin says, "I DON'T BELIEVE IT, A TALKING MUFFIN."

The children laughed. The teachers laughed. And Mr Terry realised that he already had all he could ever wish for.

# Teacher's Notes
# Mr Duncan's Story

## Background
This actually happened to me. My car wouldn't start one evening and when we got it started – eventually – the last thing the caretaker said to me as I drove off was, 'Don't stall on your way home!' I virtually prayed all the way home. And when I did get home and turned the car off, it wouldn't start again. A close shave, if ever there was one. As the Headteacher of a faith school, I encourage the children to have prayer at the centre of their day. But it is very easy to say and much harder to do. We are all so busy. It takes a certain sort of discipline. When things are going well there is a tendency to forget God, and the part He has played in that happiness. More likely, we remember to turn to Him when things are going badly.

## General themes
Making time for prayer: do any of us ever do this enough? Is it only ever when we are in need of something that we turn to God? How must this make Him feel?

## What do Christians believe?
Christians believe that prayer is central to their relationship with God. A prayer doesn't have to be perfect words, learnt by heart. What is important is spending time talking with God, offering praise; thanking him; asking for help and guidance; saying sorry and opening your heart to hear His response. Jesus taught his disciples how to pray, urging them to be humble and private in prayer (Matthew 6).

## Prayer
*Father, help us to remember to turn to you in prayer, when things are going well and when things aren't so good. Thank you for listening to us as we put our trust in you.*

## The story
Why was Mr Duncan's wife surprised when hearing of the things he intended to do? Was he doing them for the right reason? Or maybe the reason didn't matter … .

## PSMC links
- How many of us have ever said to someone if you do this for me, I'll do that for you. Many people have this kind of relationship with God at times in their lives. True friends, like Jesus, don't want to make that sort of bargain with us. It should be enough that we are friends: what I can do for you I will – out of friendship, not because I stand to get something in return.

*Modern Christian Assembly Stories*

© Gary Nott and Brilliant Publications Limited

*This page may be photocopied for use by the purchasing institution only.*

# Mr Duncan's Story

Mr Duncan was the heart-throb of Year 6. Dashingly good looking, he reminded the grandparents who gathered at the afternoon gate of a young Errol Flynn. Most of the parents and none of the children had ever heard of Errol Flynn, but they all knew the teacher was easy on the eye. Then there was his car, his pride and joy, a BMW black coupé. He had owned it from new. The car was now 15 years old and truth be told, like Mr Duncan, it had seen better days.

It was one cold December morning that he first noted a problem. A high screeched whining when he had turned the key in the ignition. Ouch, it almost hurt. What might it be? The engine would then burst into life and he would quickly deposit all doubts to the back of his mind. It would be something simple – he felt sure!

The days sped by. Each morning, the car was a little more reluctant, less willing to give a smooth start. But he put off a trip to the mechanic. It would cost him money, money he would rather spend on something else. Then one night he came out of school to find the car would not start. Dead as McDonald's on Christmas Day. He turned the ignition key and there was no response. Nothing. Shucks, he thought, the last thing I need on a cold dark night after a long day at school. He made his way back into the building, in search of the caretaker, Mr Jones. That man knew all about cars. He might know what to do. Was it the battery? Or something more serious?

'We'll have a little look,' said the caretaker, striking a reassuring tone. 'Might be something simple,' he added with a wink.

The two men stepped out into the cold winter air. Their breaths bit into the air like knives into warm butter. It was freezing.

For 30 minutes they stood in the cold, shifting from one foot to the other – trying to fix the car and stay warm at the same time. Then Mr Peters, the early years teacher, walked by.

'Why don't we give it a push?' he suggested. 'Put it in second gear, try to convince the engine that it is feeling better.'

Mr Jones and Mr Peters pushed the car backwards, towards the end of the school car park. It was heavy going. Then Mr Duncan slipped the car into second gear and at Mr Jones' signal, the caretaker and Mr Peters began to push the car along at speed. Then at a shout from Mr Peters, Mr Duncan tried to start the car and, with a lurch, it sprung into life; the engine was running.

'Now,' said Mr Jones leaning into the car, 'go straight home and don't stop.' He added with laughter, 'you might not be able to start again!' Mr Duncan smiled weakly and revved the car. The engine responded noisily. The gates to the car park opened automatically and Mr Duncan drove out. He was suddenly nervous. Mr Jones' words – meant to be a joke – rung in his ears, 'Don't stop, you might not be able to start again!'

He drove to the end of the road and prayed that there would be no car waiting to go when he needed to turn right at the junction. No, nothing. He slowed down to turn but didn't actually need to come to a stop. As he drove down the next road he suddenly found himself talking aloud to God. He prayed that the traffic light at the end of the road, which he knew would be waiting for him, would be green. It was. He said a silent prayer of thanks. Now waiting ahead, a row of traffic could be seen, waiting for something to get moving. He again said a prayer, this time that the traffic would start to move before he caught up with it. It did and though he had to slow down, again he didn't have to stop. At the next set of traffic lights, the lights were red. Now he would have to stop. He slowly pulled the car up, but rather than put the car into neutral to rest, he kept the engine turning over as he waited with his handbrake on. He was worried that he would stall the car and cause the engine to stop. Beads of sweat broke out on his forehead and Mr Duncan offered up yet more prayers.

'Dear Lord,' he found himself saying to himself, 'please turn the traffic light green now – if you do, I promise to be kinder to my brother.' He closed his eyes. The lights turned to amber. He edged cautiously forward and got moving again. He breathed a sigh of relief.

The car was now making straining noises and Mr Duncan groaned. What if he were to break down here on this busy road, with no Mr Peters or Mr Jones to push him to get him started again? He swallowed hard. He had not felt this nervous since his wife had been expecting their first child. He would feel such a fool to break down and be stranded, with other motorists honking at him to clear out of the away. How embarrassing that would be. He found himself mouthing prayers again.

'Dear Lord,' he voiced, 'if you let me keep going, I promise to phone my mum more often to see how she is.' The traffic in front of him was moving faster now. His prayers might be working. Mr Duncan knew that a busy roundabout lay ahead.

'Dear Lord,' he prayed out loud, 'please let me go straight over the roundabout without having to stop for anyone. If you do I promise I will go to Church on Sunday.' He approached the roundabout. There was nothing waiting to his right and he was able to sail across without stopping. He was almost home. Suddenly from the bonnet he could see steam rising into the dark night air. He gripped the steering wheel hard.

'Please God,' he repeated one more time, 'please let me get home without having to stop.' He looked up and was relieved to see ahead the road that would lead to his house – to safety! Turning into his drive he brought the car to a stop, turned the ignition off and rested his head on the steering wheel. He was spent. Exhausted. Out of curiosity, he turned the key in the ignition. Nothing! The car was dead again. If he had had to stop on the way home, he wouldn't have been able to start again. A wave of relief swept over him. He was so pleased to be home. Tomorrow, he could phone the car assistance people and they would send a mechanic to fix things.

He walked into the house and poured himself a stiff drink. He flopped down into his favourite chair and loosened his tie and kicked off his shoes. 'Phew,' he called to his wife, 'you wouldn't believe the journey I just had.'

Nothing. No response. His wife must still be out with the children. He leant back in the chair and suddenly thought that his journey home had been the first time in a long time that he had had a conversation with God. He didn't like the way it made him feel. He had called upon God when he had been in trouble, but when in his usual day did he ever find time to speak to the Lord? He realised he didn't anymore, at least, only when he wanted something. He had got into a groove: one where he paid less time to God than he should. He suddenly felt guilty. He downed the last drop of his drink and then went to the phone. He dialled his mother's number.

'Mum, how are you?' he said, 'I've been meaning to call.'

Five minutes later he was busy emailing his brother. Then when his wife and children came in, the first thing he said to them was that they would be going to church that Sunday.

'Good,' said his wife, 'I've missed going.' Later over dinner she said to him, 'What's brought all this on – phoning your mother, emailing your brother, planning a trip to church.'

He smiled. 'It all started,' he said, 'when my car wouldn't start … .'

God had been there for him that evening – he felt sure of it. Going forward, he decided that he would always be there when God called upon him.

# Teacher's Notes
# Benny's Story

## Background
I have only ever permanently excluded one pupil. I didn't enjoy the experience but I felt as though there was no other way forward. He had been caught on a dark winter's evening attempting to break into our school. He had matches on him and told the police he wanted to burn the school down. I shuddered. When we dug deeper, we discovered that he had a grudge against a classmate and had wanted to inconvenience (my word) him by burning his school down. I felt sorry for his mother, who didn't know which way to turn.

## General themes
Benny is offered a way out of deep trouble. Often there are people prepared to help us when, on the surface, we don't appear to deserve such help.

## What do Christians believe?
Christians believe that God's forgiveness comes freely, with no strings attached. You only have to open your heart and ask for it. He gave his only Son so that all sins may be forgiven: 'Everyone has sinned and is far away from God's saving presence. But by the free gift of God's grace all are put right with him through Christ Jesus, who sets them free.' (Romans 3:23–24)

## Prayer
*Merciful Father, thank you for sending your son, Jesus, to die for our sins. Thank you for forgiving us when we say sorry with a loving heart. In the same way, help us to truly forgive others who say sorry when they have wronged us.*

## The story
Have the children ever done something naughty – as naughty as Benny was in the story? Do children do things like this in real life or only in stories? Why did the caretaker offer Benny a way out of the situation? Did Benny deserve it? What did Benny do that showed he was perhaps sorry for his actions?

## PSMC links
- Have the children ever been offered a way out of trouble? Did it come with strings attached or was it offered freely?
- What would they have done in the caretaker's position?
- Did Benny deserve to be punished?

*Modern Christian Assembly Stories*

# Benny's Story

Benny was slow in class. A tiny boy, most of the other children in Year 6 towered over him. They would make fun of his size and the high pitched, babyish voice which belied his years – he was eleven but seemed much younger. It was easy to pick on him, too easy. His mother couldn't cope with life. She drank – and then some. Benny would let himself in at home; she would be out, drinking. Toast for tea with baked beans or spaghetti. Benny had learnt to get on with things on his own. He would go out after tea, spend time wandering the streets, seeing what was out there. He had to be back in by nine and Mum had given him a large round faced alarm clock to carry round with him, so he knew what the time was. Sometimes, he would meet up with Wilson and his mates. Wilson was cool. Everyone liked him. Sometimes he was friendly to Benny, sometimes not. It depended who else was around. If Wilson had an audience, Benny was in trouble – it was easy to make fun of the little boy with his clock and whiny voice.

Benny could still remember what had started it. Benny couldn't understand something in maths – co-ordinates – and the teacher, Mr Finch, was irritated. 'But we've done this before,' the teacher said in desperation.

Wilson sniggered. That made Benny feel worse. Mr Finch persevered. Benny began to cry, he couldn't help it. Later, at break, Wilson and a group of his hangers-on gathered round Benny.

'Crying in class,' said Wilson, 'it doesn't get much worse than that. You should be in Year 2!' Benny ran off but they chased him, whooping, pretending to cry. Benny seethed. He suddenly hated Wilson.

That night Benny sat in his bedroom, throwing a ball against the wall and catching it mindlessly. He was a good catch. Something he could do, he thought. He wondered where Wilson was now. How could he get back at him? Slowly, a thought came into his head. He could break into school and trash Wilson's locker. Dare he? Why not? The Year 6 classroom was tucked away at the back of the building. That would serve Wilson right, wipe the smile off his face.

Benny scrambled under his bed, looking for something. His fingers groped in the space and then touched what they were looking for, his baseball bat. He left the house with the bat and his alarm clock. It was already dark.

Mr Davey, the caretaker, lived on the site. Benny noticed the lights were on in his living room as he crept down the path, keeping his head low. He skirted round the outside of the school to where the Year 6 classrooms lay in darkness. It was so quiet. He fumbled his way forward. He felt the side of the building. If only he had a torch he thought, but, of course, their home was too disorganised to have such a handy item. His hands reached the glass of the corridor windows.

This was it. Wilson's locker stood in the corridor inside; he would bust it open and smash all the stuff that lay inside. Now or never! Taking his baseball bat firmly in his hand he let fly. The sound of the window glass breaking broke the silence. It was deafening and Benny dropped to the ground like a stone. Would anyone have heard? Surely, someone would have – it had been such a din. Nothing. Just the sound of some traffic from the road. Benny straightened back up cautiously and then feeling braver, took the bat by the wrong end and used the handle to pop the remaining glass out of the frame. In a flash he was in. He

© Gary Nott and Brilliant Publications Limited
*This page may be photocopied for use by the purchasing institution only.*

**Modern Christian Assembly Stories**

# A way out of trouble

# Benny's Story

felt for the light switch on the wall. There it was – bingo! He blinked at the light that suddenly poured into the corridor. He saw the lockers standing against the wall and found Wilson's. Taking the baseball bat firmly in his hand, he hit the lock hard. The door sprung open. Wilson's locker lay undone. He quickly pulled the contents onto the floor and jumped on them. Taking the bat he pushed the items out into the space on the carpet. There was a watch, some pens and some Match Attax cards. He smashed the watch and pens and pocketed the cards. That would teach him, he thought.

He turned the light off and sprung back through the window. Crouched down on the path, he could suddenly hear someone coming. He shuffled on his knees into nearby bushes, trying his hardest not to make a sound. He made himself as small as he could. In the darkness, he could see a torch beam. It opened up all before it. He could hear mumbles under a breath when the beam hit the broken window.

'Vandals,' muttered a voice.

Benny recognised the caretaker Mr Davey's voice. He liked Mr Davey. He had always been friendly to Benny when he had seen him about school. Suddenly, a twig snapped beneath Benny's foot and the torch chased the echo in Benny's direction. He breathed in, trembling, for he was scared now. What had he done? This was serious. Then without warning, his alarm clock began to ring.

'What the ...?' uttered the caretaker.

Benny stood up.

'Benny,' whispered Mr Davey, shining the torch into the young boy's face. You gave me such a fright, an alarm clock going off here in the dark. What are you doing?'

Benny stopped the alarm, which had pierced the night air.

Then he burst into tears.

Instead of shouting, the caretaker came and stood by him and gave him a hug. He was a kind man and Benny was a sad figure standing there in the darkness.

'What made you do such a thing?' the man asked.

'I was angry,' he replied. 'Angry with Mum; angry with Mr Finch; but, most of all, angry with Wilson.'

Wilson. Mr Davey knew the name well. If ever there was a boy who got under the caretaker's skin it was that boy. Always ready with a cheeky quip. Far too big for his boots.

'I don't know what to say Benny,' said Mr Davey. 'I've already phoned the police. They'll be on their way.'

The caretaker looked at the boy.

'Quick,' he said. 'Scarper.'

Benny didn't need telling twice. He scurried up the path back towards the street.

Later, two policeman stood with Mr Davey surveying the scene. 'Kids,' said one of the officers. 'Long gone. Only had time to smash one locker open, must have been disturbed by something.'

'Yes,' agreed Mr Davey.

Back in his room, Benny slid down beneath the sheets. He had been silly; he knew that now. If it hadn't been for Mr Davey's kindness, he would be in big trouble. And all because of Wilson. The boy wasn't worth it. Benny realised that.

At school the next day, Wilson was moaning as to why his locker had been the one to be smashed open. Benny said nothing but offered Wilson some of his own Match Attax cards to replace the ones that he himself had taken. 'Cheers, Benny,' said Wilson. Benny said nothing and – more importantly – neither did Mr Davey.

# Teacher's Notes
# Danny's Story

## Background
As a child I hated sports days. I was no good at them. At least, I imagined I wouldn't be – I actually didn't do one before I was ten. I was overweight; I was preoccupied with what classmates might say about my size when dressed in kit. I look at the children in my own school who get so excited about the prospect of sports day and it makes me realise how some people can hate something that others love – fairground rides are another, more obvious, example.

## General themes
We can sometimes dread something and, before we know it, we have got it all out of proportion. The thought of it often turns out to be worse than the actual experience.

## What do Christians believe?
Christians believe that God is always at their side, in good times and the not so good ones. All fears and worries should be offered up to Him. 'Do not be afraid – I am with you! I am your God – let nothing terrify you! I will make you strong and help you. I will protect and save you.' (Isaiah 41: 10)

## Prayer
*Loving Lord, sometimes in life we are worried. Sometimes we are scared. Sometimes bad things happen. Help us to remember that you are with us always and nothing will happen that we cannot face, with you by our side.*

## The story
Was it a good thing that Danny was forced to take part in sports day when he clearly didn't want to? Was the PE teacher being mean?

## PSMC links
- Have the children ever dreaded something? Did it turn out as bad as they thought it would be? A visit to the dentist perhaps, an exam?
- Do we gain anything from going through with something that we might dread?

© Gary Nott and Brilliant Publications Limited
*This page may be photocopied for use by the purchasing institution only.*

# Danny's Story

Danny was fat. His mum said he was big boned, that he would shake off the weight as he grew taller. Danny wasn't so sure. The other kids made comments about his size. They called him Fudge (though he wasn't sure why) and, from time-to-time, Tubbs. It bothered him. He covered his size with a baggy jumper. His trousers were made for boys much older than he, and Danny had to have them taken up – the legs made shorter. His size made him feel different, apart. It was true he liked his food (chocolates and crisps) but he didn't eat much more than his brother, who was as thin as he was fat. It didn't seem fair. 'You take after Dad's side of the family,' Mum would say. 'They all have a big frame. Look at Uncle Barry, he's a giant of a man.'

Danny particularly disliked PE. He didn't like getting changed and having to expose his chubby thighs in tight shorts and his oversized tummy in a poky vest. He could sense the girls were laughing at him, and some of his mates too. The year he had joined the juniors, he had stressed about doing a forward roll. He couldn't do it. He just couldn't. His size didn't help. Mum helped him practise at home but he hated PE lessons – they were embarrassing.

Then, there were sports days. Danny's worst nightmare. In Year 3 he faked a cold to get out of the day – yes, in the middle of summer. Mum believed him. At least, she said it was a shame for him to miss out but he wasn't to worry; he could spend the day at home. He had been put down for the egg and spoon race – I ask you. Mums and Dads all there to see him busting out of his kit, trying to get to the end of the track and get his spoon over the finish line first. What would he do when next year's event came round? Still there wasn't time to worry about that now and he pushed the thought to the back of his mind. But it was there troubling him. Even on Christmas Day, during lunch – he thought of it when the family were all busy discussing what they were looking forward to next year. How would he ever get out of Year 4 sports day?

The day approached. He said he had forgotten his kit. It was a lame excuse. Mrs Williams sighed in despair. She didn't have anything spare that would fit Danny. He was such a big boy, she commented, rather thoughtlessly. They tried to contact Mum to get her to bring something in but it was no use – she was out shopping. Danny smiled quietly to himself; he had asked Mum to make the journey into town to get him the latest toy with his pocket money.

In Year 5, Danny thought, God smiled on him. Just when the children had got changed, and Danny thought he would have to go through with it, the heavens opened and there was a torrential downpour – sports day was cancelled. Danny couldn't believe his luck.

The year passed – autumn turned to winter, spring to summer. Danny was now a little taller but still wider than the other kids. The boys now got changed separately to the girls. That was a relief but he still had to face revealing his stomach to the other boys – who would point and shriek.

Then one day, Simon Jenkins said, 'Danny, you've got boobies. Man boobies!' The other kids laughed – all except Pete, Danny's best friend.

'Don't take any notice Dan,' he said. 'They need to get over themselves.' Still, it hurt. Danny laughed to show it didn't bother him, but it did. Mum suggested a diet. But he felt fed up with his size, and whenever he felt fed up Danny liked to eat – and then some.

Modern Christian Assembly Stories

# Danny's Story — Being overweight/Difference

Mr Reynolds, their Year 6 teacher, was a hard man. Sporty, he expected the children to like games and be good at them. Danny could tell Mr Reynolds didn't like him much – he wasn't the teacher's sort of lad. Sports day – Mr Reynolds kept banging on about it. Would he never change the subject?

At the end of the week, with Sports Day not far off, Mr Reynolds asked to see Danny's mum. She was quiet on the way home – as if she had something on her mind. When they got in she sent Danny off to freshen up, said there was something she wanted to talk to him about before tea – before Dad got in.

'Yes Mum,' said Danny, back downstairs, 'there was something you wanted to talk about.'

'Yes,' she said looking awkward, hopping from one foot to the other. 'Look,' she said, 'Sports Day.'

Danny groaned. 'Do we have to talk about it?' He suddenly decided to come clean with Mum, tell her how he felt. Once he had started, he couldn't stop. It all just poured out. He felt better afterwards.

'Oh, Danny,' said Mum. 'The teachers have been chatting in the staffroom and with the help of Mrs Carter and Mr Donaldson, Mr Reynolds has figured out that you have never taken part in a junior school sports day. Not ever. He says, "sport is for everyone; no matter what shape they are."'

'Please Mum,' said Danny. 'Let me bunk off for the day.'

'I can't Danny,' said Mum. 'That's why Mr Reynolds wanted to see me. There are to be no excuses this year: no summer cold, no forgotten kit – you are going to have to go through with it.'

Danny swallowed hard.

He looked at Mum, who was frowning at him.

He realised all at once that he was going to have to front it out: pointing parents, giggling girls, barking boys – they would all be there. He would have to take part in a race and there was no getting out of it.

The big day finally arrived.

Danny looked out at the morning sky. It was clear blue. No chance of rain, he thought. It had been his only hope.

At school, the place was abuzz. Sports Day was something the staff and other children looked forward to. The children marched out to the field to the cheers of the waiting parents. Some of the Year 6 girls were acting as cheerleaders. Danny's heart was heavy. He flopped down on his chair, aware that other kids were laughing at his size. He sat with his arms crossed, wishing the ground would open up and swallow him. Nothing doing.

Then Mr Reynolds called out Danny's name. The boy approached the starting line, dreading the starting whistle. Which race had he been entered for: egg and spoon, sack, obstacle? Each one would see him having to haul his large frame over the grass, all the time embarrassed at the laughter that was bound to float his way.

'Here,' said Mr Reynolds, 'catch!' He threw Danny a rope. A rope, what could that be for? 'New event,' said Mr Reynolds. And then leaning down to whisper to Danny, he added, 'Just for you'. Turning to the assembled parents, the teacher announced that they would finish Sports Day this year with a Tug Of War. 'Now,' said Mr Reynolds to Danny, 'stand there and hold on to your rope. And when I say pull, pull.'

Two teams were quickly formed with Danny at one end of the rope. When Mr Reynolds said 'Pull', Danny did exactly that. And using his size to his advantage, he began to step backwards, taking the rope with him. Despite the opposing team's efforts, Danny pulled clear and a roar from the crowd signalled that Danny's side had been triumphant. Danny's teammates gathered round him, slapping him on the back. 'You were awesome, Danny,' said

Dave Carter.

Mr Reynolds approached the boys. 'Well done, Danny,' said the teacher. 'Sport is for everyone, whatever your shape or size. Today you are a winner. Remember that feeling Danny – it's a good one.' Danny smiled. His sports day had been a success, a big fat one!

# Teacher's Notes
# Samaya's Story

## Background
'You can stuff your prefect badge!' These words are stuck in my memory. They were uttered by an irate parent who thought we had overreacted to a misdemeanour by her Prefect child in our school. We are called upon many times in a typical week about the appropriate sanction for some misbehaviour. Parents sometimes agree with our actions; at other times they don't. The children are often exposed to their parents' low opinion of the school and those who have sought to keep law and order!

## General themes
We can sometimes dread something and before we know it, we have got it all out of proportion. We are all tempted to cheat or even steal or lie when we are young. We make mistakes. Sometimes, these mistakes can have serious consequences that we would not have foreseen. Mums and dads often come to our defence, even when they know we were in the wrong.

## What do Christians believe?
Christians believe in living an honest life. As Paul wrote in his second letter to the Corinthians; 'Our purpose is to do what is right, not only in the sight of the Lord, but also in the sight of others'. (2 Corinthians 8:21) Moses was handed the Ten Commandments as a guide for the life God wants his people to lead.

## Prayer
*Lord God, it is not always easy to say sorry. Give us courage and a humble heart when we need to apologise for something we have done wrong, unkind words we have said, or something we should have done but chose not to do. It is not always easy to know the right thing to do. Help us to listen to you and live honest lives.*

## The story
Samaya cheats because she wants to do well – she feels under pressure. As it turns out, she should have had more confidence in her own ability – she had the correct answer in the first place.

## PSMC links
- Have the children ever done something wrong and then regretted it? How did their parents react?
- Whose parents support the school and whose tend to take their children's side? What do the children think about this?
- Is it difficult to have confidence in your own abilities? Do some people find it easier than others? If so, why do the children think that is?

© Gary Nott and Brilliant Publications Limited
*This page may be photocopied for use by the purchasing institution only.*

# Samaya's Story

Life isn't fair, thought Samaya. These first few days in Year 6 had been difficult. Mrs Jones had chosen her monitors and Samaya had not been selected. She had such high hopes for Year 6; the previous year had been such a disappointment. Annie and Lucy, Clive and Pete, they had all been chosen but there had been no job for Samaya. 'Never mind,' said Mum. 'There are many months ahead. Let's see what happens.'

Samaya sighed. Life wasn't like that. At least, her life wasn't. She was always the last to be picked in the playground, always overlooked for the teacher's jobs. She hadn't been chosen to be a bridesmaid when her cousin married, or for an altar server at Church. Then Mr Peterson announced on Monday morning that they would be choosing prefects that week, Special Ambassadors for the school. 'This could be your big chance,' said Mum.

'Don't be silly,' replied Samaya. 'Why would they choose me?'

But they did. Samaya was astonished. 'Really,' she said to Mrs Jones. 'Me?'

Going up in assembly to collect her badge was the proudest moment in her time at St Cuthbert's. The watching children clapped. Samaya's heart raced.

In December, came the end of term exams. The tables were spaced out and the children were to sit on their own. The atmosphere was tense. The children could sense this was important; SATs were only a short time away. Samaya had tried hard this term but she wasn't a natural mathematician; she struggled. Fiona McNeil was sat to her left, Jimmy Johnson to her right. Mrs Jones paced in between the rows. The last question was particularly tough. It was a tricky word problem. Samaya thought it was a subtraction sum. She did the calculation. Her answer was 347. There were only five minutes remaining. It was time to check through all her answers. She still wasn't sure about that last question. Absent-mindedly, her gaze fell upon Fiona's answer sheet. She saw Fiona had put down 348. Her heart sank and her mind stuttered, like a car exhaust exploding. Fiona was better at maths than she. What was she to do? She didn't want to cheat but she knew the test was important: she simply had to do well for Mum and Dad were counting upon her. Mrs Jones was at the opposite end of the classroom. She looked at Fiona's paper again out of the corner of her eye. And then she glanced up at the clock. Less than one minute to go. Samaya had no time to think. She quickly crossed out her seven and copied

*Modern Christian Assembly Stories*

136

# Samaya's Story — Honesty is the best policy

Fiona's eight.

'Pens down,' announced Mrs Jones.

Samaya lent back in her chair. She had never cheated at anything before. She didn't know how she should feel. Pleased that she had got the right answer? Or disappointed that it hadn't been her own work?

On Friday break. Mrs Jones asked to see her. Mr Smithson was there too.

'Samaya,' said Mrs Jones, her face crumpled by a heavy frown. ' I'm not sure how to say this to you. But I'm disappointed. I've marked the maths tests and I think you cheated. I think you changed your answer to the last question, copying Fiona. I'm right aren't I?'

Samaya didn't know what to say. She flushed red. Her reaction said more than a whole heap of words. She may have cheated, but Samaya was not dishoneSt

'Yes,' she mumbled. 'I panicked. I just wanted to do well.'

'This is serious,' said Mr Smithson.

At the end of the day Samaya was to be found sitting with her Mum in Mr Peterson's office.

'I don't know what got into her,' said Mum. 'But we all make mistakes, don't we. Not that I am saying she shouldn't be punished. She should.'

Mum looked disappointed.

Samaya wished the office floor would open up and swallow her, such was her embarrassment – how foolish she had been?

What would her punishment be? she wondered: detention, a written apology to Fiona, to Mrs Jones?

'I have decided that Samaya can't stay a prefect,' said Mr Peterson. To do so, would give out the wrong message to other pupils.' Samaya was dumbstruck.

Mum's face dropped. In that moment, she turned from apologetic to angry. She turned crimson.

'Take away her prefect badge,' spluttered Mum. 'Don't you think you are overreacting?'

'No, I don't think I am,' said Mr Peterson. Mrs Jones was staring at the floor. She didn't seem to want to look at Mum or Samaya.

Mum pushed her chair back and grabbed Samaya by the hand.

'Come on,' she hissed. Then turning to Mr Peterson, she said, 'You can stuff your prefect badge!'

―――――――――――

Samaya and Mum didn't talk on the short walk home. Once inside the house, Samaya went to her room. She buried her face in her pillow and began to sob.

It was true, she thought. Life wasn't fair.

She had been so pleased to become a prefect but now her happiness lay in ruins, like shattered glass.

The next day at school, Samaya spent the day trying to avoid people. She went to the library at break time and said she felt unwell at lunchtime and so was sent to the medical room.

She was quiet in class, withdrawn.

The next morning, she told her mum that she was still poorly, when she wasn't.' You need a day in bed,' said Mum. In the afternoon, Mum brought her some hot soup. It tasted good, warming.

'What is it love?' asked Mum. 'Is it this prefect business?'

'Oh Mum,' said Samaya.' I've never cheated in my life. It was a spur of the moment thing. I wasn't thinking. And I was so proud to be a prefect.' Then, in a heartbeat, she added, 'Could I change schools?'

'That's a bit drastic love. I'm going to make a phone call. You stay here and snuggle down below the duvet.'

Mum made her call. She was on the phone for ages.

The door opened and Mum crept in. 'I've been talking to Mr Peterson on the phone,' she said. 'I've told him how miserable you feel and

# Honesty is the best policy — Samaya's Story

he has promised to reconsider. He's going to speak to Mrs Jones and phone me back.'

Samaya's heart leapt. Would Mr Peterson change his mind?

The next hour seemed an age. Then the phone rang. Samaya hung on to Mum, who was doing a lot of listening, rather than talking – unusual for Mum. Samaya scanned Mum's face looking for clues as to how things were going. But her expression gave nothing away.

Finally she thanked Mr Peterson for his time and put the phone down.

She turned to Samaya. 'Mr Peterson has spoken with Mrs Jones and they've decided to give you a second chance. You can have your prefect badge back tomorrow.'

Samaya shrieked in delight. Life was fair, after all. She knew she deserved a second chance, and here it was.

The next day she made a beeline for Mrs Jones in the playground. 'Thank you Miss,' she said.

'We all make mistakes Samaya,' she said. 'You made one and so did we. The punishment did not fit the crime. I thought you might like to write Fiona an apology today for copying her work.'

'Absolutely,' said Samaya, 'I'd be pleased to.'

'And then when you're finished, you might like to write one to yourself. And if you do, tell yourself to have more confidence. You had the answer right, Fiona had it wrong. When you changed your answer to hers, you changed it to an incorrect one. That was how I knew you had cheated.'

Samaya managed a half-smile.

It didn't matter.

She was a prefect again.

# Teacher's Notes
# Nicola's Story

## Background
I once sat down to school Christmas dinner and worked my way round the table of assembled pupils, asking what they would be doing on Christmas Day. There must have been half-a-dozen children, and I quickly discovered that none of them lived at home with mum *and* dad. Many of our young people have had to go through the split of their parents at a tender age, which can be very damaging. Some take it personally, seeing it as a reflection upon them. If we are thinking about events in a child's life that can cause misery and stress, separation of partners is perhaps the most prevalent.

## General themes
The pain of separation: the anguish is made worse by a child's natural disposition to think they may be at fault.

## What do Christians believe?
Jesus was brought up by a loving mother and step-father. However, he experienced pain and anguish in his earthly life, for example when his friend, Lazarus died.

## Prayer
*Dear Lord, it sometimes feels like life is full of worries and disappointments. You know what sadness feels like. You know what it feels like to be worried. We have faith that you are with us through our sad and happy times. Thank you for our families and all those who love and care for us. Help us to be patient and loving when family life is tough.*

## The story
Nicola finds out from classmates that her parents are to divorce. She worries what this will mean. Her life is turned upside down. It is her teacher who manages to calm her fears – giving reassurance where it is much needed.

## PSMC links
- This is a sensitive issue. You may have children whose parents have separated who do not feel comfortable discussing it. However, some may be open and candid – this may, in turn, help those who are not.

# Nicola's Story

Nicola knew that something wasn't right. She had heard Mum and Dad arguing long into the night and then they had stopped going out together as a family: at half-term, Dad had taken them to the zoo and, on a different day, Mum had treated them to the cinema. That was odd, different. In the past, her parents had always been inseparable, but here they now were going different ways. Nicola was in Year 5, her younger sister Natalie, in Year 3. It worried Nicola. The shouting, in particular. Then one morning when she came down to breakfast, Dad was gone. Mum said she would talk to them after school that day; that Dad had gone to stay at Uncle Jim's for a few days. Nicola was quiet at school that day. Miss Jenkins, her teacher, sensed that there was something wrong. 'What is it Nicola?' she asked. Nicola said nothing. She didn't know if it was a secret that her Dad had left.

That afternoon Mum picked them up from school and took them to McDonald's for tea. They each ordered a Happy Meal and Mum had coffee. She asked them about their day at school. But Nicola didn't want to talk about that. She wanted to talk about Dad. Mum said that Dad was going through a difficult patch. Nicola didn't know what she meant. Nanny and Granddad had a vegetable patch. Was that what she meant? Surely not.

'Sometimes,' Mum said, 'mummies and daddies stop loving one another.' Did that mean that they were going to stop loving them too? 'No, of course not,' said Mum, who suddenly looked tearful. Nicola bit into her cheese burger but it didn't taste like it usually did. She struggled to swallow the mouthful – it stuck in her throat.

They drove home in silence. It had started to rain. The weather outside mirrored how Nicola was feeling on the inside, miserable. When they got in, Mum said they were to have their baths and then have an early night. It had been a long day, she said. The house seemed funny without Dad there, empty. He was usually there to bathe them and read them a bedtime story. Instead, Mum came to read. She kissed Nicola on the forehead and told her to sleep tight. Nicola buried herself below the covers – she didn't want her little sister to hear her sobs.

The next day, Mum followed them into school to talk to their teachers. They stood at the classroom door and spoke in hushed tones. Nicola guessed they were talking about Dad. During the day, Miss Jenkins came and sat quietly next to her. 'You know Nicola, if there is anything you're worried about, you could always talk to me about it.' Nicola said nothing. She didn't know where to start.

That night, Mum answered the phone. Listening in the living room, Nicola could hear Mum shouting down the phone. It must be Dad, she thought. Afterwards, Mum came into the room. 'It's nothing to worry about,' she said. 'Mummy and Daddy just have some things to sort out.'

On Friday, there was a surprise for the girls. Waiting at the school gate to collect them was their Dad. 'Daddy, my Daddy!' exclaimed Nicola. Dad gave them both a big hug and they disappeared off into the night. Dad took them for tea at Pizza Hut. He seemed so jolly, so full of smiles. He was busy making jokes, when there didn't seem to be much to be joking about. 'Mum said you don't love each other anymore,' blurted out Nicola. Dad frowned, his smile vanishing for the first time.

'She didn't mean it,' he said. 'She's not thinking straight. 'Look,' he said, 'sometimes

# Nicola's Story — Divorce

mums and dads stop getting on. Sometimes they can work things out, sometimes they can't.'

'What if they can't?' asked Nicola.

'Let's not go there,' said Dad. 'We'll just have to wait and see.' But Nicola didn't want to wait and see. She wanted things to go back to how they were before the arguments started. Dad sighed. 'I know it's hard,' he said. 'You're going to have to be patient. You and me both.'

It was a Tuesday when Tommy Talbot said it. They were at the painting table, making pictures in the style of Monet. 'You don't have a dad anymore,' he said. 'My mum says your parents are getting divorced.' Nicola hadn't heard the word before. Divorced, what did it mean? Nicola burst into tears. Miss Jenkins was very sweet. She cuddled Nicola and told her not to worry and that Tommy shouldn't have said what he did. Later that day, during Circle Time, the teacher asked the children if anyone was worried about anything. Nicola saw her chance.

'Tommy said my parents are going to get divorced,' she repeated and started to cry again. 'I still don't know what that means,' she said, fighting off her tears.

Miss Jenkins sighed.

'Listen,' she said, 'sometimes mummies and daddies decide that they don't want to live together anymore.'

'Does that mean,' said Nicola in a trembling voice 'that my Dad won't be my dad anymore?'

'Of course not,' said Miss Jenkins, throwing Tommy a disappointed look. 'Just because mums and dads sometimes decide to live apart, they don't stop being mums and dads. That's a job for life!' she added with a reassuring smile. She suddenly looked sad, like she was remembering something painful.

'Look,' said Miss Jenkins. 'There are all sorts of families. Peter lives with his Granny, whom he loves very much.'

'And I'm fostered,' said Clive. 'I live with Simon and Alison. I call them Mum and Dad sometimes.'

Miss Jenkins looked a little uncomfortable. The children were just being themselves, honest – but it was sometimes surprising what they would say. 'My Mum and Dad are divorced now,' ventured Daisy. 'My Mum has a boyfriend. He's called David. I didn't like him at first, but now I think he's okay.'

'Look,' said Miss Jenkins. 'There are all sorts of families. Some children live with mum, others dad. Some live with an aunty or grandparents. Some are fostered. It doesn't matter what sort of family we belong to. What is important is that we have someone at home whom we love and who takes care of us. Mums and dads never stop loving their children; they can't always be with them though.' And then she added, with a slightly uncomfortable look, 'My Mum died when I was six.' The children shifted awkwardly on their seats. They didn't know what to say. 'It didn't mean that I stopped loving her,' said Miss Jenkins, 'or her me.' Nicola suddenly realised that there were worse things than Mum and Dad not getting on anymore. After all, she still had them both – just at different times.

The class were quiet. It had been what Miss Jenkins called one of their 'deep' conversations. If anyone was left with any questions, she said, she would try to answer them as best as she could, whenever they felt like asking them.

That afternoon, when Mum picked Nicola up from school, Nicola gave her a huge squeeze. 'What was that for?' Mum asked.

'Nothing,' replied Nicola, 'no reason.' But Mum looked pleased and Nicola felt happier than she had in a while.

© Gary Nott and Brilliant Publications Limited
*This page may be photocopied for use by the purchasing institution only.*

# Teacher's Notes
# Harry's Story

## Background
I have met many characters over the years. Some have been irritating and loveable in equal measure. This story was written with no one child in mind; there have been many who never knew when to stop asking questions!

## General theme
Everyone is different. Sometimes we can find somebody's personality rather grating. It is important to try to see the good in everyone. It is the kind thing to do.

## What do Christians believe?
Christians believe that God loves each and every one of us equally. It is more difficult to love those who don't treat us well or who we find annoying or who don't seem to be living as God wants them to. Jesus showed his followers how to treat others with compassion and love.

## Prayer
*Father in Heaven, You made us all in your image. May we always seek to see the good in other people. Give us patience and love in our hearts at all times.*

## The story
Harry has a natural curiosity about everything and everyone. He doesn't always find it easy to accept the answer he has been given. Despite this, his teachers are fond of him because they sense that he can't help it – it's how his brain is wired.

## PSMC links
- We all have different personality traits. Sometimes, someone's particular ways can make them harder to get on with. How can we best move forward in such circumstances?
- Is it ever right to tell someone what it is about them that we find annoying – or should we just go and play with someone else? Which is the kinder thing to do?

# Harry's Story

Harry liked to ask questions. Not just like you or I might ask a question – perhaps to while away the time or occasionally to try to answer a thought that had popped into our heads. Harry would ask all sorts of questions constantly. Sometimes, he liked to ask what his teachers called the big questions. Where does Santa go on holiday? How come polar bears live at the North Pole and penguins at the South?

Then, more irritatingly, there was his favourite 'little' question: just the one word – one single word – *why*? If Mr Daynes said to Harry, 'We are not using paints today in art,' Harry would come back at him in an instant with the question, 'Why?' If Mrs Harries said we aren't having hymn practice today, Harry would again ask, 'Why?'

Harry always had to have an explanation for everything. The doctor said his brain was wired differently. Harry, he said, had a condition. It was called Asperger's. His mum and dad didn't bother him with the word but he knew he was different.

His condition meant he had an enquiring mind. It also meant he took things quite literally. If Grandma said her feet were killing her, Harry thought Granny's life was in danger. If a teacher asked him to wait a minute, he would look at his watch so that he could time himself accurately. The other kids didn't get it. Sometimes they laughed. Other times, they didn't get the joke, even if the teachers did. Harry just appeared a bit of a pain, especially when he wound up the teachers, who often despaired of him.

Friendships weren't easy for Harry. He couldn't take turns. Although many people had tried to teach him over the years, he could never grasp the idea. This meant problems in the playground. The children would play games and sooner or later Harry would not be able to take his turn. At that point he would lash out and become tearful. This would make the other children angry. There would be a stand-off: Harry on one side of the playground, pacing; the other boys to the other side, grumbling.

The Isle of Wight trip was the highlight of the children's time in Year 6. In early June, they would set off on the three-hour trip to the island. It was a long journey. Harry found himself sitting next to Bradley, opposite Mr Daynes and Miss Harries. The teachers knew they were in for a long coach journey! There would be questions from Harry – and then some.

'Are we going to be on the road long?' enquired Harry.

'A couple of hours,' replied Miss Harries.

'So it's 9.05 am now,' said Harry looking at his watch, 'so we'll be there at 11.05.'

'Well, near to that time,' sighed Mr Daynes. 'Maybe not exactly at that precise minute.'

'When we say a couple of hours, Harry, we mean approximately that. Not exactly.'

At dinner time that evening, Roy, the hotel owner brought out the first course of soup – tomato. Harry's favourite. Harry devoured his portion and his hand quickly shot up. 'Yes?' asked Roy, all smiles. 'Can I have some more?' enquired Harry.

'No,' said Roy.

'Why?' asked Harry.

'Because you'll be tucking into fish fingers and chips shortly.'

But Harry wasn't satisfied.

'They haven't finished their soup yet,' pointed out Harry. 'There's time for me to have more.'

Roy smiled.

'No,' he said.

'Why?' said Harry.

'We've been here before son,' said Roy. Moving off quick smart.

The hotel owner hadn't met a boy quite like Harry before.

Harry had a difficult time in his room that first night. The children had walked to the beach and played on the sand. When they returned, they all wanted a shower. The boys in Harry's room decided to draw lots to see who would shower first. Harry didn't like the sound of that and so had stripped off and jumped in the shower before the other boys knew what was happening. Taking a turn, it wasn't something that Harry understood. After dinner, Harry approached Mr Daynes. 'I want to go home,' he announced. 'I don't like the boys I am sharing with.'

'You can't go home Harry,' replied his exasperated teacher.

'Why?' shot back Harry.

'Because you can't,' the teacher insisted.

'But why?' asked Harry. 'I don't like it, I want to go home.'

Mr Daynes looked at Harry with a resigned expression. He was a kindly man but nevertheless Harry could push him to the boundaries.

'Because,' said Mr Daynes, drawing breath, 'there's no ferry back to the mainland before Friday.'

Harry appeared stumped.

'If I could get you on a boat,' the teacher said, gaining confidence, 'I would. But I can't: there's no boat.'

Harry looked like a balloon that had had the air let out of it. Deflated, crumpled. He knew there was nowhere for him to go with this questioning of his teacher.

The week came and went. Harry continued to ask for more at dinner time. Roy felt able to reject his requests, just sometimes mind you! On each day trip that they went on, Harry was always ready with his questions: Why did Queen Victoria like the Isle of Wight? What caused the dinosaurs to become extinct? But by the end of the week Harry had changed, just a little. He had realised that he couldn't jump the queue of room-mates; the other boys insisted that he take his turn. With no teacher, or parent to give in to his demands, Harry simply had to bite his tongue, take his turn, get on with it. Similarly with his teachers, he became resigned to the fact that they would tire of his questions 24/7 and refuse to entertain him further.

On the journey back to school they played a quiz, Mr Daynes at the coach microphone. The teacher tried to make it enjoyable for the characters and characteristics that had surfaced during the week. He came to the final question: Who has asked more questions than anyone else this week? The children smiled. They knew the answer was Harry. Harry smiled.

'Why did you include that question?' the boy asked his teacher.

'Because,' his teacher replied, 'although your constant questioning can be a bit of a pain, it's what makes you – you,' said the teacher; 'and Harry, we are all very fond of you. One thing's for sure,' the teacher said with a wink, 'you're never boring!'

'Would you take me on another school trip?' asked Harry with a grin.

'Yes,' said Miss Harries and Mr Daynes with one voice.

'Why?' said Harry.

'Why not?' answered Mr Daynes with a wink. Harry couldn't think of anything to say to that. His teachers smiled a triumphant grin.

# Teacher's Notes
# Darren's Story

## Background
Not a week passes that I am not required to make a judgement call with regard to keeping children safe at home. Sometimes, there can be as many as half-a-dozen such occasions in the one week. I don't always get it right. I endeavour to follow the guidance given to me as a Headteacher but the guidance is constantly changing. It's never easy ... .

## General theme
Why do some parents mistreat their children? What can a school do to keep children safe at home?

## What do Christians believe?
The Christian message is one of love. We are encouraged to be slow to anger: instead to love those around us with all our hearts. But the Christian message is also one of forgiveness. Should Darren forgive his dad? (What do the children think? Be prepared for some surprises!)

## Prayer
*Loving Lord, please be with all those who suffer, through illness, loneliness, bereavement, hunger, violence in the home or homelessness. Thank you for the charities and those people who work for them tirelessly to bring happiness and change to people's lives.*

## The story
Darren's recount to his teachers is probably true. However, he doesn't want to get his dad into trouble. Often children will change their story when their parents are present. The child will want the mistreatment to stop but it takes a very courageous child to speak out against a parent.

## PSMC links
- Is there an adult to whom the children would speak in school, if they were worried about something at home? If there isn't, why is that?
- Shouldn't all adults in school be approachable in such circumstances?

© Gary Nott and Brilliant Publications Limited
*This page may be photocopied for use by the purchasing institution only.*

# Darren's Story

Mr Smith had already endured a difficult morning. The Headteacher of St Anne's Primary, he was used to seeing a great many problems pass across his desk. However, nothing had prepared him for 25th June. Miss Davies, his Deputy, entered his office with a worried look clouding her face.

'I think we might have a problem,' she said.

'What is it Lynne?' said the Headteacher.

'It's Darren Gibson. He says he can't walk on his foot. Miss Tierney says she thinks it might be broken. Only, Darren says his dad pushed him off the bed this morning.'

'If he has a broken foot there will be swelling,' said the Headteacher.

'Yes,' agreed his Deputy, 'and there is. He can't stand on it.'

Mr Smith sighed.

He had been worried about Darren in the past. The boy's father often appeared rough with him. There had been concerns voiced by teachers and even other parents.

'We'll have to get him to Casualty. We can quiz him on the way.'

'Do we tell his dad?' asked the Deputy.

'We do, but not for an hour or so. It will give me time to get him to the hospital and raise the issue with Social Care.'

They left the office and made for the medical room. There was Darren sitting with his leg raised on a chair. He had a cold compress that Mrs Tierney was holding lightly against his skin.

'Okay, Darren,' said Mr Smith. 'It's a short car trip to the hospital. When we get there, we'll have someone take a look at you.' Mr Smith helped Darren to his feet – well to one foot. Putting Darren's arm round his shoulder, the Headteacher helped Darren hop to the car. Miss Davies opened the back door, so Darren could slide in.

'Ouch,' he said. 'It hurts.'

'Yes,' said the Deputy Head, 'we think you may have broken a bone.'

Mr Smith slid into the driver's seat and Miss Davies sat beside him. They set off. Mr Smith started to talk to Darren. He wanted to know more about the push.

'What happened exactly this morning, Darren?' he asked.

'Dad pushed me off the bed,' the boy mumbled.

'How come, pushed?' asked the Headteacher.

'He was angry with me because I had been cheeky, so he pushed me. My foot hurt, it felt squishy.'

'Didn't Dad say he would take you to the doctors?'

'No,' replied Darren. 'He said to get ready for school or I'd be late.'

Miss Davies frowned, not that Darren could see, sitting in the back of the car. Mr Smith caught her eye. This was a difficult situation.

They drove into the hospital car park and found a space. Miss Davies disappeared inside and emerged in a couple of seconds with a wheelchair. The two adults helped Darren into it and Mr Smith pushed him inside. There was a long queue, which they joined. The first person to see was the receptionist, who asked them to take a seat and wait for Darren's name to be called. Mr Smith wanted to talk to Darren a little more.

'Are you sure Dad pushed you on purpose? Because he was angry?'

Darren looked uncomfortable. Did the young boy sense where this might be going?

'Yes,' he mumbled. 'I've already said.'

Eventually, Darren's name was called. The

Modern Christian Assembly Stories

# Darren's Story

doctor was nice. He spoke slowly. How did this happen he asked Darren. 'My Dad pushed me,' Darren replied.

The doctor said Darren would have to have an X-ray – a special picture, which would photograph the bones inside his foot. There were several different ones, said the doctor. He then asked to see Mr Smith to one side. The two men spoke in hushed tones. Then the doctor walked off in the direction of the main desk.

'Where's he going?' asked Darren, looking troubled.

'Just to arrange the X-ray,' replied the Headteacher. A porter arrived and said that he would take Darren to the X-ray ward.

'Will it hurt?' Darren asked Miss Davies, who suddenly felt sorry for the boy. He looked so vulnerable.

'No, not at all,' said the porter, who was a cheery chap.

Mr Smith asked to see Miss Davies and they stepped to one side so Darren was out of earshot.

'The doctor is asking the receptionist to phone the Police and Social Care,' he said. 'They will send someone along to speak to Darren. I need to phone his dad to let him know where he is and ask him to come down to be with him. We just have to hope the Police arrive before his dad. But there are no guarantees.'

Mr Smith went off to phone Darren's dad. Miss Davies would accompany Darren and the porter. They were gone some time and then all at once they were back.

'We have to take him to the children's ward now,' the Deputy Head said. 'It's just through there.'

The Head and Deputy went with Darren but had to wait till a nurse buzzed them in. The door opened automatically.

They sat with Darren who had been lifted on to a bed. They had to wait for the doctor to find out if a bone was broken.

It was a stressful wait.

Darren looked as if in he were in some considerable discomfort; he also looked worried. Mr Smith could guess why.

Suddenly, a lady and gentleman who they hadn't seen before appeared. The lady asked to see Mr Smith. They returned shortly. The woman was all smiles. 'I am a police officer, Darren,' she said gently. 'This is my colleague, Peter. We want to talk to you about what happened this morning.'

Suddenly Darren's dad appeared and walked up to the group. Mr Smith jumped to his feet, looking nervous. 'Hello, Mr Gibson,' he said. 'Before you speak to Darren, I need to explain where we are at.'

'What do you mean?' said Darren's dad.

'Well it's just that Darren said this morning you had pushed him off the bed.'

'Yes,' said Mr Gibson, looking at the two

plain clothes policemen suspiciously. 'We were having a bit of rough and tumble, a laugh, that's right isn't it, Darren?'

Darren nodded.

'Let's go and get a cup of coffee Mr Gibson, so Darren can explain what happened and I'll explain who's who.'

Mr Smith expertly guided Mr Gibson to the door and they walked through. Darren's dad looking back at his son anxiously.

The two officers turned to Darren. 'Well Darren, what did happen this morning?'

'Like Dad said,' said Darren, 'we were having a play around. It was an accident.'

Miss Davies inhaled sharply. 'That's not what you said to Mr Smith and me. Is it?'

'I was wrong,' said Darren. 'I was angry with Dad because he had sent me to school.'

Darren's dad reappeared with Mr Smith. 'Well,' said Mr Gibson sounding angry now.

'Darren says that you were playing around. He *had* said you pushed him in temper because you were angry with him.'

The doctor reappeared. 'Well Darren, he said you have broken a bone all right and so we are going to need to treat it.'

On the journey back to school, Mr Smith and Miss Davies sat without talking. 'I'm not sure we handled that correctly,' said Mr Smith, breaking the silence at last.

'No,' sighed the Deputy Head.

'I guess we will never know what really happened.'

'No,' said Mr Smith, 'but I worry that Darren was telling the truth first time round – when he said his dad had pushed him in temper. And if he did, will he do it again?'

'I think Mr Gibson will have learned his lesson, if he did act in temper. I like to think he wouldn't try anything like that again.'

'Yes,' the Headteacher said. 'Let's hope so.'

It had been a long day and truth to tell, Mr Smith would be pleased when it was over.

Back at the hospital, Darren's Dad gave him a hug and whispered 'I'm sorry' in his ear.

Darren gave his dad a squeeze.

# Teacher's Notes
# Comfort's Story

## Background
I recently had a touring singing group come to the school to work with some singers. The problem was that on arrival, they announced they only wanted to work with boys. Their intentions were good: they wanted to raise the profile of singing with children less likely to sing. But you should have seen the faces of the girls when they were told they weren't to be involved. We almost had a mutiny. Football is often a point of contention for girls in the school: some feel like they are overlooked in favour of the boys.

## General theme
Do we assume that some pastimes are better suited to either boys or girls? Is this reasonable?

## What do Christians believe?
Christians believe that we are all given gifts and talents that we should use to bring glory to God and for the good of others.

## Prayer
*Loving Lord, we thank you for giving us all different talents and skills. Help us to recognise that we are all different but all valuable in your sight. May we use our skills and talents to help others and to bring you glory.*

## The story
Comfort has a passion for football. She encounters some opposition when she tries to show that girls can enjoy the game as much as boys. Her ultimate aim is not for a separate team for each but a mixed team of equals. How likely do the children think it is that her dream will come true?

## PSMC links
- Can the children think of some activities that are associated with boys rather than girls – and vice-versa?
- Have the girls ever wanted to do something that is more closely associated with boys? How about the boys – have they been in the position of wanting to do something that is associated with girls?
- If the boys hesitated to try a particular activity, what was stopping them? Are they confident enough to share their thoughts or is there a stony silence? Peer pressure is a strong force.

© Gary Nott and Brilliant Publications Limited
*This page may be photocopied for use by the purchasing institution only.*

Modern Christian Assembly Stories

# Comfort's Story

Comfort loved her football, and she was fond of her teacher Mr Albert, who in turn, liked her. However, one autumn, pupil and teacher found themselves on a collision course and the focal point of the clash was the beautiful game itself.

Mr Albert organised the football team. The boys were drawn from Years 5 and 6. That September, Comfort had become a member of the School Council. At her first meeting, the usual themes were explored: could there be a school disco and that perennial favourite, could they have more non-uniform days? But Comfort had other ideas. She was waiting for her moment and then all at once it came. 'Comfort, what would you like to say?' asked Miss Simpson.

Comfort took a deep breath, 'I think we should have a girls' football team!' Miss Simpson looked uncomfortable. Comfort had practically shouted. And she had always seemed such a sensible girl too.

The boys on the council hung their heads and began to grumble. A girls' football team? What a silly idea. But the girls sitting round the table had other thoughts. 'What a great idea!' exclaimed Chantelle from Year 4. The meeting broke up with children talking ten to the dozen; the boys against the idea, the girls for it.

It wasn't long before Mr Albert got wind of the suggestion. Miss Simpson told him all about it over tea break. Mr Albert was shaken. There was a boys' team, yes; but girls? Why, he didn't know the first thing about girls' football. No, no, no, they couldn't agree to that! But Comfort had other ideas. 'Why not?' she said to Mr Albert, when she encountered him in the corridor.

'Because at St Limes, we only have a boys' football team. It has always been like that and it will always be the same. At least, as long as I am the teacher in charge of football!'

At that point, Comfort knew that she had glimpsed the future: Mr Albert may be the teacher in charge of boys' football but the children needed someone new to lead girls' football in the school. Comfort thought about the teachers who were available. Her preference was Miss Lilywhite, who coached the girls' athletics team. If there could be girl runners, why not girl footballers?

Miss Lilywhite was excited, Comfort could tell. She wanted to talk team selection and tactics. Comfort thought the conversation was running away with them. Surely the first step was to ask the girls who might be interested in joining a team? It might be that none would. Miss Lilywhite put a sign on the PE notice board, asking all girls who were keen to come

*Modern Christian Assembly Stories*

to the Hall at break time on Tuesday. Comfort could hardly sleep that night. Would the idea have caught on? Some girls had expressed an interest in what was going on but still, a team, who would have thought it?

The next day dawned bright and Comfort felt nervous over her cornflakes. Would a crowd show? Comfort needn't have worried. There were girls from every year group, all looking excited. Miss Lilywhite announced that there would be trials the following day on the field at 12.30. Comfort was excited. Miss Lilywhite was excited.

The trials were fun, Miss Lilywhite saw to that. You had to dribble with a ball the full length of the field and then shoot into a goal that was protected by Suzanne Jenkins, from Year 6. The girls shrieked with excitement. The boys who had gathered round, groaned.

'The only problem,' says Miss Lilywhite, 'is that we don't have any teams to play against. Which other schools in Dipson have a girls' football team?'

The next day Miss Lilywhite made some calls and organised a match for 1st October against St Cuthbert's.

On the day of the game, the girls were nervous. They were playing away from home and it was difficult to relax. If you weren't relaxed, said Miss Lilywhite, you wouldn't play your best. The ball came to Comfort and she miskicked, so nervous was she. The ball flew to the feet of one of the St Cuthbert girls who ran with it and took a shot on goal: 1–0.

After that, things got worse. The match seemed to be racing by and the girls could not find their rhythm. By half-time, they were 3-0 down. At the interval, they handed round oranges and Miss Lilywhite gave them a pep talk. You need to keep possession, she said. As soon as you get the ball, you give it away. The opposition can't score if they haven't got the ball. The second half was better. The girls tried to slow things down and to keep hold of the ball like their teacher had said. They didn't score but neither did St Cuthbert's, who ended the second-half in the same position as the first – 3-0 up.

'Well done girls,' said Miss Lilywhite.

'But we lost,' said Comfort.

'Yes, but let's look for the positives.'

'The positives,' said Comfort, 'were there any?' She felt deflated.

'Yes,' said Miss Lilywhite. 'Lots. It was a game of two halves – yes, you lost the first half – but you were unbeaten in the second.'

It seemed a funny way of looking at things but Comfort could see the point Miss Lilywhite was making. So did the other girls, who began to look forward to their next match. It was a home fixture against St Peter's.

'Now remember,' said Miss Lilywhite, 'relax and keep hold of the ball. You win football matches through having lots of possession.' The first half was tight. No goals were scored. Then in the second half, the girls seemed to relax into their stride. Comfort kept pushing forward and with ten minutes to go the ball landed at her feet just outside the area. She took aim and struck the ball with all her might. Goal!

The girls held out and were the victors. Comfort was delighted. Things had gone well, even better than expected. Mr Albert, who had been watching from the sideline, made his way over. 'Comfort,' he proclaimed, 'that was tremendous. Well done. You saw things through and have won the day. St Limes now has a girls' football team and one that can win games. You've done spectacularly well. I'm proud of you.'

'No, sir,' relied Comfort, with a cheeky grin. 'I won't have won until we have a 'mixed' team – boys and girls.' Mr Albert groaned, it was going to be a long year … .

# Teacher's Notes
# Lottie's Story

## Background
I received a letter from a mother who was on the verge of adopting saying it was exciting times for the family. It got me to wondering. How would I have felt as a boy if my parents had announced we were to be joined by another child – an outsider? I must confess that I think I would have been resentful, not wanting to share my mum and dad with others – there were times when I was jealous of my own brother! This story has a twist – because Lottie discovers that the child joining the family is disabled. This challenges her perceptions of what her family would come to look like.

## General theme
Are we good at sharing? Or do we have limits – we will share some things but have difficulty in some areas.

## What do Christians believe?
Christians believe that when they encounter someone in need, be it for companionship, food, shelter or care, they are encountering Jesus himself: 'Whenever you refused to help one of these least important ones, you refused help to me.' (Matthew 25: 45) Christians believe in sharing!

## Prayer
*Loving Lord, you have given us so many things to be grateful for. Help us to be willing as we share and always act with a loving heart.*

## The story
Lottie is confused. She doesn't know what to think. Having your world change can seem exciting for some people, but for others it causes anxiety. Lottie finds that she can talk to Granny, who has wise words to reassure her.

## PSMC links
- How do the children think they would react if their parents announced that they were to adopt or foster a child? Can they put themselves into Lottie's shoes? Lottie feels threatened – she worries that her parents might love the new baby as much as her. Does that tell us anything about Lottie?
- Why do adults adopt children when they already have a family? Is it a good thing?

# Lottie's Story

Lottie was an only child. Her friends all had brothers and sisters but in Lottie's world there was just her. Growing up, she had often wished for a brother to race, or a sister with whom she could dress up. But now she was 11 and Mum and Dad had told her solemnly that they had given up trying for another baby: they said it just wasn't going to happen and they should all accept that and move on. Lottie could tell her parents were disappointed and that made her feel odd inside: wasn't she enough for them? Then one Sunday morning, Mum and Dad said they wanted to see her. They had something to talk through with her, they said.

'Lottie,' started Mum, 'we are thinking of adopting a baby.'

Adopt.

Lottie wasn't sure what the word meant though she had heard it. Her parents carefully explained. Some children couldn't live with their parents. 'Why?' asked Lottie.

'Oh, all sorts of reasons,' said Dad. 'Sometimes they just have nothing left inside to give and so other families give the boy or girl a forever home.'

'How would you feel about it?' asked Mum. Lottie wasn't sure. On one hand, she had kind of gotten used to being the only kid in the house – the centre of Mum and Dad's world; on the other hand, she had always wanted a brother or sister.

'What will it be?' she asked. 'A boy or a girl baby?'

'We don't know yet,' said Mum, laughing. 'And we don't know for sure that it will be a baby either – some boys and girls have already started to grow up when they are first adopted.'

Lottie wasn't sure. A baby would be one thing but a child who was four or five or maybe even older? She had a number of questions. Where would they sleep? Would Mum and Dad love them more than they loved her? What would Granny say? Where would they go to school?

'Whhoa, slow down,' said Dad.

'Yes,' said Mum. 'We have to apply to the people who control these things.'

'Apply?' questioned Lottie. 'You mean like when I applied for St Joseph's?'

Mum laughed. 'Yes, sort of,' she replied. 'You don't just get to adopt. You have to ask and then someone called a social worker will come and talk to us about why we want to adopt and how we would provide a safe and loving home for a baby or little child.'

Mum and Dad didn't mention it again and Lottie didn't like to. She thought if she didn't talk about it maybe the problem would go away. And that's how Lottie saw the suggestion: it was a problem, a problem that was worrying her. Try as she might, she couldn't help but feel unhappy at the thought. This was her mum and dad; she wasn't sure that she wanted to share them with what would, after all, be a stranger. Mum mentioned it next. They were doing the weekly shop when she announced that a lady called Sarah would be coming to visit them next week. Sarah was a social worker. She would ask some questions, find out a little more about them.

'Will she want to speak to me?' asked Lottie, nervous at the thought.

'Of course,' said Mum. 'We're a family.'

Lottie didn't say anything more. But she couldn't help thinking that was her point: they were a family, *already*; they didn't need anyone else. Mum could tell by her silence that she was in a bad place.

'Listen Lottie,' she said. 'Haven't you ever

# Adoption

## Lottie's Story

thought that there was someone missing, someone we still were to meet?'

'No,' said Lottie. 'Well, yes, when I was little but now I'm used to how things are.'

'Oh Lottie,' said Mum. 'Let's just see where the journey takes us. Trust Daddy and me – we won't do anything you are unhappy with.' She gave Lottie's hand a squeeze. Lottie blinked back tears. She felt miserable. This adoption thing was hanging over her and she couldn't seem to change the way she was feeling. It was spoiling things.

Sarah came with a man called David. They wanted to speak to Mum and Dad alone first and to get a feel for their home, they said. Lottie waited in her bedroom till she was called.

'Hello Lottie,' smiled Sarah.

'Mum and Dad have been telling us why they would like to adopt someone. How do you feel about it?' Lottie took a deep breath. She looked at Mum and Dad, whose eyes were fixed upon her.

'Well,' said Lottie, 'I guess it could be fun.'

'You don't sound too sure,' said David.

Lottie said nothing.

Mum and Dad shifted awkwardly in their seats.

'It has been just we three for eleven years,' said Dad. 'It will take some getting used to.'

'Yes,' agreed David. 'Look Lottie,' he ventured with a smile, 'some boys and girls are excited about the thought of having a new brother or sister whilst others are less sure. It would mean you having to share Mum and Dad with someone else. Some boys and girls find that thought difficult. That's natural. Not to worry.'

'We'll leave you to talk some more over the next few weeks and then maybe, if you are all sure, we can start to think about who might be a good match for you.'

'What would happen then?' asked Lottie. 'I mean if we decide to say yes.'

'Let's not run before we can walk,' said Sarah. 'Take a few weeks to talk things through and we'll give you a call in a little while.'

Mum and Dad were disappointed with her, Lottie could tell. They tried not to show it.

Granny asked for Lottie to spend the day with her. Lottie enjoyed their chats. She could tell Granny anything.

'Well,' said Granny, 'what's worrying you? Are you worried that Mum and Dad might love a new brother or sister more than they love you?'

Lottie gulped. Could she be honest with Granny? 'No,' she replied, 'I know they wouldn't do that. But I am worried that they might love a new baby as much as they love me! I know that sounds selfish but it's just how I feel.'

'Oh, Lottie,' said Granny. 'I can't tell you that Mum and Dad would love you more. That wouldn't be fair on the new baby. But it doesn't mean that they would love you any less. They feel that they have enough love for you and someone else.'

'Have you thought that you might grow to love your new brother or sister as much as you love Mum and Dad?'

'No,' Lottie admitted, she hadn't thought that.

She felt confused but just a little better. Granny had given her more to think about.

Mum and Dad said that the adoption people had someone in mind. A four year old boy called Jonathan. Would Lottie like to meet him?

She agreed. Reluctantly.

She still didn't know how she felt.

They took a long car journey to the home where Jonathan was living.

Lottie sat in the back of the car in silence.

When they got to the house, Lottie followed Mum and Dad in. They were met by Sally and Terry – Jonathan's foster parents. They all heard Jonathan before they saw him.

# Lottie's Story — Adoption

He was playing with his toys on the floor. But something was wrong. Lottie wasn't sure what it was. Jonathan didn't look or sound his age. He sounded like a toddler and he started crying when Sally tried to introduce him to the family. This wasn't going to be easy.

Mum and Dad tried to play with him but it was hard work. He seemed different.

On the way home Mum explained that Jonathan had something called 'global delay.' It meant that he didn't understand things a child of four would normally grasp; he struggled to walk and talk. And he would get upset easily.

Lottie hadn't thought that her new brother or sister would be different to other children.

When they got back home, Lottie went to her room whilst Mum and Dad talked in the kitchen. Dad called for her.

'Listen,' said Mum, 'Jonathan is a little different. He has some problems. But he needs love. Do we think we could give him that love?'

'Take some time to think it through, Lottie. If you're not sure about things then we'll stay as we are.'

Lottie thought it through that evening.

She came down to Mum and Dad later and said:

'Not all people are shiny and new and neither are all children.' She had learnt that at school.

'Exactly,' said Mum. 'But everyone deserves to be loved.'

'Yes,' said Lottie, 'they do. I think I'd like Jonathan to be my brother.'

Mum and Dad gave her a hug. 'It's going to be an adventure,' said Mum.

'An adventure,' agreed Lottie. 'One for four!'

# Teacher's Notes
# Luke's Story

## Background
Dementia is a cruel disease. Unlike other illnesses, the person can appear fit and healthy; but the personality of the person we know and love can disappear in front of our very eyes. Grown-ups find this difficult to handle and children too can be slow to adjust – it doesn't seem right that this could happen to someone we care about.

## General theme
What happens when someone who is elderly grows sick and won't get well again? How do we cope?

## What do Christians believe?
Jesus showed huge sadness when his good friend Lazarus died. He experienced sadness and pain, just as his followers do now. Christians believe in the message of eternal life: 'I am the resurrection and the life. Those who believe in me will live, even though they die.' (John 11:25)

## Prayer
*Heavenly Father, we bring before you all those who are suffering and in pain. Give strength, love and compassion to those who care for the sick and the elderly. We remember those we loved who have died and entrust them to your heavenly care.*

## The story
Luke's dad finds his father's illness difficult to cope with; he can't visit his dad, as he finds it too upsetting. Adults aren't always able to do the right thing. Luke has fond memories of his granddad, who now appears very different from the person he once was. Luke is able to enjoy a last hug from the man he loves and this may ultimately be something he remembers into adult life.

## PSMC links
- Have any of the children lost a grandparent? Do any of them feel comfortable talking about it?
- How important are memories? They can help us to keep the person alive in our hearts.

# Luke's Story

Luke could remember when it had started. It was Christmas. Granddad couldn't remember the words to his favourite Christmas songs. Granny said he had had too much to drink. But Luke was sure it wasn't that. Granddad wasn't a big drinker but he did love to sing – especially at parties. It was later at Easter when Dad said that Luke might find Granddad a little changed when he saw him. On the journey down to Devon, he asked Mum what Dad had meant. Mum frowned and clicked her tongue disapprovingly in Dad's direction. 'Pops is just getting older,' she said. Was she tearful? Luke thought so. It was true, Granddad looked different when Luke saw him. He hadn't shaved – that wasn't like him. And he spent the afternoon just sitting in his chair watching the television; he didn't take much notice of Luke, which was unusual. He had always wanted to tickle Luke and swing him round ever since he was little. Granny carried on as if nothing was wrong but she was talking more loudly and slowly to Granddad, who seemed to be getting on her nerves; she was impatient with him when he couldn't decide if he wanted a cup of tea or not.

'Oh, go without,' she chided him.

'Mum,' scolded Dad. 'Don't talk to Pops like that.'

Granny made a fuss of Luke but seemed strained and worried when talking to Mum later in the kitchen. They stopped talking when Luke walked in, which was odd – they never did that. Dad spent most of the afternoon sitting by Granddad's side, holding his father's hand. Luke had never seen his Dad do that before. Was Granddad ill? he wondered.

No one spoke a great deal on the drive back home. A cloud seemed to have descended upon them. Back at school, Luke couldn't shake his worries about Granddad from his mind.

'What's the problem, Luke,' asked his teacher, Mrs Mayo. He told her. She listened. She put her arm round him and despite his best efforts he burst into tears. He felt better afterwards, relieved to have shared his worry with someone. Mum and Dad seemed unapproachable. Whenever he mentioned Granddad they changed the conversation. It was awkward. He didn't want to upset his parents but he was worried. Mrs Mayo asked to see Mum. On the way home, Mum asked if there was anything he wanted to ask her.

'Is Granddad dying?' asked Luke.

'No,' replied Mum. And then she added absent-mindedly, 'That might be easier.' Luke was shocked. Mum, realising that she had said something she wished she hadn't, turned away. Luke sensed that she was fighting back the tears.

That evening, Mum and Dad sat Luke down. Granddad was ill, they said. He had something called dementia.

'Will he get better?' asked Luke. His parents looked down. Finally Dad said, 'No, son, he won't. Gradually he will get worse. We don't know how quickly the condition will move.'

'He has got very forgetful, I'm afraid. Some days he doesn't recognise Granny and can't remember where he is.'

'Then there are days,' added Dad, 'when he will say something that surprises Granny. Last week he said he could remember the holiday we all had by the sea when you were younger.'

Luke was upset. He didn't know what to think.

'When will we see Granddad again?' he asked.

'During the summer holiday,' said Mum. 'I am going to take you down to see him and

© Gary Nott and Brilliant Publications Limited
*This page may be photocopied for use by the purchasing institution only.*

Granny when Daddy is away on business. Daddy doesn't like to see Granddad in this way; it upsets him. But I feel we should go. What do you think, Luke? Would you like to see Granddad?'

'Yes,' said Luke.

On the drive down Mum was preparing him, he could tell. 'He might not recognise you, Luke. And he will quickly tire. So we won't be staying long. Just a couple of hours or so.'

As they drove up to his grandparents' cottage, Luke was suddenly nervous. He didn't know what to expect. He loved his granddad so very much but it was odd to be here without Dad.

Granny came to the door.

'How is he?' asked Mum immediately.

'Not too bad, out of breath most of the time,' she said. In the hallway, Granny suddenly smiled. 'I caught him staring at the kettle yesterday morning. He said he couldn't remember how to make a cup of tea. You have to laugh,' she added. 'Or else you'd spend all day crying.' Catching sight of Luke's worried face, she took her grandson in her arms and hugged him. 'Don't look so worried Darling,' she said. 'It's still Granddad. He just doesn't seem himself. But we remember how he was, don't we,' she added, wiping away a tear.

'Now, come on, he's in the front room and is looking forward to seeing you, I'm sure he is. I've told him you're coming. It's sad that your father didn't feel able to come. It makes me feel so wretched.'

Luke took a deep breath and followed his Granny into the room. Granddad was sitting near to the window. He was thinner than when Luke had last seen him and looked strained. However, when he saw Luke, his face broke into a broad grin. 'Why it's David come to see his old Dad,' he said. Luke stood rooted to the spot. He was confused. Granddad was calling him by Dad's name. What could he mean?

His mother stooped down to whisper in his ear, 'He thinks you're Daddy when he was a boy.'

Granny and Mum held their breaths.

'Yes it's me,' said Luke, playing along.

His Granddad swept him in his arms and gave his the tightest hug. Then the old man burst into tears.

Luke and his Mum spent the afternoon on the settee, whilst Granddad stared into the garden through the window. When it was time for them to go, he didn't even look up. He seemed to have forgotten they were there and Mum thought it best not to agitate him.

Some weeks later, Mum woke Luke early. 'It's Granddad,' she whispered. 'He died unexpectedly in his sleep, quite peacefully,' she said. Luke began to cry. 'Listen,' said his mother, 'you made him so happy when we visited, letting him think you were Daddy when he was a boy.'

'Did I?' said Luke.

'Oh yes,' said Mum. 'He had so much fun seeing his little boy again. And with the hug he gave you, you had your granddad back again!'

# Teacher's Notes
# Mr Reynolds' Story

## Background
We all see the world differently. This story is based loosely upon events that happened to me when I began to lead a church school. I was expecting everyone I met to be kind. How naive I was. It is always hard when one feels unappreciated. Life is full of disappointments and I guess a measure of us as 'reasonable' people is how we deal with the setbacks that come along.

## General theme
Is it easy to be offended when someone doesn't like the things that you do, especially when you are trying hard to please?

## What do Christians believe?
Jesus suffered rejection. Not everyone accepted the truth that he brought. Christians are taught to love everyone and it is not always easy to love those who are unkind to us. That is a true test!

## Prayer
*Lord, help us to be strong in the face of disappointment. May we always remember to turn to you when things get a bit tough and not try to struggle on by ourselves.*

## The story
Mr Reynolds perhaps has his priorities wrong. He wants to be liked but doesn't appreciate that not everyone will like his way of going about it. He takes this personally.

## PSMC links
- It is a hard lesson in life that 'we cannot please all the people all the time.'
- Have the children ever heard this phrase? Can they explain it?
- Does everyone always like what they do? How does it feel when someone doesn't appreciate their actions when they are trying to be nice?

# Mr Reynolds' Story

Pat Reynolds had come to St Joseph's full of promise and ideas. He wanted to be the best Headteacher the school had ever known. He worried about how he could make himself known to the families who made up the school. This was his first headship and he wanted to make a good impression – being popular was important to him. The previous Headteacher had told him that the families of St Joseph's were difficult to reach, distant; some were even hostile. There were so many families –over 400 – how could Pat possibly get to know them all? He tried standing at the school gate first thing in the morning and at the end of the day. But people always seemed in such a hurry; there was never any time to talk properly.

So he hit upon two ideas. Firstly, he would write a newsletter each week that would include a personal reflection on something he felt important – let the parents know what he was thinking. Secondly, he would open up an email account entitled tellpat@stjosephs.com. He would encourage parents to email him with their thoughts and concerns. In these ways he hoped to form a bond between the parents and himself. He thought this was important. Parents would be more likely to support their children with their homework and reading if they felt like they belonged and if the Headteacher was interested in them.

Pat enjoyed writing the weekly newsletter. He included lots of news items and his weekly reflection too. Entitled 'Thought for the Week', it generally had a spiritual message; it was a time to talk about God. And Pat tried to make the thought come to life by telling the parents about his own family: Tracey, his wife, and his three children, David, Chloe and Ben. He shared their ups and their downs, in a style that was intended to amuse and entertain.

That week had been difficult and long. There had been a number of problems to solve. His teachers were tired for it had been a long half-term. The children were worn out too and that made them more difficult to deal with. Still, it was half-term holiday next week and as he drove home that evening, Pat relaxed at the thought of having a week off from the hustle and bustle, a chance to recharge his batteries.

He let himself into the house and was greeted by his three children, who were pleased to see their father. He relaxed with a cup of tea and after dinner opened up his emails. He stopped in his tracks. There sitting in his tellpat email box was a message that said simply:

> Why do you always talk about your family in the newsletter? Surely there are kids who attend St Joseph's about whom you could write?

Pat felt his stomach lurch. He was disappointed. No, stronger than that. Shocked. This was personal. He had only made reference to his family with the notion of making himself seem human, likeable.

Should he tell his wife? No, she would only worry. He went to bed that evening troubled. Who amongst the parents would have been so unkind as to say such a thing? And were other parents thinking that too? No, surely not. At least, he hoped not. All at once, he felt embarrassed and silly. What had made him think people would be interested in stories about his family?

Half-term came and went. He tried not to think about the setback he had suffered but the thought was never far from his mind.

How should he respond? Was it best to

**Modern Christian Assembly Stories**

ignore it?

As Pat drove into work on Monday morning, he had decided upon his course of action. He would reply to the parent whom he judged to have been unkind via this week's 'Thought for the Week.'

He thought hard about what to write. He needed to get it right. He wrote:

> Last week, I upset someone and they in turn upset me. From time to time, I make reference to my family here in this weekly 'Thought'. I do so to try to make a point I am making come alive. I will try to do it less often because the last thing I would want to do is upset anyone.

Pat felt better when he had written it. It was like he had got something of his chest. That Friday, as he drove home, he wondered how the parents who read his latest 'Thought' would react? And what about the person who had been unkind to him? Would they read it? Would they reflect upon their words? Would they conclude that they had been wrong to email Pat with such unpleasant thoughts?

He had his dinner and sitting down with a cup of tea logged into his email account to see if he had any messages.

What he saw there made him smile. There were ten messages sitting in his in-box, all saying similar things:

> We like the fact you talk about your family in the newsletter.

> Thank you for sharing tales of your family – more of the same please.

Pat felt happier.

The following week Pat didn't talk about his family in his 'Thought for the Week'. Nor the week after. But in that third week, David had done something funny at school that he wanted to share with everyone.

On Monday morning, he logged into his email account absent-mindedly. There sitting in his in-box was a second nasty message – it was from the same person:

> Yet again, you couldn't resist talking about your family, could you? What makes you think we are interested?

Pat sighed. In his heart of hearts, he had hoped that the mystery parent would have had second thoughts and even regretted their post, thinking that they had been wrong. But clearly, not.

What to do?

Should he reply?

He sat and thought.

He spoke to his wife that evening. She could see he was troubled. 'Listen,' she said, 'you can't hope to please everyone, all the time. There will always be people who like what you do and others whom you displease.'

Pat sat and thought.

It was true.

His mistake had been to think that everyone would like his stories; moreover, that they would all like him. There were always going to be people in life who didn't like what you had to say, who didn't like you. That was true for everyone – even Headteachers. He had to accept it and move on. He felt brighter as he skipped down the stairs.

'Take the positives out of every situation,' his wife had said. Well Pat would do just that. Some people liked what he had to say and in future he would remember that he was writing for them. Popularity, he had decided, was overrated! In future he would focus on being the best headteacher he could be, not the most liked. There was a difference. He knew that now and it was a lesson he wouldn't forget in a hurry.

# Teacher's Notes
# Gary's Story

## Background
Every good assembly collection needs a Christmas story; this one has two. This first one aims to capture the children's imagination for everyone loves a surprise at Christmas! Indeed, the children will have all sorts of thoughts as to what Gary's present might be and you might like to stop the story mid-flow and ask for some guesses. The love that the brothers have for one another hopefully comes through – it's a true story and one my brother and I still chuckle over when we remember back – our dad still doesn't know … .

## General theme
Christmas is a time for surprises. People will go to great lengths to keep someone guessing as to what the gift might be. Sometimes we spoil things when we don't know when enough is enough!

## What do Christians believe?
Christians believe that the greatest ever Christmas gift was God himself, in human form. A tiny baby, born in Bethlehem, as prophesied by Isaiah: 'A son is born to us! A child is given to us! … . He will be called "Wonderful," "Counsellor," "Mighty God," "Eternal Father," "Prince of Peace."' (Isaiah 9:6)

## Prayer
*Father in Heaven, we thank you for sending us the most precious Christmas gift ever, Jesus, your Son. May the true message of Christmas remain in our hearts always.*

## The story
Gary's dad loves him. He wants him to have a surprise. Gary ends up ruining this when he plays his brother up. Gary's brother doesn't mean to spoil things but he is provoked. How does the brothers' love for one another shine through in the ending to the story? How many secrets were there in this story?

## PSMC links
- Have the children ever had to keep a secret? Were they able to?
- Why do we take such pleasure in surprising someone with something?
- Do adults like surprises as much as children?

# Gary's Story

Christmas was Gary's favourite time of year. He loved everything about it: the pantomime, the turkey dinner and, of course, the presents. That year, he had been looking forward to it as much as any other year. But that was before Dad made his announcement. When they were on holiday in Cornwall during the summer holidays, Dad had suddenly said that Santa would bring Gary something unexpected that year.

'A surprise?' questioned Gary. 'You mean I don't get to choose my present?'

'No,' said Dad. 'I don't want the usual Christmas list for Santa. Instead he will bring you something you haven't asked for. A complete surprise!'

Gary wasn't so sure that this was a good idea. But Dad's mind was clearly made up. He clapped his hands together with glee, a twinkle in his eye.

When he went back to school in September, Gary asked Dad if he had been joking. 'No joke,' said Dad. 'This year I am determined that you won't know what Santa is bringing you as your number one present!'

In early December, the Christmas tree was put up. Gary enjoyed seeing it and the cards too that arrived during the weeks preceding Christmas. Dad put balloons up in the corners of the living room. It was getting exciting. And then one morning, as he left for school, Gary noticed that gifts had appeared under the tree. Santa had come early. 'You'll have to wait till Christmas morning to open them,' said Dad.

In the middle of the pile stood a small box shaped present, wrapped in jolly paper. That must be it, thought Gary. My surprise gift.

When Dad and Mum and Paul, his brother, were safely out of the way he picked up the present. He felt it. A solid box seemed to lie underneath the wrapping. No clues there then. He shook it. No rattle. Still no clues. Then he smelt it. Nothing. What could this mystery gift be? He held it up to the light. Could he see through the paper? No. Nothing doing. This was a surprise that he couldn't figure out.

Gary decided to work on his brother Paul, who was ten years older than he. 'You must know Paul,' he said, 'what surprise Dad has planned.'

'Yes, I know all right,' said Paul annoyingly. 'But I'm not going to tell you. Dad wants this to be a surprise and a surprise is what it is going to be!'

'You must know Mum,' tried Gary, later. But Mum wasn't telling either. 'Your dad wants it to be a complete surprise this year Gary,' she said. 'Don't go on. Just wait. Be patient.'

But Gary was no good at waiting: he was impatient to know what the surprise gift was. There were still five days left till Christmas. He couldn't bear the suspense.

Then Christmas Eve arrived. Gary's mum and dad were going out for dinner. Paul was to babysit. Paul had continued to get on Gary's nerves these past few days. 'Want to know your surprise?' he would tease. 'Shan't tell. Is it a toy, a book? – who knows?' He laughed. 'Well, I do, of course,' he would add, and then dissolve into giggles.

It was only 7 o'clock. Still two hours to go until Gary's bedtime. The wait was killing him. He picked up the present wrapped in gold and shook it. Still nothing doing! No clues. Zilch!

Paul came into the room. 'Put down that present,' he ordered in his most grown-up voice. 'I'm in charge, do as you're told!'

Gary began to muck about, pretending to dance in front of the tree. As he jiggled and giggled, he slipped and fell backwards.

'Look out,' cried Paul, 'if you're not careful you'll land on it and smash your radio!'

Gary crumpled to the floor. The secret was out. Paul had let slip the surprise. His brother looked mortified.

'Gary,' he whispered, 'whatever you do don't tell Dad that I've told you. He so wanted you to have a surprise this year!'

Gary didn't know how he felt; the wind had gone out of his sails. He felt deflated. After weeks of guessing, he suddenly knew what his surprise was. And although he was pleased to have a radio – he had always wanted one – he was at the same time disappointed to have ruined things.

Paul looked white. He was afraid that Dad would be very angry with him.

'Don't worry,' said Gary, 'I'll pretend that I don't know.'

'You'll never be able to pass it off,' said Paul. 'Dad will guess.'

'No he won't,' insisted Gary. 'Trust me.'

The next morning Gary came down to Christmas and the tree with his parents sitting round to attention. He opened the smaller gifts first. He could tell from their shape and feel what they were: an annual, a toy lorry and a board game. Then he came to the mystery gift.

Except it was no longer a surprise. He looked up and saw Dad's expectant gaze. He was loving this moment – Gary not knowing what he was about to receive.

Gary played along.

He shook it and smelt it, took the weight in his hand.

'No,' he said. 'I don't know what it is … .'

He slowly began to unwrap the parcel. First the top layer, then the bottom. As the box emerged with a picture of the radio inside printed upon it, Gary's face was a picture. No one watching would have guessed that Gary was unwrapping anything other than a surprise. Gary looked up. His dad seemed delighted.

'You see,' said Dad.' I told you it would be a surprise.'

'Yes,' agreed Gary. 'You did.'

He looked up and caught sight of his brother Paul's face. He could tell he was urging him to keep the secret.

'It was a surprise, Dad. The best surprise I could have wished for.'

Gary's dad smiled.

Paul heaved a sigh of relief.

Christmas had never been so pressurised!

# Teacher's Notes
# Dominic's Story

## Background
I can remember as a child being told that our pet budgie had flown to freedom out of the living room window. Looking back, I am guessing this was itself a story. The budgie had died and my parents were trying to spare me the pain – we have never discussed it, and I prefer to persist with the story of a great escape! It got me thinking. What would happen to a child who managed to 'lose' the school pet … .

## General theme
We all make mistakes. Sometimes, looking back, we find it hard to explain just how we came to be so foolish – often, it just seemed like a good idea at the time. Panic can set in! Panic can give way to desperation – we are often desperate to get ourselves out of a tricky situation. Sometimes, we will go to extraordinary lengths to do so … .

## What do Christians believe?
Christians believe that there is nothing God will not forgive, if forgiveness is asked for with a true and honest heart. In the Lord's Prayer, Christians ask: 'forgive us our sins, as we forgive those who sin against us'. So it is important to have a forgiving heart towards others, if you are seeking God's forgiveness for your faults.

## Prayer
*Dear Lord, give us the courage to own up to our mistakes and say sorry. It isn't always easy to admit we have done wrong or not done something we know we should have. Thank you that there is no end to the forgiveness you offer.*

## The story
Why does Dominic get the bird out of the cage whilst travelling on a bus, of all things?
Are Dominic and his dad being dishonest when they replace the bird?

## PSMC links
- Have the children ever done something foolish that they later couldn't explain – try as they might?
- Has anyone ever tried to conceal their mistake? Did they get away with it? Is it best to come clean, or is it reasonable to try to keep people from news that will only disappoint?

# Dominic's Story

When Mrs Solomon had announced Class 4S were to have a pet, Dominic was as excited as his classmates. His mum had always said he couldn't have a pet of his own. 'I know what will happen,' she had said, 'you'll grow bored with it and then I'll be left to care for it.' Dominic thought this unfair but Mum wasn't going to budge; he could see that. The class were to have a choice: a fish, a hamster, a budgerigar or a stick insect.

'I fancy a budgie – a blue one,' said Gemma at break time. Dominic was undecided. He wasn't sure that birds should be kept in cages. It seemed cruel. They must want to fly but there they sat, day in, day out, cooped up. He would rather they had a stick insect.

'Ugh,' said Rosie, 'a stick insect. They give me the creeps.'

They were to vote on Friday and Mrs Solomon would buy the pet over the weekend. They were each given a piece of paper and asked to write their choice down. It was to be a secret vote, said Mrs Solomon. She didn't want anyone's choice to be influenced by how their classmates were voting. The children were excited. This was fun. They each placed their voting slip into a box and Mrs Solomon started on the task of putting the slips into four piles. Two piles had more votes than the other choices. Mrs Solomon counted.

'Well Class,' she said, 'the chosen pet is a budgie.' There were smiles from some of the children. Dominic looked around. He thought most of the girls had voted for a bird. Gemma was grinning from ear to ear.

On Monday morning the children entered the classroom straining their necks in order to see their new pet. They spied a cage on Mrs Solomon's desk. It had a white towel over it. The children took their seats and Mrs Solomon called the register.

'Now then,' she said. 'I want you all to be quiet; we mustn't startle Monty.' Monty, it was a cute name. Carefully the teacher lifted the towel. There was the sound of fluttering as the bird flew from one side of the cage to the other. Dominic couldn't help but admit he was a beauty – yellow and blue with a white spot on his forehead.

Monty's cage was carefully placed in their quiet area. It would be the best place for him, said Mrs Solomon. The class started their morning activities and more than one child glanced over in Monty's direction during the morning – Dominic included. The week came and went, and before they knew it, it was Friday again.

After lunch, Mrs Solomon called them to the carpet. 'Each weekend,' she announced, 'someone different will take Monty home with them. He will need to be fed and watered on Saturday and Sunday and there will be no one in school to do it. Each Friday morning I will pick someone's name at random and then give their parents a call to check they are okay with the class pet coming home to stay. This morning I picked someone's name out of the hat and have spoken with their mum. I am pleased to say that this weekend Monty will be going home with Dominic.'

Dominic's jaw dropped. He had been chosen and even more surprisingly his mum had agreed to have a feathered visitor.

At the end of the day, Mrs Solomon handed the cage over to Dominic and his mum, together with a pack of bird seed. 'Look after him,' said the teacher. 'We'll see him back in school on Monday morning.'

'What changed your mind, Mum?' Dominic asked as they made their way to the bus stop.

Modern Christian Assembly Stories

'It's only for a weekend,' she replied. 'We'll have him just the right amount of time – you will want to take care of him rather than leave it to me.'

When they got on the bus, people looked at them, smiling to see the budgie in his cage. Monty sat on his perch and didn't move. He seemed rooted to the spot. Maybe he was nervous, thought Dominic, who sat resting the cage on his lap. Dominic's gaze was fixed upon Monty. Monty tilted his head and stared back. The bird looked sad to Dominic. The boy looked at his mother, who was paying him no attention whatsoever as she looked out the window. With very small movements, Dominic slowly opened the cage door and slid his hand around Monty. He would take the bird out and give him a quick stroke. Out Monty came and Dominic sat stroking him. Suddenly his mother glanced in his direction and saw that the bird was out of its cage. She shrieked and, startled by the sound, Monty pecked Dominic's finger in fright. Dominic was in turn startled by the bird's action and released his grip. Monty flew up and bounced off the ceiling. He flew around the crowded bus, threatening to perch on one of the many ladies sitting on the lower deck. There were screams. Dominic thought there may as well have been a tiger on the loose for all the fuss the travelling public was making. But Dominic didn't appreciate that a bird on the loose in a confined space can be a frightening experience for some – however small the bird. The bus driver called out to ask what all the commotion was about. He was trying hard to concentrate on driving and the sound of his passengers in uproar was making his job difficult. Then the bell rang –more than one passenger wanted to get off. Dominic stood and ran forward with the cage, holding it in Monty's direction but before he could reach the bird, the bus had stopped, the doors had opened and Monty had flown out into the teatime sky.

Dominic sat back down and looked sheepishly at his mother. 'I knew having a pet would mean trouble, but I never imagined that.' The woman sitting in front of them began to laugh but Mum wasn't laughing and neither was Dominic. They got off at their stop and walked home without a word.

---

That night, Dominic sat staring at the empty cage. The realisation that he would have to go to school on Monday morning and tell his teacher what had happened left him cold. His classmates would blame him for the loss of their pet and who could argue with that? He had been so silly to get the bird out of his cage but it was too late now for second thoughts.

In the morning, Dad woke him and told him to get washed and ready for breakfast. He realised this was no dream. It was Saturday morning and the events of Friday loomed large

# Getting out of bother — Dominic's Story

in his mind. 'We are going out,' announced Dad.

'Where to?' asked Dominic.

'You'll see,' replied Dad.

Dominic was slow to get dressed. He had butterflies in his stomach. He was dreading Monday and couldn't shake the thought of it from his mind.

Dad drove them to town. He parked the car and they walked down the High Street. Dominic still didn't know where they were going. Suddenly Dad turned into a shop. Dominic realised it was a pet shop. 'Your mission Dominic Turnbull,' said Dad, 'should you choose to accept it, is to find a budgie that is the spitting image of Monty. That way you can take it into school on Monday and no one will be any the wiser.'

Dominic looked at Dad. It was a plan; he couldn't argue with that. They made a beeline for the caged birds. They had all sorts and several budgies, but none were yellow and blue.

'Don't despair,' said Dad seeing Dominic's crestfallen face. 'There's another pet shop at the top end of town. We'll try there.'

They hurried – almost ran to the shop. It was smaller than the first and Dominic's heart sunk. Dad gave his hand a squeeze.

Inside they made their way past the rabbits and guinea pigs, fish and puppies, and then spied the bird cages. There was just the one bird, sitting in a cage: it was a blue and yellow budgie.

'Look Dad,' cried Dominic with a mixture of relief and excitement, 'he's perfect.'

They paid and Dad took charge of carrying the bird to the car. 'We don't want any mishaps en route, do we?' and then added with a wink, 'to lose one budgie is a bit of bad luck, to lose two would be careless.' Dominic laughed.

That weekend they enjoyed having the budgie at home, although Mum was keen to point out that Friday's experience had put her off having a permanent pet for good.

Dominic walked into school that Monday morning with the cage firmly under his arm. Mrs Solomon took the bird from him, asking if he had been a good boy over the weekend.

'Oh yes,' grinned Dominic, 'no trouble at all.'

Nobody seemed to notice that the bird sitting in the cage had no white spot on his forehead and Dominic, who hadn't given that detail any thought, settled down to his day in class. Maybe Mum was right, a pet wasn't for them!

# Teacher's Notes
# Mickey's Story

## Background
This happened to me. During examinations, my teachers came to me looking ashen. A child had slipped out a mobile phone during an exam; they hadn't thought to ask the children if they had a mobile in their pocket – calculators, crib sheets – yes – a device with access to the world wide web, no. I had to phone the examination board and ask them how I should proceed. Sticky moments … .

## General theme
Sometimes we find ourselves in 'hot water' and we didn't see the trouble coming. When we look back, we can honestly say that we could not have foreseen the difficulties that might arise from our actions. It is called innocence; sometimes unkindly termed naivety.

## What do Christians believe?
Christians believe that God gives them the strength to deal with any situation and they are reminded of the need to call on His strength in times of need.

## Prayer
*Loving Father, Thank you for your precious love – a love that never lets us down. Help us to have the strength and courage to admit when we are wrong. May we always be quick to say sorry and quick to forgive others.*

## The story
Mickey doesn't mean to cause any problems. The only thing he might be guilty of is carelessness. He could reasonably have been expected to realise that a mobile wouldn't be a good idea to have out during an examination. But he is young. He is not worldly-wise. He manages to extricate himself from difficulties, but he surely won't forget the lesson the incident has taught him.

## PSMC links
- Sometimes, children don't see the problems that an adult might spot in a particular situation. Inevitably, children can feel aggrieved when confronted with an adult's interpretation of events if that interpretation differs from how they see the world.
- Has this ever happened to children in the class? Have they ever been in the situation when they have said: 'It's not fair, I was only … .' Experience is a valuable commodity: when you are young, you don't have much of it and life can be very confusing as a consequence.

# Mickey's Story

Could there be anything harder than answering questions in SATs, thought Mickey.

Mr Rodgers and Mrs Price had prepared the children well for their end of year exams. They had spent weeks practising and the children were as ready as they were ever going to be. The test papers arrived in school on Monday and the two teachers sat reading the test instructions over coffee at morning break on Tuesday. There were a lot of rules to follow. The papers had to be kept secure in a safe place and not opened before the time of the test.

'There's an awful lot to take in,' remarked Mrs Price, with a deep sigh.

The teachers were nervous. So much depended on the outcome of the tests! The parents were expecting the children to do well and Miss Richards, the Headteacher, was keen to ensure the school did its very beSt

'Do you think they're ready?' asked Mr Rodgers.

Mrs Price didn't answer.

The day of the first test arrived. Every adult knew what was expected of them. Some were to help children with reading. Mrs Donaldson was available to walk children to the bathroom, should they need to go to the toilet during an exam. The children all knew the drill. They were allowed their pen and ruler and a sharp pencil to draw with. They had also been given permission to take a mascot into the exam room – something that might help steady their nerves.

Mickey had a picture of his granddad, who had died the year before. When he looked at it he felt better, less nervous. He carefully placed the picture on his desk. He was sitting opposite Michael, who had a cuddly toy to keep his spirits up.

Mrs Rodgers asked if anyone had any questions. No one did. 'The time,' she said, 'is 9.30 - you have 45 minutes. If you need anything during the exam, please put up your hand and someone will come to you. Good luck everyone. You may begin.'

Mickey opened the paper. The first question seemed straight forward. After weeks and weeks of practice papers, this seemed different. This was for real and they were each seeing the questions for the first time. Samantha Davies started to cough. Mickey looked up. Five minutes had gone. He turned through the pages of the paper, there were thirty questions in total. His mind began to wander. He looked at the last question; he couldn't make head nor tail of it. Suddenly Mrs Price was at his side. She turned the pages back to the beginning and prodded question four with her fat finger. He looked up at her. She was straining not to say anything because that wasn't allowed. He knew that; she knew that. She looked irritated and the message was clear: stay focussed, tackle the questions one by one – just like you have been taught.

He got himself back into the zone and worked through the next few questions one by one. Mrs Price moved away from him and went to answer a question from Annie Palmer. He was most of the way through the paper now. This next one was tricky. He glanced over at Michael, who seemed to be on the final page. How long was there left? Mrs Price was standing in front of the board, talking to Zoe. He couldn't see the displayed time. He began to panic. Was there enough time left to complete the paper? Without a thought, he slipped his mobile phone out of his pocket to see the time. He was suddenly conscious of Mr Rodgers standing over him. The teacher didn't look

*Modern Christian Assembly Stories*  © Gary Nott and Brilliant Publications Limited
*This page may be photocopied for use by the purchasing institution only.*

# Mickey's Story — Making mistakes without thinking

happy. Without saying anything, he motioned to Mickey that he was to give him his phone. Mickey did. Why would Mr Rodgers want it?

'Five minutes remaining,' said Mrs Price. Mickey looked back at the paper. Mr Rodgers had made his way over to his colleague and had bent over to whisper something into her ear. She looked displeased and glanced in Mickey's direction.

'Pens down,' said Mr Rodgers.' Time's up.'

Then Mrs Price added, 'You may go to break. All except you, Mickey. We need a word.'

Mickey sat in his place. He suddenly felt very ill at ease. The phone.

'Mickey,' said Mrs Price. 'I am disappointed in you.'

Disappointed? What had he done exactly?

'Your mobile,' said Mr Rodgers. 'You are not allowed a mobile phone in an exam, you know that. You could have been cheating. You have access to the Internet.'

'Did you cheat Mickey? Think carefully before you answer?' said Mrs Price.

'No,' said Mickey. 'I was just checking the time. You were in the way; I couldn't see the time displayed on the whiteboard. I didn't know you weren't allowed your phone. You didn't say at the start of the exam that we weren't allowed them. You said no calculators or notes. You didn't say anything about mobiles.'

It was true. They hadn't. But neither teacher had ever stopped to think they should be saying no phones either. It was a new one on them. The truth was it had never occurred to them.

'Step this way, Mickey,' said Mrs Price. 'We'll need to talk to Miss Richards.'

Mickey sat outside the Headteacher's office. He could hear the adults' voices from inside. Try as he might, he couldn't help but panic. His mouth went dry and he squeezed his hands together. Was he going to be labelled a cheat? What would his parents say? Or the other kids, for that matter?

Inside the Headteacher's office, the adults stood poring over the test instruction manual as if it were the first time they had seen it. Both teachers were nervous. This was serious; they knew that much. Then they read it, in the middle of page 5, it said in italics: 'If it is thought that a pupil has gained an unfair advantage, then a phone call should be made to our dedicated number where an allegation of cheating can be reported.'

'Well?' said Mrs Price. 'What shall we do?'

The teachers and Miss Richards fell silent.

If Mickey had cheated, then there was nothing else for it but to report it. They realised what this would mean. The parents of all the children in Year 6 would hear about it. There was a chance that each child in Year 6 would have their exam papers disqualified for the Authorities might decide that if one pupil had cheated, others might have done the same. Questions would be asked of them, the teachers. Why hadn't they done their jobs properly? Each of the adults felt sick to their stomachs.

Mickey, sitting outside in reception, was staring at Granddad's photo. What would he say if he were there? He thought back. He suddenly remembered the time his sister Lucy had been accused of bullying another girl in her class. Granddad had refused to believe it. He had insisted they all stay calm and talk the problem through. What had Lucy done that might have accidentally upset the girl in her class. Yes, stay calm, he thought. How can I prove that I wasn't cheating? He suddenly remembered the history feature on his internet browser.

He knocked tentatively at the Headteacher's door.

Mrs Price opened the door.

'I think I can prove that I didn't use my phone to cheat,' pleaded Mickey. 'You can check my internet history and see when I last logged on.'

'Come in,' called Miss Richards. 'I'll have to make a quick call to your mum. She will need to give me permission to look at your phone.'

Miss Richards made the call. Mickey strained to hear what his mum might be saying on the other end of the line. Miss Richards looked like she was having a difficult conversation; her face was red, her cheeks pinched and she was writing on a pad that sat on her desk. After what seemed like an age she put down the receiver.

'Mum has said we can look at your phone Mickey. Go on, show us.' Mickey's fingers were wet with sweat and he slipped on some of the keys but he managed to pull up the internet history.

Mrs Price looked carefully. 'It indicates you haven't logged on to the web at all today,' she said.

Mickey felt his heart leap. He was in the clear.

'Wait,' said Miss Richards. 'It is possible that someone could have communicated with Mickey in the exam room by text. Look to see what the last text message received was.'

'It was at 8.30 this morning,' said Mr Rodgers. 'It's from Mickey's Dad. It simply says, "Good luck today!" And,' added the teacher, 'Billy replied at 8.33 saying, "Thanks dad, I'll need it."' That had certainly been true, thought Mickey with a wry smile.

The adults seemingly let out a collective sigh of relief and Mickey realised that they were as pleased as he that his innocence had been proved.

'What have you learnt from today Mickey?' asked Miss Richards.

Mickey stopped to think. 'I have learnt that there are worse things than having to answer the questions in an exam,' he said. 'Being suspected of cheating in one is far worse.'

Mr Rodgers and Mrs Price glanced up to the Heavens. It had been a long day.

# Teacher's Notes
# Daniel's Story

## Background
The first time a child spends any length of time away from home can be daunting. For many, it is their first school residential trip. However, if it happens to be a stay in hospital, the child may have two things to confront: homesickness and the anxieties associated with the procedure. I can remember having my tonsils out at the age of seven. I was in hospital for a week; it seemed like an age. I made it to the last night and then crumpled into tears; I knew that I couldn't break down before that point because I had to keep going.

## General theme
Feeling homesick can be all consuming. Once you feel it, it is hard to shrug off. It can affect adults as well as children although it probably hits home hardest when one is young – especially the first time one has spent time away from home. It can affect boys as easily as girls: confident children as much as those who are less so.

## What do Christians believe?
Christians are taught to trust in God and have faith, especially during difficult times. The friends who took their paralysed friend to Jesus for healing showed ultimate faith in His ability to help their friend (Luke 5).

## Prayer
*Jesus our friend, please be with all those who feel homesick or alone. We especially remember those children who are in hospital at this time and their friends and families. Help us to remember that we are never truly alone, as you have promised to be with us always.*

## The story
Daniel tries to be brave. He almost pulls it off – he makes it to the last evening in hospital before showing Mum and Dad how he is feeling.

## PSMC links
- Have any of the children ever felt homesick? How did they try to deal with it? The best advice I have been able to share with children who were feeling that way, was to take it day-by-day – not to focus upon anything but getting through the day, whilst remembering that time flies by and before we know it we are back home!

© Gary Nott and Brilliant Publications Limited
*This page may be photocopied for use by the purchasing institution only.*

Modern Christian Assembly Stories

# Daniel's Story

Daniel had had a sore throat off and on for much of December. In the New Year, Mum took him to the doctors. He had to open his mouth wide and the doctor placed a plastic instrument upon his tongue. He pressed down firmly, so much so that Daniel thought he would gag.

'Hmm,' remarked the doctor, 'I want Daniel to see a specialist at the hospital. His tonsils are inflamed and we may need to remove them.'

On the way home Daniel was quiet. 'Penny for your thoughts,' said Mum.

'What will happen next?' he asked. 'I mean, after I have been to the hospital.'

Mum was slow to answer. She seemed to be thinking carefully about what to say. 'You might need an operation,' she said finally.

Daniel felt his stomach lurch. He didn't know what this would mean exactly but it didn't sound good.

'What's an operation?' he asked. He had heard the word before but was unclear.

'Sometimes,' Mum said, 'when we are ill we need an operation. We go into hospital and the doctors mend our bodies.'

'How?' persisted Daniel.

'Well,' said Mum, sounding uncomfortable, 'they might take something away that is giving us problems.'

Daniel fell quiet once more. Mum looked at him.

'Don't look so worried,' she said.

But he was. He didn't like the sound of it at all. Take something away. He wasn't sure how they would do that.

The weeks came and went. The sore throats continued. Then on to the doormat dropped a letter from the hospital. It was an appointment for Daniel at Outpatients.

The doctor Daniel saw was nice enough. He did the same thing pressing Daniel's tongue down but Daniel was ready for it this time; he knew it wouldn't laSt

'Yep,' he said, 'they're going to have to come out. Not tricky, easy to do – nothing to worry about.'

But worry, Daniel did. Mum packed him a bag on the Sunday before he was due to go into hospital. He had butterflies in his tummy – like the day before an exam. Mum gave his hand a squeeze. 'You'll be fine,' she said. Daniel didn't reply.

The next day came too soon. Daniel's mum and dad were both taking him into the hospital; Dad had taken time off work. The hospital ward was bright and colourful, with lots of fun paintings on the walls. Daniel sat on the bed and Mum sat on a chair – there was no chair for Dad, who stood hopping from one foot to the other. The three of them waited and waited.

Then a doctor appeared. 'Sorry to keep you hanging on,' he said. He asked lots of questions about Daniel, which Mum answered. Dad kept Daniel distracted by talking about the coming cup match between Arsenal (Daniel's team) and Chelsea. Daniel had been an Arsenal supporter since Infants but had never seen them play – the tickets, said Dad, were too expensive.

'Okay,' said a nurse who appeared and started to draw the curtains around the bed. 'It's time to say goodbye to Mum and Dad, and pop your clothes off. I have a gown for you to wear.'

Daniel swallowed hard. He didn't want to say goodbye to Mum and Dad. He suddenly felt alone and vulnerable. Mum gave him a kiss on the forehead and Dad patted his shoulder.

Later, the nurse reappeared. There was a man with her; he was to push the trolley bed.

He tried to make Daniel laugh by cracking a joke. Daniel forced a smile. He was nervous, scared even. The porter swung the trolley bed into a small room. Everything was white: the ceiling, the walls and the floor. It was dazzling. A doctor appeared and told Daniel to expect a little prick in his arm. He was to count backwards from 3 – he wouldn't make it to 1, said the doctor with a wink. Daniel was so scared he thought he might wee. He felt the prick and started to count.

Later, Daniel came round and was promptly sick. Deftly, a nurse had guided him to a nearby bowl. It was silver and shiny. 'All over,' she said with a smile. 'We'll have you back to the ward soon; just now, you're in the recovery room. You'll feel sleepy but try not to give in; it's best to stay awake. You might feel sick again.' As if on cue, Daniel reached for the bowl again. He felt a little better after. He was suddenly conscious of the pain in his throat. It felt as dry as sandpaper. Daniel nodded off to sleep and when he awoke he was back in the children's ward. Mum was sitting next to his bed. 'You've been asleep for ages,' she said, squeezing his hand. 'How are you feeling?'

He felt groggy.

He bit his lip – he was determined not to cry; it would only upset Mum. Dad arrived. 'It will be Friday before you know it,' he said with a weak grin. The time came to say goodbye to Mum and Dad. Granny would be visiting too the next day, they said. Daniel felt miserable. He didn't like being in hospital on his own. It felt lonely.

On Tuesday morning, Daniel woke early. Everyone seemed to get started early in a hospital. He looked at his watch; it was only ten past six.

His throat was still sore.

The nurse (who was called Angie) said he was to keep drinking – it would help. She gave him a wash in his bed.

Later, she brought him a breakfast of bran flakes. 'It will be good for your throat,' she said. 'It helps to toughen it up.' Daniel wasn't so sure. As he tried to swallow the bran flakes, it hurt. He listened to the hospital radio and read his book. The day dragged on: visiting time was at 2 o'clock. Mum arrived with Granny and they both tried hard to take his mind off how he was feeling. Mum went looking for the nurse to ask if there was anything he could have for the pain. He was allowed a thick green medicine. It didn't taste like the medicine his mother gave him, but the nurse said it would do the same job.

Daniel was brought another bowl of bran flakes.

'When I had my tonsils out,' said Granny, 'they gave us ice cream to eat all day. How things have changed.'

That night when Granny and Mum had gone, Daniel realised that what was making him miserable was not his sore throat (although it didn't help matters). No, he realised that he was missing home. It was the first time he had spent time away from his family. He didn't like it. Wednesday and Thursday dragged by. He was determined not to show Mum and Dad how he was feeling. Then on Thursday evening, with one only one night to go before he went home, he could keep his brave face no longer: he began to cry. Once he had started, he couldn't stop. Then Mum, seeing how upset he was, got tearful, which made him feel even worse.

'Come on,' said Dad. 'You're nearly there – it's Friday tomorrow.'

Daniel took a deep breath. 'I want to come home,' he mumbled.

'You will,' said Dad. 'And there will be a surprise waiting for you. For being such a good boy.'

'A surprise,' mumbled Daniel. He had stopped crying. What could it be?

———

The following week back at school, Daniel was asked by Miss Chambers to share with the class how he had found being in hospital. He hesitated. He didn't want to tell them about being homesick; he didn't want anyone to laugh. Instead, he told them about Angie, the nice nurse, and the endless bowls of bran flakes that he had been given to eat.

'What was the best bit?' asked Katy Danvers.

'The best bit?' said Daniel. 'You must be joking, there wasn't a best bit. I was in hospital!'

Afterwards, he thought he could have told them about the tickets to see Arsenal that his Dad had bought as a surprise treat. But he had rather enjoyed the attention the class had given him as a kind of wounded soldier. They had thought he was brave; he could tell. That was the best bit – better even than the Arsenal game.

# Teacher's Notes
# Anna's Story

## Background
This is based on a true story that a colleague and good friend told me. It is a Christmas story and you can never have too many of those. I am always keen to ensure that the children know that for some people Christmas is a sad time: a time when they are acutely reminded of what they don't have – whether it be friendship, money or health. The great thing, of course, is that although you may be suffering one year, it won't be too long before another Christmas comes along, bringing for most people a fresh opportunity to enjoy the season – sadness passes, unhappy times get forgotten. You never know what next year will bring … .

## General theme
None of us are protected from unhappy times but it is possible to overcome great sadness. Sometimes the sadness is so huge, that people doubt they will be able to carry on. But invariably they do. Time of course is a great healer.

## What do Christians believe?
Christians believe that God sent his Son, Jesus, to Earth to save them. They celebrate his birth at Christmas with joy. It is their duty to share God's love and compassion with everyone they meet and to share their earthly possessions with those in need: 'Command them to do good, to be rich in good works, to be generous and ready to share with others.' (1 Timothy 6:18)

## Prayer
*Generous and loving God, we thank you for all blessings. Be with those who are lonely, hungry or distressed. May they feel your love surrounding them.*

## The story
The old lady in the story could have been bitter and wallow in her misfortune. Instead, she enjoys the happiness of others – at no time more than Christmas. She is grateful for small mercies – such as Christmas lunch with a neighbour.

## PSMC links
- Life is full of disappointments. How do the children feel they would have felt if they were in the old lady's shoes? Would they have managed to be so positive? What effect does hearing the old lady's story have on Anna?

# Anna's Story

The build up to that Christmas had been like any other. It was busy and exciting. Working in a school as a classroom assistant, Anna saw just how much Christmas meant to the children. December was filled with all the usual traditions: the nativity performance; Christmas lunch; and the parties. On the last Friday, the children said their goodbyes and were swallowed up by the winter evening as they left for home, happy and tired.

The next day, Anna woke early. There was plenty to be done. Now school was finished, it was a first opportunity to focus upon her own family and their preparations for the big day. It was Christmas Eve. She would go to the market that morning and buy the last few presents to be put around the tree. Mollie, her daughter, was only two but already had a clear idea of who Santa was. Seven year old Jake was so excited he felt he might burSt

They made their way around the bustling market, Mollie in the buggy, Jake by her side. It was hard going. The crowds were bigger than she could remember them. They bought the last minute vegetables and fruit and made their way to the toy stall. It was surrounded by young children who pressed ever closer forward, urging their parents to make one further purchase.

Then out of the corner of her eye, Anna spied her. Wrapped in a big coat she sat watching the crowds from a nearby bench as they went about their business. She must have been fifty or so. Anna saw sadness in her eyes, which were a startling blue. Was she one of the homeless folk who could be seen throughout the year, begging for a few pennies? They always stood out at this time of the year. Suddenly a young family pushed past her and when she looked to the bench, the woman was gone. But she had made an impression on Anna. Maybe it had been her eyes, so startling in colour but so sad.

Christmas came and went and the New Year quickly gained pace. The spring dawned with the appearance of daffodils and the children at school presented a wonderful retelling of the Easter story. May brought the Year 6 residential trip and Anna was asked to accompany the children. She didn't think she would be able but then John, her husband, took the week off from work to look after Mollie and Jake and Anna enjoyed a week of abseiling, canoe fun and sing-songs by the camp fire. The summer holidays flashed by in a blur and before anyone knew it, the autumn term had arrived. The leaves on the trees turned brown and began to fall and then soon it was December again and Christmas preparations were afoot.

It had been a thought at the back of Anna's mind all year. Would she see the old lady again this year? But with the hustle and bustle of school, there wasn't the time to dwell upon it. Christmas Eve again saw the family in the market, her husband John was with them this time.

'Fancy a coffee?' he asked mid-afternoon, just when they were beginning to flag.

'Heavenly,' replied Anna and then turning round she saw her. She was seated at the same bench as last year. Wrapped in the same coat, with the same startling eyes.

'Get me two,' she said.

'Two?' replied her husband, incredulous. 'Are you thirsty or what?'

'One of them is not for me,' she replied with a smile. Anna had had an idea.

When her husband returned she asked him to look after the children for a few minutes and taking her courage in her hands, she approached the old woman. Her husband looked on, bemused. What was his wife doing? Did she know this woman? Was it a friend from school? She looked like a homeless person, down on their luck. But there was something different about her. He wasn't sure what it was. He turned the children towards the next market stall and they continued with their Christmas shopping.

'I thought you might like a coffee,' Anna said, giving the lady a bright smile.

'That's a kind thought, dear,' she replied. She looked cold.

Anna sat down next to her and without a second thought, cuddled up next to the woman to give her warmth.

'It's as busy as ever,' remarked Anna. Now she had got this far, she wasn't quite sure what to say next. She wanted to find out a little more about the woman. Was she needing help? She looked so alone.

What the woman said next was unexpected.

'I love this time of year,' she said. 'The smiles on the children's faces, the love that families show for one another, couples hand in hand.'

Then without thinking, Anna blurted out: 'But you look so alone, sitting here. I saw you last year and I struggled to forget the pain on your face.'

'Ah,' said the woman, 'you're right. There is some pain. For I was once one of the crowd. Happily going about my business with my family, looking forward to Christmas with all its promise.'

'Whatever happened,' asked Anna. 'Where is your family now?'

'Lost them,' said the old lady. 'Wasn't anyone's fault. A burst tyre on the motorway. The car spun out of control and crashed. I was pulled from the wreckage but my husband and children died. I lost all that I held dear that day.'

Anna didn't know what to say.

They sat there sipping their coffee in silence. It had begun to snow.

'But I'm not bitter,' said the old lady. 'Like I said, it wasn't anyone's fault. It was just a twist of life. I have my memories and when I see the smiles of folk at this time of year, it is a comfort – I remember back to my happier days.'

'How will you spend Christmas?' asked Anna.

'Oh, I'm lucky,' replied the woman with a smile. 'I have a good neighbour and she invites me to spend Christmas lunch with her. I could be alone. I'm not. I know many aren't so fortunate.'

Anna stood up and leaning forward kissed the woman on the forehead.

'Thank you for the coffee, darling,' she said. Anna smiled and turned away. She blinked back a tear.

When she caught up with John and the children she gave them all a big squeeze.

'What was that for?' enquired her husband. 'Nothing,' she replied, 'just counting my blessings.'

The following Christmas Anna looked for the woman, but didn't see her. Nor the next. In fact, she wasn't to see her again, though each year she looked. But she didn't forget her – not her eyes of deepest blue, nor her story – a story that whilst sad filled Anna with hope. Whatever happened to us in life, we would all have our memories to keep us company. It was a comforting thought.

# Teacher's Notes
# Archie's Story

## Background
My own son struggled to ride a bike. It made him feel left out when friends came calling on their bikes. We took him to classes and he tried his hardest, but something wasn't clicking into place. He lost confidence and sold his bike. Later, an occupational therapist recommended that he come to learn at a special course that was being run for children who struggled with balance. He learned within the space of two days. And once he got it that was it. As they say, 'You never forget how to ... .'

## General theme
What are we to do when we try hard to learn to do something and fail? Do we have to accept that there are some things that we will not be able to do?

Most of us want to feel included. It hurts when we feel left behind or out of something. What comes easily to one person may be a struggle for another. This is a hard lesson to learn in life.

## What do Christians believe?
Jesus knew what it was like to be the outcast, the one who didn't fit in. He came to a world that mocked and rejected him. Christians believe that God is the source of all strength and that all troubles should be shared with him, through prayer.

## Prayer
*Dear Lord, You know that we sometimes struggle, with learning new things, with keeping promises, with being a good friend. Help us to remember to turn to you when we find things difficult. May we always keep our eyes open to see those around us who are struggling with something we could help them with.*

## The story
Archie desperately wants to feel included at the start of the story. Later, in learning to ride a bike, he grows in confidence. At the end of the story, when faced with the prospect of a new challenge, he is upbeat. Confidence is a wonderful thing; with it, most things are possible.

## PSMC links
- Have the children heard the phrase, 'If at first you don't succeed, try, try again!' What have the children found difficult to do? Can they think of a time when they have persevered with something? Is it always possible to master something – or will there be times when it is better to admit defeat and move on. Can we expect to be good at everything? Does it matter if we are not?

# Archie's Story

It had started at Oliver's party. Archie had been looking forward to it for weeks. Then when he arrived, he was disappointed to see that the other boys – Jack, Aaron and Daniel – had all brought their bikes. Archie didn't ride – couldn't ride. He had tried to learn the summer before, but he just couldn't get the hang of it. Mum hadn't said the other boys would be bringing their bikes. Perhaps she hadn't known. He spent the afternoon, watching them spin round, doing wheelies. He had felt left out until eventually Oliver's mum had told them to do something else so Archie could join in. They chose a game of football: Archie's second least favourite thing to do. But at least he could kick a ball so things had looked up for a while. On the way home in the car, he quizzed Mum. Had she known it was going to be a bike party? Yes, she admitted, she had. But she hadn't wanted to say anything because she hadn't wanted him not to go – he had been looking forward to it.

Some weeks later, Dad suggested they have another go. There was no point, argued Archie, moodily. 'Well if you feel like that about it,' snapped Mum, 'why not sell your bike?' She hadn't meant it, of course. She said it because she was frustrated by Archie seeming to give up and this when they had spent good money on the bike.

But the idea took hold. Archie could be quite stubborn. He could buy some Skylanders with the money, he said. The bike was placed on eBay where it sold – a man came and collected it one Saturday morning. Nothing more was said about it.

A few weeks later, Mrs Jacobs, Archie's teacher asked to see Mum.

'We are a little concerned about Archie,' she said, peering at Mum over a pile of books that were waiting to be marked.

Mum asked in what way, concerned?

'Archie seems to have problems with balancing and running,' the teacher said. 'The children play running games and Archie is invariably last. He's been getting quite upset about it. He is reluctant to join in when we do PE; he lacks confidence when on the apparatus.'

Archie's mum was taken aback. Archie hadn't mentioned anything. It troubled her to think that he had been getting upset and to make matters worse, he hadn't shared how he was feeling with her.

'And,' said Mrs Jacobs, who suddenly hesitated, 'he has fallen off his chair on more than one occasion.'

'Fallen off his chair?' said Archie's mum. 'Don't all children do that?' She felt a little cross. She wasn't sure Mrs Jacobs was being fair.

'Not as often as Archie,' said Mrs Jacobs, who suddenly looked uncomfortable. 'We'd like to have someone look at Archie, an occupational therapist. She will be able to tell us what is going on.'

Archie and his mum walked home in silence. Over tea, Dad brought it up with Archie in conversation. Had he been getting upset in the playground? Archie began to cry; he bit his bottom lip, which was trembling. Dad put an arm round his son's shoulder. He felt guilty. Why hadn't he known Archie had been sad at school? He wanted to protect his son from unhappiness; he felt he had failed him.

That evening, the three of them had a good chat about things. Archie felt better afterwards and as Mum tucked him up in bed, he smiled. 'That's good to see,' said Mum. 'You know Archie, no problem is too big for us to handle together.' She kissed him on the forehead and

# Keep trying — Archie's Story

turned off the light.

A few weeks later, a letter arrived in the post. It was an appointment for Archie to see an occupational therapist. 'What will happen?' he asked Mum.

'I'm not sure, but it will be nothing to worry about,' she replied.

But Archie did worry. He couldn't help it. It was the way he was wired.

The day of the appointment arrived. Archie had been asked to come in a tracksuit. He wondered why. What sorts of tests would he have to do? He didn't have long to wait before he found out. It was a morning when he had to run, jump, balance – in all sorts of ways, often as fast as he could. He had to hop on one leg, then the other; he had to walk along a straight line, then a crooked one. Afterwards, he was asked to sit down and had to place pegs in holes and move counters from one side of a board to the other. He hardly had time to draw breath. Towards the end of the morning, he had to do some handwriting.

He thought he was done.

'Okay,' said the occupational therapist, 'well done Archie. I'd like to end the morning with some simple questions to find out a little more about you.'

Archie sighed. Questions, when was this going to be over? And what was the point of it all?

'Come on,' said Mum. 'Nearly there.'

'Archie, what do you find most difficult?' asked the therapist.

Archie thought. 'I'm not as good as others at running,' he said. 'I'm always first to be caught.'

'Anything else?' she asked.

'No, I don't think so,' said Archie. 'Maybe maths.'

'Have you ever found anything particularly difficult?'

Archie said without pausing for breath, 'Riding a bike. I can't.'

The therapist put down her pen. 'Okay Archie, that's enough for one day. Well done. You did really well. You tried with everything I asked. Not everyone does that. Thank you.'

Archie felt pleased. It was nice to hear that he had done well at something. He didn't hear that very often.

A few weeks later Mum and Dad were called into school to see Mrs Jacobs. She said that they had received the report from the occupational therapist, who said that Archie displayed the traits of someone who had dyspraxia. It was a long word, difficult to say. What did it mean? they wondered.

'It means he will have difficulty with co-ordination. Moving and balancing.'

It was as if a light bulb had been turned on. When Archie had struggled to learn to ride a bike, it wasn't something that he could help. He was bound to find it trickier than other children.

'Is there anything we can do to help him?' asked Mum.

'Oh yes,' said Mrs Jacobs. 'There are exercises he can do and it's possible to learn to ride a bike at special lessons run by a small team who work with children with dyspraxia.'

The lessons were scheduled for half-term. Archie would have five mornings to learn. He was determined to crack it. He would be lent a bike to ride for the lessons. The first thing the instructor did was take the peddles off. 'Let's get you used to the feel of a bike before we try and do anything else with it,' he said. This was different. Archie got used to sitting on the bike, keeping himself upright on the seat. Only then did they put the peddles back on. On Wednesday morning, Mum took a phone call. Would she like to come and pick Archie up?

'Oh dear,' she said. 'Has he given up again?'

'Given up?' said the instructor. 'No, he's riding. He's done it – there's no more I can teach him.'

When Mum arrived at the centre, Archie was riding proudly around the gym. He had the biggest smile on his face that you could imagine. Mum's heart leapt.

Some months later, Archie arrived for Jack's party. He had brought his bike with him. His mum was dismayed when she saw his friends clamber out of their parents' cars – they hadn't brought their bikes. Instead, each boy had a gleaming scooter. Mum exchanged a look with Archie. How was he going to react? But Archie was smiling. 'Great,' he said, 'that's what I will learn to ride next. It may take me a little longer than most kids, but I'll get there.'

Mum smiled. Archie had his confidence now and nothing was going to change that.

# Teacher's Notes
# Ashan's Story

## Background
When I was at primary school, I had lots of girlfriends. We never kissed, at least I don't remember doing so. But classmates were 'going out' with classmates; I was 10 and that was the 1970s. Funny, but I can still remember their names, 40 years later: Jenny, Suzanne, Tracey and Linda. We never actually 'went' anywhere in those days. You were just known to be 'an item' and when there was a party, you danced together. Working with children nowadays, I occasionally am told who fancies whom and just occasionally we are made aware of a pairing. Nothing changes! Young love … .

## General theme
Peer pressure. We have all experienced it; it is only much later that we learn the 'term'. As we mature into young adults, we face many challenges. We think we must behave in a certain way – dress, act or speak. It is only much, much later in life that we have the confidence to be who we want to be: we become less concerned about what others think.

## What do Christians believe?
Christians believe that God loves them for whom and what they are. He knows their failings and their faults and still loves them. 'Accept one another, then, for the glory of God, as Christ has accepted you' (Romans 15:7). Christians are commanded to 'love one another.'

## Prayer
*Dear Lord, thank you for the talents and gifts you have given us. Help us to work hard and use our talents wisely. Give us the courage to be ourselves and give us strength when we feel pressurised to fit in with how others want us to be or want us to look. Thank you for the things that make us the same, and the things that make us different.*

## The story
Ashan has to reconcile what others expect of him with what he wants to do himself. He finds this challenging. At the end of the story, he find his true self and is rewarded for his courage. And, courage is not too big a word. Being young is hard and as one moves into teenage years (which seem to start in Year 5 these days!), one learns a great deal about oneself.

## PSMC links
- What sort of person do the children think Ashan is? How would they describe his character?
- What does this story tell us about courage? Answer: it comes in all shapes and sizes!

# Ashan's Story

Each Friday, Mrs Wright would share the weekly newsletter to parents with her Year 6 class. This particular Friday (the last in May) would, she knew, cause quite a stir. Mr Davis, the Headteacher, had decided there would be an end of year prom. Joanne Dougall, scanning the back page, was the first to spot it. 'We're going to have a prom,' she shrieked. The class erupted into a cheer. Mrs Wright smiled, pleased to see their excitement. Ashan shouted in delight alongside everyone else; then turned to Adam, and mouthed 'What's a prom?'

'It's a party,' said Adam. 'The kind teenagers have. Normal parties are boring.'

Adam frowned. They weren't teenagers, so why were they having that kind of party? But he didn't say anything; it seemed a popular idea that had caught his classmates' imagination.

When he got home that evening, Mum was busy giving their dog a bath.

'We're going to have a prom,' he said.

'A prom?' Mum replied. 'That's an American idea; you usually have those when you're older. Whose silly idea was that?'

'Mr Davis' I think,' he said, 'but Mrs Wright seemed to be in on it.'

'It will just end up being a party,' said Mum, then seeing Ashan's face, added, 'for goodness sake, don't worry about it. You don't have to go if you don't want to.' But Ashan knew he would have to go. He wouldn't want to feel left out.

On Monday, the boys at break time played football as normal but shouted about the forthcoming prom as they ran around. There seemed to be a buzz about it.

On the way home, Adam turned to Ashan and asked who he was going to ask to go with him. Ashan was puzzled. 'I guess I'll go with you,' said Ashan. The two boys went everywhere together. Adam laughed. 'No,' he said, 'it's a prom. You have to ask a girl to go with you!'

Ashan swallowed hard. 'A girl!'

'You're joking. We're eleven, we don't ask girls to parties.'

'We do now,' said Adam. 'It's a prom.'

Ashan walked on without speaking. His brain had gone into overtime and he had butterflies in his stomach.

That night after tea, Ashan sat on his bed, hugging his knees. He realised why he had been unnerved at the first mention of a prom. He was used to parties where they played games like pass the parcel and musical statues. He had sensed there would be dancing and that would be bad enough. But to ask a girl to the party, he had never imagined for one second that he would have to do that. He cringed at the thought. Sitting there on the bed, he blushed.

There was a knock at the door. Mum popped her head around.

'What's the matter with you, skulking around up here?' she asked.

'Nothing,' he replied. But Mum wasn't so easily fooled.

'What worrying you,' she said, plonking herself down next to him. 'I know when there's something wrong.'

'It's the prom,' he said. 'Adam says you have to ask a girl.'

'Does he now?' said Mum. 'My little boy is growing up,' said Mum, ruffling his hair. She looked at his red face and could see he didn't appreciate what she had said.

'I'm sure you don't have to if you don't want to,' she said.

'But you do,' said Ashan. 'I don't want to be the odd one out.'

Mum could see he didn't want to talk further about it and she let herself out quietly.

**Peer pressure** — **Ashan's Story**

Life, sighed Ashan. There you were going along nicely and then wham! Something out of the blue would come along and smack you right in the face.

He thought about the girls in his class. Who was nice enough to ask to the prom? And more importantly, of those, who would be likely to say yes if he asked them. There was Annie: she was pretty and funny but he wasn't sure she liked him that much. Then there was Meryl Corker: she was even prettier than Annie but there would be a number of boys wanting to ask her. She would be able to take her pick and Ashan wasn't sure she would pick him.

The next morning on the way to school, he mumbled something to Mum.

'Say again,' said Mum, 'I couldn't hear you.'

'Do you think I'm good looking?' he said a little louder.

'You're the most handsome boy in the whole world,' she said with a squeeze of his shoulders.

'Don't be silly Mum,' he said. But she could tell he was pleased. She had said the right thing. She breathed a sigh of relief. He had been quite touchy of late.

It was raining and so they had indoor break. 'What will you be wearing to the prom,' asked Adam. Ashan looked at his friend. They had been best friends since the infants, but Adam was beginning to get on his nerves. His friend sat grinning at him and said, 'You'll have to wear a suit. Everyone will be in a suit.'

Ashan had only one suit. He had worn it to his cousin's wedding in April. He had felt like a penguin but Mum had insisted. He didn't fancy the idea of wearing one to a school party – he had always preferred jeans and a smart shirt for parties.

'Have you asked a girl yet?' continued Adam.

'No,' admitted Ashan. 'Have you?'

'Yes, Annie,' his friend said. Ashan didn't need to ask whether Annie had said yes; he could tell from Adam's happy face what the answer had been.

That night at home Ashan was at his most miserable. Mum sent Dad to talk to him – man to man.

'Look,' said Dad, 'what is it exactly that is bothering you about the party?'

Ashan looked at his Dad. He could tell him anything.

'It's not a party, it's a prom. I don't want to go to a prom because I don't like dancing,' he snapped.

'Well don't go then,' said Dad.

'But I don't want to be left out,' replied Ashan.

'And, I don't want to ask a girl to go with me,' he added. Ashan now found himself on a roll.

'Well don't then,' said Dad.

'But I don't want to be the odd one out,' he almost shouted. 'And then there's the suit, I hate wearing a suit. But everyone else will be in one and I don't want to look different.'

Dad didn't say anything. The two of them just sat there. Ashan now looked crumpled. It

*Modern Christian Assembly Stories*
186

© Gary Nott and Brilliant Publications Limited
*This page may be photocopied for use by the purchasing institution only.*

had taken a lot of energy to tell Dad how he was feeling and now he was spent.

'Look,' said Dad. 'I only have one piece of advice to give you. As you get older, you realise that you don't have to do the things you don't want to do – just because everyone else is doing them. Think about it ... .'

The evening of the prom arrived. Mum and Dad hadn't mentioned the subject since Dad's chat with Ashan. Their son appeared at the living room door. He was wearing jeans and his party shirt. 'I decided to take Dad's advice,' he said, 'partly, that is. I don't want to feel left out so I'm going to the prom. I won't dance, I am not wearing a suit and I haven't asked a girl.' His parents smiled. They were proud of their son but didn't say it. They didn't need to, he could tell how they felt.

When he arrived at the school hall, he felt a little awkward. He took a deep breath and went in. He was looking for someone he knew. He felt embarrassed to be on his own. The class were up dancing. Suddenly Meryl was standing in front of him.

'Hello,' Ashan, she said. 'You look different, nice different.'

Ashan blushed and shifted from one foot to the other.

'Are you on your own?'

'Yes,' replied Ashan.

'Me too,' said Meryl.

'How come?' asked Ashan.

'No one asked me,' Meryl replied.

Ashan realised that none of the boys had dared ask Meryl because they thought they would be turned down.

'Would you like to dance?' she asked.

What was it Dad had said about not having to do the things you didn't want to do? That was when he realised. He did want to dance after all.

And so he did.

Ashan was growing up and finding out new things about himself along the way. It wasn't always fun, but it certainly wasn't boring.

# Teacher's Notes
# Damien's Story

## Background
My parents had an elderly neighbour who didn't like school children sitting on his garden wall. He made his feelings clear. One summer's evening, my parents sitting in their neighbouring bungalow suddenly felt a wall of heat. On looking out of their window, they realised that the boys had set fire to the neighbour's trees that bordered his wall. Sometimes, it is hard to stop ourselves being annoyed by the actions of others. Having someone sit on your wall was irritating but the children hadn't been doing any harm. Things got out of hand because of the way the neighbour reacted to them.

## General theme
We all like our own personal space. When people encroach on that space, we can all feel uncomfortable – but for some people it can become all consuming. Whether it be someone walking on their grass or sitting on their wall or playing their music loudly – they can't bear what they see as rudeness.

## What do Christians believe?
Christians believe that they are called to show love to all, not just those people they like and get on with. It is much more difficult to love those who appear 'unlovable' or seek to upset us, yet that is what Jesus did during his time on Earth and it is an example that Christians will try to follow. 'Love your enemies and do good to them; lend and expect nothing back.' (Luke 6:35)

## Prayer
*Dear God, thank you for the love you showed in sending your Son to earth to show us how you want us to live. Sometimes it isn't easy to love others, especially those who aren't kind to us. May we look for opportunities today to show your love to others, in what we do and what we say.*

## The story
At which point in the story does Damien's attitude to Mr Roberts change? Why is that?
What is it about being told what not to do that Damien doesn't like?

## PSMC links
- Nobody particularly likes being told what to do. But our actions sometimes offend or irritate others and we all need to be mindful of how we are making others feel. Common courtesy makes the world go around.
- Can the children remember a time when they have made someone else feel uncomfortable by their actions? Would they have known?

*Modern Christian Assembly Stories*

# Damien's Story

Damien was enjoying being in Year 6. The Year 6 children were at the top of the school, the oldest and the biggest: it felt good. The younger kids looked up to them. The Year 6 pupils were cool! In the summer term, Mum had said that he could walk to and from school on his own. It would be good preparation for secondary school, she said. He walked with Toby, Patrick and Luke. On the way home they would stop off at Mr Patel's newsagents where they would buy drinks and crisps. Along the way home there was a row of houses sitting at the bottom of a steep hill, which was quite a climb. The houses had pretty gardens and each had a low wall that ran parallel to the pavement. One of the gardens had four small laurel trees and it was on a Friday evening in late June that the boys stopped to sit on the garden wall to drink their drinks and eat their crisps. The trees gave them welcome shade. It had been a busy day in school. They were rehearsing for their end of term production. They were doing Barnum, the musical story of a great circus owner. Damien had the part of an acrobat.

'Look at me,' he urged and standing on the wall, began to walk along it as if he were on a tightrope. Suddenly the upstairs window of the house opened and a man called down gruffly to them.

'Oi, you horrible lot, off my wall.' The boys looked up and spied the man. He was old.

'Come on,' said Luke. 'Let's move on.'

Reluctantly, Damien jumped down. He looked behind him as they moved off, staring at the man, who was now closing the window.

Damian hadn't liked being told what to do. They hadn't been doing anyone any harm. 'What was that old geezer complaining about?'

The weekend came and went. School on Monday was a chore. It was still hot and the day wore on. The boys stopped off to buy their cold drinks on the way home.

'You've been annoying old Mr Roberts,' said Mr Patel, with a wink.

'Mr Who?' asked Toby with a puzzled look.

'Mr Roberts, he lives at the foot of the hill. He was in here buying his paper this morning and said some yobs had been mucking about on his wall.' Mr Patel was chuckling. 'I recognised you four from the description he gave. He's a cantankerous old so and so. He wasn't amused.'

But Mr Roberts wasn't the only one who wasn't amused. Damien's face looked like thunder.

As they emerged into the sunshine, Damien turned to the others.

'Who's he calling yobs? What an old misery.'

As they past Mr Roberts' house, Damien sat down on the garden wall. 'Come on,' he said and then added with a mischievous grin, 'let's take the time to enjoy the shade of these lovely trees.'

Reluctantly the other boys sat down; they weren't looking for more trouble. But they could tell Damien was in no mood to budge.

Damien swigged from his can of drink.

The boys sat in silence and waited. Sure enough, within a few minutes, they heard the top window of the house open and a voice cried down to them.

'I told you lot last week, off my wall!'

'Don't anyone move,' hissed Damien. 'What can he do. He's just an old geezer. We're not doing anyone any harm. He's bang out of order!'

Silence. Then they heard the window slam shut.

'Come on,' said Damien. 'We've made our point.'

© Gary Nott and Brilliant Publications Limited

*This page may be photocopied for use by the purchasing institution only.*

Modern Christian Assembly Stories

## Respecting others — Damien's Story

The boys walked away. 'Walk slowly,' said Damien. 'He'll be watching us.'

Tuesday came and went. Damien's friends had put the incident out of their minds. But at the end of the day, they sensed Damien had not. He mumbled something about 'that old geezer' as they entered the shop.

'Here they come again,' said Mr Patel. 'The local wild boys. You've been on his wall again, haven't you. He was in here this morning and groaning. He says if you do it again, he's going to phone the school and make a complaint.'

As they emerged into the afternoon sun, Luke was the first to speak.

'We've had our fun,' he said. 'Let's give it up now.'

'You must be joking,' replied Damien. 'He's out of order. This is a wall we are talking about. What harm are we doing?'

'But it's his wall,' said Toby.

'If you want to chicken out, that's fine by me,' said Damien. 'But I'm going to sit on it. I fancy a rest before we climb that hill and he's not going to stop me.'

Patrick sighed. Damien was being obstinate. But he didn't want to let his friend down and he certainly didn't want to be labelled a chicken. As they approached the wall, Damien strode forward and parked himself. The other boys followed suit and waited. Nothing. Damien casually looked over his shoulder up at the window. The curtain twitched.

'He's there,' said Damien. 'We must be winding him up good and proper.' He chuckled. His friends said nothing.

'Come on,' said Toby. 'Let's move on, point made.'

Damien slowly drained his drink and stood.

He stretched and after burping loudly, he sauntered off in the direction of the other boys – hands in his pockets, whistling.

The next day, Luke, Toby and Patrick caught up with each other in the playground at break time. Damien wasn't there; he had been in trouble in maths with Mr Sydney and had been kept in.

'Have you noticed that Damien is getting weird,' said Toby. 'He seems determined to get himself into bother.'

'My mum said he's getting too big for his boots – thinks he's fourteen.'

None of the boys wanted to say anything to Damien about his recent behaviour. Truth be told, they were a little intimidated by their friend – he had gotten so cocky of late.

As they walked home, the three boys knew what was coming. Damien would want to sit on Mr Robert's wall. They would have to go along with it; none of them wanted Damien to tell others that they were chicken.

They walked along the path and following Damien's lead sat down one by one on the wall. Damien started to swig his drink. Suddenly from behind one of the trees, old Mr Roberts jumped out. Damien leapt up in fright, spilling his drink down his front. He shrieked (Toby thought later that he had sounded rather like a girl!).

'What are you doing you mad old fool?' he shouted.

Mr Roberts was brandishing a walking stick.

'I've told you before, stay off my wall – you young hooligans!'

Without thinking, and more in panic than anything else, Damien threw what was left off his drink in the old man's face. Mr Roberts lunged forward and hit Damien across the arm with his stick.

The old man was frail and the smack wasn't hard but Damien began to wail.

'You're for it old man, you can't hit children with sticks. Come on,' Damien shouted to his friends, picking up his bag. The four boys walked off, leaving a worried looking Mr Roberts behind. Only Toby looked back. Damien was intent on getting home to tell his parents what had happened.

Damien's mother listened carefully to him.

# Damien's Story — Respecting others

She waited for Dad to get home and then they made a call to Damien's Headteacher. They wanted advice as to how to proceed. Dad was on the phone for ages. He came up to Damien's bedroom later and sat down on the bed next to Damien. They were to go to school the next day when things would be sorted out. He asked Damien if he had told them all they needed to know. Damien repeated to his father how they had been sitting on the wall when the old man had leapt out and hit him. Damien's dad looked angry. Damien's Headteacher had told Damien's parents to contact the police, which they did. The police were too busy to come out that night but said two officers would meet with Damien and his parents at the school the next day. They took details of the incident over the phone from Damien's dad.

The next day, Damien and his parents walked into the Headteacher's office. Standing at the desk were two police officers. Sitting in the corner, was Mr Roberts. Damien hadn't been expecting to see him. The boy had imagined police officers would visit the old gentleman at his home. He hadn't realised he would have to face him. 'Sit down, Damien,' said his Headteacher.

Damien stared at the old man. He looked tense and worried.

Damien's Headteacher frowned.

'We've been speaking to Mr Roberts about what happened yesterday,' she said. 'He tells us that you have been annoying him by sitting on his wall. Is that true?'

Damien looked at the floor.

He looked up again at Mr Roberts. Now he looked at him again, he realised that he looked a lot like his granddad.

'Listen,' said Damien's Headteacher. 'Mr Roberts shouldn't have hit you. That is serious. But we all make mistakes. You're a big boy now. What do you think should happen next?'

Damien looked down at the floor again. He felt uncomfortable. He looked up at Mr Roberts and realised that the old man looked frightened. Damien thought back over the past few days. He had been a pain. He knew it. He hadn't liked it when he had been told he shouldn't do something he wanted to do. The thought occurred to him that Mr Roberts might be somebody's granddad. How would his grandchildren feel if they could see him sitting here, looked scared?

Damien's dad suddenly spoke. 'I think Damien is probably thinking that we should forget about it, aren't you son?'

'Yes,' mumbled Damien.

Having said goodbye to his parents, Damien went back to class.

That evening as the boys walked home, they passed Mr Robert's house. Damien looked up at the window and saw the curtain move. Instinctively, he waved up at the window. Mr Roberts suddenly appeared and waved back. Damien grinned. It was good to be friends with the old man. The four boys went charging up the hill, laughing and shouting. Mr Roberts went down to his kitchen whistling and made himself a nice cup of tea. Kids, he thought and smiled.

# Teacher's Notes
# Tommy and Jacob's Story

## Background
Do not decide against telling this story because you think it far fetched. Would a pupil ever bend over and pull his pants down to expose his bottom to his teacher? Surely not. Well, it happened to me. I had my wife (a teacher in my school) in the car with me when the ex-pupil decided to make his grand gesture. I reported it to the community police and the ex-pupil and his parent duly expressed regret, I was told. However, I wonder if they burst out laughing once the officer had departed. It was a naughty thing to do but even I break into a smile when I now recall it. Is that wrong of me? The children will be shocked when you tell the story; they will only laugh at the end if you indicate that it is acceptable to laugh! Go on … .

## General theme
Parents often fall out when their children clash. Sometimes, before the parents are back on speaking terms – and sometimes they never are – the children have long forgotten their differences and are the best of friends once more. Children, it would seem, are far quicker to forgive and forget.

## What do Christians believe?
Christians believe that they are called to love everyone, even those who dislike or despise them. God shows His forgiveness to those who ask and Christians are taught not to hold grudges.

## Prayer
*Dear Lord, Thank you for the good times we have with our friends. You know that friendships are not always easy and that sometimes we disagree and fall out. Help us to be the first to say sorry, even when we feel it shouldn't be up to us. May we never be too proud to admit we were wrong and ask for forgiveness.*

## The story
The story has several layers. In a sense, it is about the recurring theme of bullying in schools. Added to this, is the dimension of social media and the ways in which people use it to communicate – a growing problem in schools.

## PSMC links
- Who was at fault in this story? Tommy, Jacob, Tommy's mum or Jacob's? Or did they all do things that could be said to have contributed to the difficulties. Can the children identify what each character could have done differently?

# Tommy and Jacob's Story

Tommy Carter and Jacob Walker had been in the same class since Infants. Tommy was tall, Jacob was short. Jacob was bright; however Tommy found lessons hard. The two boys rubbed along. They weren't close friends but everyone played with everyone and so they spent time in each other's company each day. Truth be told, each was a little jealous of the other: Tommy wished he was as good as Jacob in lessons; whereas, Jacob would have liked to be tall, like Tommy.

The boys were now in Year 6. At the weekend, it was to be David's party. The children were looking forward to it. It was a ten pin bowling party. Jacob was good: his aim was accurate and he quickly built an unbeatable lead.

'Not bad, shorty,' remarked Tommy, when Jacob fist pumped the air when it was announced he was the winner. That was the start of it. Jacob didn't like being small.

At school the following week, they had tests. Jacob liked doing well at school. It made him feel better about his size, which – after all – he couldn't help. Mrs Talbot read the results out on Friday afternoon. Jacob had come first. Tommy scowled. Jacob gave a wink in his direction. Who was feeling small now, he thought.

Things went downhill from there.

In the playground on Monday morning, Tommy was still feeling sore at Jacob. He persuaded the other boys not to play with him. When Jacob came in their direction, the boys ran off. It was mean and Tommy knew it, but he couldn't help himself, Jacob was so smug.

They played without Jacob all week. Tommy was a big lad and the other boys didn't want to upset him. On Saturday morning, Tommy received a text message from Emmanuel. Check out Jacob's mum's Facebook page, it said.

'Who's that?' asked Mum.

'Emmanuel,' said Tommy. 'He says to look at Jacob's mum's Facebook page.'

'I wonder why,' said Mum.

Walking towards the computer, she logged on. She was a Facebook friend of Mrs Walker. She scanned down the page and then she saw it. A post that shouted out at her.

My son is being bullied. Click to find out more.

She clicked and a video message started to play. It was Jacob talking to a camera. He was describing how he was being picked upon by the school bully. They sat listening, Tommy and his mum, and then Jacob did it, he named Tommy as the culprit.

Tommy's mum went red. She clicked her tongue, something she always did when she was annoyed. She turned to Tommy.

'Well,' she barked. 'Is there any truth in what he is saying?'

'No,' lied Tommy. And then he added, 'Jacob has been making fun of me because I am not so good in tests as him.'

Mum stared at him. She could usually tell when Tommy was being less than honest. But she was perhaps too angry to tell on this occasion.

She went to the phone and dialled Jacob's mum's number. Tommy began to feel uncomfortable. He didn't like where this was headed. But he was in too deep now. He couldn't tell Mum about what had happened in the playground that week. Besides, Jacob had started it, hadn't he?

Tommy went up to his room. He had decided that he wanted a bit of 'me time'. Why had he got the boys to ignore Jacob that week in school? Stupid, stupid, stupid.

© Gary Nott and Brilliant Publications Limited
*This page may be photocopied for use by the purchasing institution only.*

# Falling in and out of friendship — Tommy and Jacob's Story

Later, he heard the phone ringing. Who would that be? he wondered.

He didn't have to wait long to discover that Mum was talking to Jacob's mum. Mum was speaking in a raised voice.

Then things went quiet. Dad would be in soon. What would he say? Suddenly, the door opened. It was Mum. She looked even angrier than she had before.

'We will see Mr Smithson tomorrow after school,' she said. 'I want this sorted. Jacob's mother should not have let Jacob talk about you online, whatever you've done. And I'm still not sure what you have done, mind you. But everyone will have seen it and that's not fair. You've been branded.' With this, she shut the door.

*Branded*. It was the first time Tommy had heard that word. It didn't sound good.

As they made their way to the school gate next morning, Tommy's mum stooped down and spoke into his ear. 'Whatever you do today,' she hissed, 'don't be mean to Jacob.'

At break time, they all played together.

Tommy didn't speak to Jacob, who in turn ignored him. The other children didn't mention the spat; they thought it best to steer well clear.

On Monday evening, they were shown into the Headteacher's office. Tommy's mum didn't give Mr Smithson a chance to speak until she had said all she wanted to say. What, she asked, was he going to do about the post online? What did the school's e-safety policy have to say about it?

Mr Smithson attempted to speak but Tommy's mum was in no mood to listen. She talked over the Headteacher, who looked flustered.

Suddenly she stood up and, taking his hand, pulled Tommy to his feet.

When they got to the car, Tommy's mum let out a sigh. 'I feel better now,' she said. 'I've made my feelings clear.' She put the car into gear, and slowly pulled forward towards the school car park gates. Some pupils were walking past, having just finished at after school football club. Jacob was the last in the line. He spied Tommy's mum and Tommy sitting waiting in the car. Tommy's mum frowned.

Then Jacob turned his back to them and bending over pulled his shorts down, cheekily exposing his white bottom to them.

Tommy's mum spluttered. She couldn't believe what she had just seen Jacob do. Jacob meanwhile, had swiftly pulled his shorts back up and had run off laughing to catch up with the other boys.

Tommy looked at his mum. He thought she was going to explode. To make matters worse, he felt himself wanting to laugh; he was having to work really hard to stop himself dissolving into giggles.

They drove home in silence.

As soon as they got home Tommy escaped to his room, where he laughed into his pillow – he didn't want Mum to hear him.

The next morning at the school gate, Mum made a beeline for Jacob's mum. The two women started an almighty argument. Everyone stopped to listen. Tommy's mum shouted about the video clip and Jacob's flash of his bottom; Jacob's mum repeated the claim that Tommy was the playground bully and was being mean to her son. Mr Smithson approached the two women. He tried to calm them down but they were in no mood to listen. Finally he had had enough and he blew on his whistle. The two women stopped in their tracks.

'Look,' he said, 'look at your two boys.'

The women stopped to look. There in the playground stood Jacob and Tommy laughing and joking with one another. They looked as though they were the best of friends.

Suddenly, the two women felt foolish. Here they were arguing about their sons when the two boys didn't look as if they had a care in the world.

'Maybe, we should all move on,' said Mr Smithson. 'The boys certainly look like they have.'

Without another word, the two women melted into the crowd.

Mr Smithson sighed. It was sometimes more difficult to deal with the parents, he thought, than it was to manage the children. Children were so much quicker to forget their differences.